"This book is superb—rich, deep, sponses to the challenges of suffering and will be read as God's great hug for all who are in pain."

Os Guinness, author of *Carpe Diem Redeemed*

"Suffering is like manure—though totally repellent, it provides compost for growth. In this thoughtful book, Ken Boa and Jenny Abel reflect on the pain experienced by the apostle Peter. Themes of grace, hope, and even joy emerge as character is forged. Such personal growth does not come cheaply, but it is eternal."

Alec Hill, president emeritus of InterVarsity Christian Fellowship/USA and author of *Living in Bonus Time: Surviving Cancer, Finding New Purpose*

"For decades, Ken Boa's writings have directed readers' thoughts toward worship, spiritual formation, and living in light of eternity. Now, in *Shaped by Suffering*—which is arguably his most profound book—he offers hope, meaning, and perspective on our suffering. In Ken's words, get ready 'to let God use our difficulties to pry our fingers off the tight grip we have on our expectations and turn our attention to a living hope—one that won't let us down.'"

Paul Borthwick, senior consultant for Development Associates International, coauthor of *Fellowship of the Suffering*

"The challenge of suffering calls for all the resources we can find, and Kenneth Boa's latest book is filled with them. Drawing extensively on the letter of First Peter, Boa vividly describes the way God uses life's difficulties to shape our characters and prepare us for eternal fellowship with him. While nothing diminishes the pain that suffering brings, he insists, we have the assurance that God is with us through it all, forming us in the likeness of Christ. The book is filled with inspiring illustrations of people who have grown in suffering, sometimes dramatically, and it concludes with a number of practical ways to apply its insights to our lives."

Richard Rice, author of *Suffering and the Search for Meaning: Contemporary Responses to the Problem of Pain*

"My good friend Ken Boa has done it again—this time with Jenny Abel. This is not only an in-depth and scholarly approach on the subject of suffering, but it is deeply pastoral. We all need encouragement in this area of life— whether personally or in helping others. This book will definitely meet that need."

Gene A. Getz, professor, pastor, and author

"I cannot think of a better person to write such a book. Ken has spent his life focusing on people and on ministry to them. He is one of the best-read individuals I know, and his love of Scripture, his knowledge of apologetics, and his deep passion for practical spirituality have touched the lives of many over the years. This is a timely book. The topic is vitally relevant and, as you will see, the message speaks to the heart as it informs the mind. The mystery of suffering hits all, and we need wise counsel to navigate through the hardships it brings. This book is a great resource and one you will want to share with others. I heartily commend it."

Stuart McAllister, global support specialist with Ravi Zacharias International Ministries

"We don't typically think of the words *suffering* and *joy* as going together. But Ken Boa teaches us that—in the context of God's goodness and sovereignty—they do. *Shaped by Suffering* contains fresh insight on just about every page, which is no surprise to those of us who have come to love Ken Boa and his work. He is truly one of the wise men of the church today, and like the wise men of old, he has a special gift for seeing the glory of God first, before the rest of us. Also like the wise men of Scripture, Ken Boa does not keep the secret to himself but shares it with the world. *Shaped by Suffering* may be his best yet."

Warren Cole Smith, president of MinistryWatch.com

"I am a devout follower of Ken Boa's writing and resources because of their ongoing impact in my personal growth and ministry, and *Shaped by Suffering* delivers a desperately needed message for our personal challenges, injustices, and afflictions. Drawing from the wisdom of 1 Peter, Ken and coauthor Jenny Abel teach us how to 'lean in' and leverage our suffering to accomplish God's ultimate agenda—to make us like Jesus and bring honor and glory to himself. I highly recommend it!"

Chip Ingram, teaching pastor and author, Living on the Edge Media and Discipleship Ministry

"Outside those who steward the message of Christ, there remain almost no resources in our culture to help people who suffer—with hope, with meaning, with purpose. Ken has done us all a great service here, bringing the truth and hope of the gospel to bear exactly where we need it to speak most. Not only does this book point us beyond our suffering to the One who suffered on our behalf, it will equip us to point others to him as well."

John Stonestreet, president of the Colson Center for Christian Worldview

"Suffering is hard, but it's never pointless. Many Christians know this to be true. But Ken Boa helps believers embrace a fresh vision for how hardship creates Christlikeness through his treatment of the Scriptures and real-world examples. This book is packed with fresh insights and a wide array of encouragement. It's theological and personal—a rare combination for a book on suffering. It's hopeful and honest—an important tool for rethinking our approach to pain. Read this book and you'll see how suffering can shape your soul for the glory of God."

Mark Vroegop, lead pastor of College Park Church, Indianapolis, author of *Dark Clouds, Deep Mercy: Discovering the Grace of Lament*

"In case you are thinking this is just another book on suffering—think again. Ken Boa has crafted a perspective on suffering that is often overlooked yet significantly relevant. Boa reminds us that suffering is not random and that we are not just vulnerable victims of the whims of fate. Understanding God's work to not just transform us but to prepare us for our eternity with him gives strength of meaning and purpose to all who journey through the dark downturns of life. This is a 'must read' for those who are experiencing difficult times, for your friends who suffer, and for any of us who wrestle with why a good God would permit pain. Thanks, Ken, for this indispensable contribution to the upside of down!"

Joe Stowell, president of Cornerstone University, Grand Rapids, Michigan

"Why is there suffering in this world? This is one of the hardest questions we face as Christians, and many books have been written to try to answer it and to provide help for those struggling with pain and sorrow. Rather than following the well-trodden paths, this book explores how God uses suffering to prepare us for our eternal home. In showing us a purpose for our suffering, *Shaped by Suffering* does something even more important than giving us a theodicy: it offers a perspective that brings hope and even joy in the midst of hardship."

Glenn Sunshine, senior fellow at the Colson Center for Christian Worldview, professor of history at Central Connecticut State University

"Suffering comes for all of us. When it does, we're filled with questions: Why did this happen? Is there a purpose behind it? Is there hope of healing? Perhaps the most important question we can work through is the one *Shaped by Suffering* takes up: How shall I respond? With rich insight, a long view of eternity, and a careful handling of Scripture, Boa and Abel offer preparation for those soon to suffer, help for those in the midst of suffering, and comfort for those who have emerged on the other side."

Russ Ramsey, pastor of Christ Presbyterian Church's Cool Springs location in Nashville, Tennessee, and author of *Struck: One Christian's Reflections on Encountering Death*

SHAPED BY
SUFFERING

HOW TEMPORARY HARDSHIPS
PREPARE US FOR OUR ETERNAL HOME

KENNETH BOA

WITH JENNY ABEL

An imprint of InterVarsity Press
Downers Grove, Illinois

InterVarsity Press
P.O. Box 1400, Downers Grove, IL 60515-1426
ivpress.com
email@ivpress.com

InterVarsity Press® is the book-publishing division of InterVarsity Christian Fellowship/
USA®, a movement of students and faculty active on campus at hundreds of universities,
colleges, and schools of nursing in the United States of America, and a member
movement of the International Fellowship of Evangelical Students. For information
about local and regional activities, visit intervarsity.org.

All Scripture quotations, unless otherwise indicated, are taken from The Holy Bible, New
International Version®, NIV®. Copyright © 1973, 1978, 1984, 2011 by Biblica, Inc.™ Used
by permission of Zondervan. All rights reserved worldwide. www.zondervan.com. The
"NIV" and "New International Version" are trademarks registered in the United States
Patent and Trademark Office by Biblica, Inc.™

Published in association with the literary agency of Wolgemuth & Associates.

While many stories in this book are true, some names and identifying information may
have been changed to protect the privacy of individuals.

Cover design and image composite: Cindy Kiple
Interior design: Jeanna Wiggins
Images: gold picture frame: © Lyn Randle / Trevillion Images
        apple and orange tree: © Colin Anderson Productions pty ltd
        tree silhouette: © christys66 / Digital Vision / Getty Images
Interior image of Barry Morrow and Kenneth Boa used courtesy of David Reudelhuber

ISBN 978-0-8308-4592-7 (print)
ISBN 978-0-8308-3647-5 (digital)

Printed in the United States of America ∞

InterVarsity Press is committed to ecological stewardship and to the conservation of
natural resources in all our operations. This book was printed using sustainably
sourced paper.

Library of Congress Cataloging-in-Publication Data
A catalog record for this book is available from the Library of Congress.

P 25 24 23 22 21 20 19 18 17 16 15 14 13 12 11 10 9 8 7 6 5 4 3 2 1

Y 37 36 35 34 33 32 31 30 29 28 27 26 25 24 23 22 21 20

This third volume in the Eternal Perspective trilogy is dedicated
to the staff and supporters of Reflections Ministries
(2020 is its twenty-fifth year) and Omnibus Media Ministries.

CONTENTS

INTRODUCTION

(Do not skip this!
It's vital for understanding the rest of the book.)

In this world you will have trouble.

But take heart! I have overcome the world.

JESUS (JOHN 16:33)

T HIS ISN'T JUST ANOTHER BOOK ON SUFFERING.
For one, this isn't a theodicy, which is a fancy word for an explanation of the age-old dilemma of how a good God can allow evil and suffering (also known as "the problem of pain," as C. S. Lewis put it in his book of the same title).[1]

This book also is not primarily intended to help you cope in the midst of suffering and pain, although it's likely to have that effect as a byproduct. Again, others have written eloquently on this important topic.[2]

If this book doesn't set out to explain why suffering exists or to help you cope as you pass through it, then what does it do? *The main*

purpose of this book is to show how God uses suffering to prepare us
for eternity—for life forever in our heavenly Father's house.

To be sure, how exactly God uses suffering to shape us, purify
us, and conform us more to the image of his Son is, to a great extent,
a mysterious process, but the Scriptures as a whole and my focus
text of 1 Peter in particular give us some good clues about how this
process works. I (Ken) hope you will come to understand better
why so many sufferers declare, in so many words, "I would never
have chosen this trial, but I also would never trade it for an easier
path because, through it, God has changed me for the better."

The qualities we most admire in people are seldom forged in
times of ease but in times of adversity. All the heroes of the faith
suffered in some way, whether in an internal or external sense,
chronically or as a result of a single crisis. Some suffered even to
the point of death. While no sane person eagerly runs into the
arms of suffering, believers in Jesus today often avoid it *at all costs*.
Our most earnest prayers are too often, "Take this painful thing
away" instead of "Use this for your glory" or "Keep me safe" instead of "Embolden my faith in this danger or threat." This book
takes a hard look at our perspective on suffering and challenges
us as believers (myself included) to see it more as God would have
us see it: from an eternal perspective.

A NOTE ON PERSONAL SUFFERING

Suffering has a universal nature, which is why it can be so
comforting to talk and listen to a fellow sufferer. As believers, we
also share the same certain outcome—eternal glory in the presence
of God.

At the same time, suffering is deeply personal. Among members
of the body of Christ, adversity takes as many forms as there are
believers. All of our experiences with suffering are unique—yours,

mine, and my coauthor's—"Each heart knows its own bitterness" (Proverbs 14:10). As a result, with a book like this you're likely wondering, *Do the authors themselves know what it's like to suffer?* Let us divulge a little of our own personal backgrounds now, knowing that more about each of us will come out in other parts of the book.

I (Ken) have primarily endured a variety of nonphysical adversities so far in my life, including relational difficulties and mental sufferings. Discouragement is one of the devil's most effective tools, and it's one I've battled in ministry. Misunderstanding of my ministry's direction, among other difficulties, has plagued me recently.

Perhaps my greatest struggle, however, has been witnessing the decline in my wife's health. While I worked on this manuscript, Karen was diagnosed with Parkinson's disease. Thankfully she has the mildest form, but it's still a difficult path to walk. Her latest diagnosis was piled on top of years of chronic pain she has endured, dating back to a near-death vehicle accident in her early twenties (not coincidentally, that accident was also the moment she first called out to Jesus). After praying for some time for healing for various symptoms, Karen and I were both discouraged to receive news about her Parkinson's. As a husband, it often feels more painful to stand by and watch my wife suffer than it would be to take her suffering upon myself, yet I recognize that I cannot fully understand the depth of her struggles—or anyone else's—and I suspend judgment (a concept I owe to Os Guinness) as we endure this time of worsening trial.

All of these experiences, together, have made me more keenly attuned to the mystery and complexity of suffering. God has used spurts of adversity to humble me and teach me the importance of his grace, of relying on him, of "numbering my days," and of cultivating a grateful attitude no matter the circumstances.

Jenny, my coauthor and editor, brings a different perspective that has enriched this manuscript. I will let her speak directly.

My suffering has taken various forms since I was little, ranging from internal fears resulting from multiple moves as a child (I was never in one school more than three years in a row) to financial strains in my family when I was young to a period in my late teens and twenties when I endured severe panic attacks and anxiety issues that encompassed both internal and physical aspects.

Most significantly, however, my husband and I (married since 2004) experienced more than a decade of unexplained infertility. The depth of despair and grief that trial brought us drove me to my knees—into the open arms of the heavenly Father—with a sense of desperation I never had before. As an overachiever and an overanalyzer, the lack of control and lack of understanding of the *why* of this trial were agonizing. *If only I knew how this ends,* I often thought and prayed during those physically and spiritually barren years in which the Lord often seemed silent. However, increasingly, in recent years he seemed to respond, *If you knew, how would you learn to trust me?* I could see my self-will being conquered one day at a time—slowly replaced with his "good, pleasing and perfect will" (Romans 12:2). It was an agonizing but necessary process that only came about with the passage of time.

Ironically, just days after Ken and I finished the first draft of this book, to my complete surprise, I learned I was with child. The years of pursuing medical options had long since ended; I had begun to pray with more frequency (especially while working on this book), "Lord, make me content as a childless wife; help me be fruitful in the ways *you* desire!"

The miracle of this child is too great for words, and yet it's much more than a child that I have received from God. The lessons he's taught me, the cultivation of trust, and the deep intimacy with Christ gained in that waiting period are priceless and well worth every ounce of pain—pain which has shaped me and still brings tears to my eyes. My prayer is that my suffering (past and future) continues to shape me *and* be used by God to minister to others. The process isn't over.

This book presents no rosy picture of suffering, nor does it resort to trivial, simplistic explanations for the reasons why we suffer. The primary goal is to help you see how God wants to use your sufferings to enlarge your perspective and lift your gaze to the One who suffered and died for you, who walks with you in your suffering, and who is coming again to set everything aright *forever*. That day is coming, and we're called to prepare for it.

DEFINING SUFFERING

When we think of suffering, our minds immediately gravitate to the more visible, outward forms. But suffering can be inward too—invisible to others, but just as real. Mental illness, fear, and struggles against certain temptations are examples of inward suffering. We have to be careful about judging by outward appearances, because a person's life might appear to be going smoothly, without much adversity, but he or she could be experiencing a deep inner turmoil of which we're unaware. In addition to occurring either inwardly or outwardly, suffering can be either self-caused (a result of our own sin or simply a stupid mistake) or inflicted by a source outside of a person—whether an invisible spiritual force (see Ephesians 6:12) or a visible agent (for example, another person, an "act of God" in nature, a chemical gone awry in the body, and so on).

Thus, I see four categories of suffering: (1) innocent and inward, (2) self-inflicted and inward, (3) innocent and outward, and (4) self-inflicted and outward. Everyone's lives feature a blend of these four categories of suffering; we may even face a blend within the same trial (a hardship may have begun due to no fault of our own, but it may be prolonged by internal struggles resulting from our own sinful reactions).

So suffering, by nature, is varied. The biblical authors (including Peter; see 1 Peter 1:6) acknowledged as much. I, like them, will use various words for suffering, as the occasion warrants: *pain, trial, temptation, suffering, distress, oppression, affliction, tribulation, burden, persecution.* In varying the language, I'm not indicating that a specific word is restricted to some special form of suffering. What one person might call "hardship" another might call a "trial." This same variety of language runs throughout Scripture. I purposely do not present a word study of the numerous terms used to describe suffering in the Bible. A study of those words would be useful for some purposes, but not in order to assign some special significance to particular Hebrew or Greek words. Rather, such a study would lead us to uncover the context of the types of suffering found in the Bible. We would discover instances of suffering resulting specifically from persecution (for faithfulness to Christ) *and* instances of general suffering, due to unknown reasons or reasons we can only account for as a result of living in a fallen world. Indeed, a study of that sort would unearth examples from Scripture of all four categories of suffering mentioned earlier.[3]

Just like the suffering you and I experience in our lives, the examples of suffering we see in the Bible don't always fit neatly into one category, nor does suffering always occur in predictable contexts. Job's suffering was innocent, inward, and outward, compounded in multiple areas and in multiple waves—and all as a result of Job's righteousness, no less! Similarly, the prophet Elijah's fear and severe depression weren't the result of failure but actually came on the heels of great success and an act of faith.

Of course, in an ultimate sense, suffering was injected into this world through the failure of the first humans, Adam and Eve, and it is through their sin that their offspring (including us today) and the very world itself are subjected to suffering. All suffering, in some sense, can be traced back to that moment. And all of us can take a lesson from their example—on how the failure to trust God can lead to widespread pain and increased suffering for ourselves and others.

The bottom line is that nobody escapes suffering, and the actual causes and forms of suffering are more varied and nuanced than we typically acknowledge. Only God knows the details of our lives fully; only he sees the full picture of both our outward circumstances and inward conditions and intentions. Regardless of our particular experience of suffering, God can and does use difficulties for our formation (conditional upon our appropriate response); he even uses suffering that is self-inflicted, though as we'll see in 1 Peter, enduring that kind of adversity is not on the same level as "innocent" suffering or suffering for the name of Christ.

PART OF A TRILOGY

This book completes an unofficial trilogy united by the theme of cultivating an eternal perspective. The first book, *Rewriting Your Broken Story*, focused on the *power* of an eternal perspective. *Life in the Presence of God*, the second book, focused on the *practice* of an eternal perspective. (That book's companion training guide, *A Guide to Practicing God's Presence*, offers a suite of exercises for helping you cultivate such a perspective.)[4] Last, this third book focuses on how God uses temporary hardships on earth to forge

Christlike character in us in *preparation* for glory. I encourage you to read the other books as well, though it's not necessary to read them in the order named.

OUR HOPE AND PRAYER FOR YOU

Finally, I recognize that you bring your own set of circumstances to this book, your own personal history of pain and suffering. That history may fill volumes, or it may be relatively short. Whatever the case may be, I sincerely hope this book encourages you to see your own struggles and pains *and those of others* in a new light: from the perspective of God's Word. May he prepare you for the suffering still to come in your life, and may he help you speak with wisdom and encouragement to loved ones you know who are suffering.

In terms of persecution as a particular type of suffering commended by God, enduring hardship for the name of Christ is, in many parts of the world, very real and already intense. A 2019 report by Open Doors USA indicates that persecution is increasing at "an alarming rate," with eleven Christians dying for their faith per day in the top fifty countries on the organization's World Watch List.[5] For others of us, persecution on this level may seem far removed from daily life, but we would do well to heed Peter's words—and warnings throughout the Bible, along with the examples of brothers and sisters around the world—so we are prepared to suffer in this manner when the time comes. We are seeing signs of growing persecution for those of us in America and the West as the twenty-first-century progresses; let us not be caught off-guard when this pattern intensifies (as I believe it will).

If you are a follower of Jesus Christ, this book is for you because Jesus promised every one of his followers would face trouble—suffering, pain, even persecution for his name—at some point in time. May you be open to the refining effect of the crucible of affliction—always aware of your status as a stranger in a foreign land. We're not home yet, but one day we will be, and no doubt will linger that, as Julian of Norwich put it, "All shall be well and all shall be well, and all manner of things shall be well."[6]

THE CRUCIBLE
OF SUFFERING

In all this you greatly rejoice, though now for a little while
you may have had to suffer grief in all kinds of trials.

1 PETER 1:6

AS MY LONGTIME FRIEND lay in his hospital bed, weak and dying in the spring of 2018, he looked up at me with inquisitive eyes, as if asking—pleading—"What do I do now?" Of all the shared years of ministry and friendship with Barry Morrow, one memory flashed in my mind and stood out from all the rest: Barry and me punting down the Cherwell River in a short afternoon getaway during a summer program at Oxford in England. It was the summer of 1996. The journey was filled with the things we both loved: reveling in the beauty of God's creation, talking of great literature, and exchanging quotes and ruminations on one of our favorite writers, C. S. Lewis.

But that pleasurable memory faded as a tinge of bitterness grew into a heavy weight of sorrow as I recalled the path Barry's

Barry Morrow and Ken Boa

life had followed in the years since that summer. Yes, Barry was a man saved by grace. He, of all people, knew it was by God's grace alone, through faith in Christ alone, that would lead him into the presence of the Father in a matter of days. He was a man who had spent a lifetime teaching and coaching others about finishing well in life, yet here on his deathbed he lay estranged from his former wife and now-grown children—alienated by the wreckage infidelity had wrought and all the lies, deceit, and cover-up that so often accompanies it. He was, by all indicators, *not* going to finish well.

The irony was obvious to everyone around him. But it didn't make the situation easy. Conquering human pride never is.

The cancer that wreaked havoc inside Barry's body was eroding the earthly shell of this man who once stood at my side as a partner in ministry. But his soul was fully alive, and there was still time. I knew exactly what Barry needed to do, but I wasn't sure if he would do it. He'd resisted my and others' past urgings to be reconciled with his earthly family.

But now was different: with nothing left to hold onto, keenly aware that he didn't have much longer to live, his heart had become tender. He was open and ready to hear the truths God had put on my heart to share. I urged Barry to make his relationships right—his relationship with God and his relationships with his former wife and children. Leave no unfinished business, I told him.

Shortly after I talked to Barry in the hospital, which wound up being my last time with him, Barry called for his ex-wife, Caroleeta, to join him at his bedside, and they spoke for over an hour. Forgiveness was requested and granted. When he called for his two grown children immediately thereafter, he spoke these words of reflection on his encounter with Caroleeta:

> It's like sitting down with someone for the first time. You know them but yet you don't. It was amazing, there was no pretense. . . . The love and forgiveness I've been shown from her, you all, and friends would not have happened apart from this [disease]. There's a great line from C. S. Lewis, who wrote a letter in *A Severe Mercy*; what Lewis is saying is God has given you a severe mercy—you would never in your life have asked for this—but you've been given tragedy, and it has saved you. We are all going to die, but if this illness had not come I would never have known of love.[1]

At that moment, Barry's daughter Anna looked in the eyes of her tear-filled father and said, "Dad, you're finishing well." At his memorial service weeks later, she remarked, "Isn't disease ironic like that? It takes all we have, leaves us in a position of surrender, and then in our brokenness and emptiness we can begin to learn of love." This profound insight is echoed by the psalmist:

Before I was afflicted I went astray,

But now I keep Your word. . . .

It is good for me that I was afflicted,

That I may learn Your statutes. (Psalm 119:67, 71 NASB)

THE CRUCIBLE

The crucible of affliction can come in the form of cancer and sickness, as it did for Barry, or in numerous other physical forms, ranging from a physical disability or injury to poverty or other difficult external circumstances to physical abuse or mistreatment on the level seen during the Holocaust, to name just a few examples. The crucible also includes countless forms of nonphysical affliction—mental, emotional, and spiritual—such as depression, anxiety, anguish over a family member's death or spiritual lostness, the sting of social rejection or loneliness, career-related discouragement—the list goes on.

Suffering can be chronic, recurring, or lasting only a moment or a season. It can be externally caused, self-inflicted (as a result of sin or poor decision making), or a combination of the two. Suffering encompasses those unwanted things in our lives we contend with as well as the lack or loss of things we wanted.

Truly, if there's one topic every human being can relate to on some level, it's suffering, and yet suffering is unique to every person not only in its forms and causes but in the ways it is experienced. I might endure the same kind of affliction as you do, but we could each react to it very differently. Adversity that paralyzes one person may only briefly faze another.

In addition to being an individualized experience, suffering is, in many ways, mysterious—something our modern science-steeped, pain-averse selves have trouble accepting. If only some over-the-counter pain medicine, or something stronger, could fix it, whatever *it* is, permanently! Yet without pain we would not know something is wrong. And that something wrong runs deeper than any temporary hardship, no matter how difficult it is, we'll ever face. Pain is, in spite of itself, a gift. Pain is not the problem itself; it's the symptom of (and even a warning signal pointing to) the bigger problem of evil in a world that God created to be good.

Although this book is not a theodicy, at this juncture you may desire an explanation of the very complex problem of evil and suffering, and how they fit within a biblical view of the world. If so, stop right now and turn to appendix 1 for a brief summary to that end.

The last thing I want to do is to downplay the complexities or difficulty of evil and suffering. I do not want to appear to be "dropping a Romans 8:28 bomb" on those going through trials, as though saying "Hang on! God is working all of this out for your good!" will suddenly dissolve the difficulty you're enduring.[2] My wife and I have personally experienced the pain and insensitivity of such comments regarding adversity in our own lives. They don't help much and in fact can be more injurious than helpful.

This book may amplify your questions about suffering because a central theme is the fellowship of sharing in the sufferings of Christ himself. The suffering of Jesus was anything but light. In fact, it was the worst the world has known, encompassing every type of affliction, even to the point of experiencing alienation from his Father for our sakes—a curse you and I never have to bear. The suffering of the sinless Christ was also wholly undeserved *in every instance.*

But this book's purpose is not to try to explain this very difficult reality (which our limited human minds will never *totally* comprehend) but to consider suffering from an eternal perspective. Specifically, I want to examine how God uses suffering in our lives—regardless of the form it takes or the reasons we're under-going it. In other words, what role does adversity play in achieving God's goal of conforming us more to the image of his Son so we'll be ready to meet him face to face?

There's no doubt from the witness of Scripture and human history that God uses difficulties of all kinds to break his people of self-reliance and self-trust, and to teach us to rely on him, trust him, and find our true hope, identity, and security in him alone. We call this the crucible or furnace of affliction. Sometimes, this is a furnace of our own making, which is not praiseworthy in itself. Even then, however, God can use that pain for good in our lives. He has a way of allowing the heat to rise just enough in the crucible of affliction to produce a beautifully molded character in us as soon as we're open to his redemptive work in our lives.

TWO OPTIONS

To be sure, adversity doesn't automatically produce something beautiful in a person's life. It can and often does have the opposite effect. Suffering can either make us bitter or make us better.

Russian writer and historian Aleksandr Solzhenitsyn exem-plified the "better" outcome. After turning against the communist Soviet regime and being sent to a labor camp in the mid-twentieth century, the atheist found Christ (or, rather, Christ found him). In addition to raising awareness of the brutalities of the gulag, Solzhenitsyn's writings have ministered to tens of thousands since then. Yet think of the millions of prisoners who suffered in those camps and grew bitter, not better; Solzhenitsyn wasn't alone, but he certainly wasn't the norm in being able to honestly say, "Bless you, prison, for having been in my life!"[3]

Suffering always changes us in some way. The person we were before our suffering is never who we are after the suffering. The critical question is not so much what happened (or what is happening) but what's our response?

Knowing who God is in advance and preparing for suffering when it comes (since Jesus promised it would come to all of us [John 16:33]) enables us to evaluate our circumstances in light of his unchanging character rather than to evaluate God in light of our changing circumstances. This, in turn, allows us to maintain an eternal perspective in the midst of our suffering. Instead of a narrow vision of what's happening to us right now, we will have a long-term view, recognizing we're seeing just a part of a much larger and very *good* story that God is writing—one that we know *will* end well—despite present appearances.

1 PETER: JOB OF THE NEW TESTAMENT

Although the theme of suffering and its use by God to grow us and prepare us for eternity runs throughout the Bible, the Pauline writings are often a go-to body of Scripture for helping us gain perspective on the obstacles we face. But the first epistle of the apostle Peter, not a Pauline letter, is often called the "Job of the New Testament"—Job being the iconic example of godly endurance of suffering in the Old Testament. *Shaped by Suffering* stays closely tethered to 1 Peter, which I believe has growing relevance and parallels to our current context.

Writing shortly before intense persecution of Christians broke out under Roman Emperor Nero in AD 64, Peter, in this letter, was preparing his readers for the suffering they would endure and some had already endured.[4] While persecution up until that time had been sporadic and localized, AD 64 marked the Great Fire of Rome, which devastated the city and was blamed (by Nero) on the Christian community, though it was likely ordered by Nero himself.[5] Discrimination against Christians heated up from there with intensifying, organized persecution—ten waves in total—by the Roman government. The pervasive mistreatment continued until AD 313, when Christianity was officially legalized in the Roman Empire under Constantine.

Nero's own reign began less infamously than it ended. After five years of "tolerable" rule, a horrifying environment unfolded—the environment Peter was readying his readers for in his epistle. *Foxe's Book of Martyrs* gives us a glimpse of the kinds of events that swept through the Roman world:

> This monarch [Nero] . . . gave way to the greatest extravagancy of temper, and to the most atrocious barbarities. . . . The barbarities exercised on the Christians were such as even excited the commiseration of the Romans themselves. Nero even refined upon cruelty, and contrived all manner of punishments for the Christians that the most infernal imagination could design. In particular, he had some sewed up in skins of wild beasts, and then worried [strangled] by dogs until they expired; and others dressed in shirts made stiff with wax, fixed to axletrees, and set on fire in his gardens, in order to illuminate them. This persecution was general throughout the whole Roman Empire.[6]

Peter wanted believers to determine ahead of time to hold fast to their faith, not allowing difficult circumstances to cloud their long-term vision or diminish their hope in God. In fact, Peter emphasized how their sufferings could actually be to their benefit, helping to prepare them for eternity. And this is exactly what happened. *Foxe's Book of Martyrs* goes on to tell us that the widespread persecution "rather increased than diminished the spirit of Christianity."[7] In the absence of earthly security and hope, believers had to radically depend on God and each other.

Although 1 Peter was written in the context of the coming Neronian persecution, the letter does not concentrate only on suffering for the name of Christ. First Peter alludes to other types of suffering as well (1 Peter 1:6 speaks of their trials as "various" [NASB]). While 1 Peter's theme is often said to be hope, adversity—as the consistent *context* of that hope—is mentioned in every chapter of the letter, with the last two of the five chapters heavily focused on suffering. This is one reason for the letter's label as the Job of the New Testament.

ORIGINAL READERS: A MIXED AUDIENCE

A general epistle, 1 Peter was written to a broad audience of Christians. Its first verse makes clear that Jews were included in Peter's original readership. In particular, he was addressing Jewish people who had been dispersed from Judea due to persecution and scattered into multiple regions of Asia Minor (modern-day Turkey): Pontus, Galatia, Cappadocia, Asia, and Bithynia. These five groups were not evangelized in the book of Acts and may very well have been in places Peter visited. Across Asia Minor, these Jews faced growing opposition from their non-Christian neighbors. Christianity was not yet officially banned by Rome at the time of Peter's writing, but it would be within about a year. Part of the occasion of the letter, then, was to warn the people of this coming vilification—emphasizing that their problems would increase, not decrease.

But while persecuted Messianic Jews were clearly among Peter's audience, the text gives us reason to believe Gentiles were among his intended readers as well. Several verses suggest this fact. First Peter 2:9 characterizes his readers as "called . . . out of darkness into his wonderful light," and the next verse says they "once . . . were not a people, but now are the people of God," suggesting a non-Jewish audience. In addition, Peter mentions "the empty way

of life handed down to [his readers] from [their] ancestors"
(1 Peter 1:18), also implying a pagan background. Peter references
that background again in 1 Peter 4:3: "For the time already past is
sufficient *for you* to have carried out the desire of the Gentiles,
having pursued a course of sensuality, lusts, drunkenness,
carousing, drinking parties and abominable idolatries" (NASB).

Peter was addressing a mixed audience, and the letter's truths
extend to believers today who are undergoing sufferings of all
(various) kinds. The one exception is suffering that is a direct
consequence of personal wrongdoing (cf. 1 Peter 2:20; 4:15). That
kind of suffering, Peter emphasizes, is not admirable or praiseworthy, but the logical, natural result of individual sin. That being
said, such suffering can still be used for redemptive purposes—this
was certainly the case in Peter's life. But through that type of suffering, we cannot be said to share in the sufferings of Christ, who
suffered sinlessly.[8]

THE AUTHOR: A TRANSFORMED MAN

Peter wrote his first epistle from what he calls "Babylon" (1 Peter 5:13),
likely a figurative designation for the city of Rome commonly used
by early Christians. A future martyr himself, killed at the hands of
Nero in AD 68 (just a few years after penning this letter), the apostle
Peter was well qualified to speak not only on suffering but also on
two other key themes of 1 Peter: grace and glory.

A supreme example of a transformed life, Peter had heeded the
call to follow Jesus early. During Christ's life on earth, Peter went
with the Lord both to the heights of his glory and to the depths of
despair. He was among the three disciples privileged to see the
manifestation of Jesus' preincarnate glory at the Transfiguration—
an event recorded in three of the four Gospels and referenced in
2 Peter 1:16, with an additional possible reference in 1 Peter 4:13.

On the other end of the spectrum, Peter denied Jesus in his final hours as the Lord was mocked and beaten before going to the cross. Peter wasn't alone in abandoning Jesus, of course; all the other disciples fled too. But Peter's denials are notable given that he was the one disciple singled out by name as confidently asserting to Jesus before his arrest, "Even if all fall away on account of you, I never will" (Matthew 26:33). The shame he felt in letting his Lord down is clear from the Gospel accounts: after Peter realized his failure, the apostle was overcome with sorrow and "went outside and wept bitterly" (Luke 22:62; see also Matthew 26:75).

Peter's fearfulness for himself *before* the resurrection starkly contrasts with his eager and courageous witness immediately *after* it, and with his ultimate willingness to die for his faith. Prior to the crucifixion, for example, we see Peter fearful of Jesus' presence in an early encounter (Luke 5:8), faltering in his faith as he starts to walk on water (Matthew 14:30-31), and (as mentioned earlier) three times denying Jesus in his darkest hours (apparently to save himself from being associated with one arrested and taken into custody). Yet this was the same man Jesus called the "rock" he would build his church on (Matthew 16:18); imagine the doubt, even confusion, cast over that promise as Peter betrayed the Lord! Would Jesus' words be fulfilled? (How many of us have asked that same question in the midst of a deep valley or crisis of faith?)

God wasn't finished with Peter, though. After the resurrection, the Gospel of John reports Peter as the first disciple to enter the empty tomb (John 20:4-6). Later, when Jesus appeared at the Sea of Galilee, Peter jumped half-dressed off his fishing boat and into the lake at the moment he recognized that Jesus was the one standing on the shore (John 21:4-8). A handful of verses later (John 21:15-17), we read of Jesus' recommissioning of Peter— three times—providing a beautiful picture of God's power to completely cover all of our failures and sins, even the most heinous ones, and to restore us for his good purposes.

Doubt of Peter's faith and character dissipates by the time we reach Acts 2, which records Peter as confidently and fearlessly announcing the good news of the risen Lord to a crowd that included Jesus' murderers. Peter's newfound confidence wasn't self-focused but Christ-centered, the fulfillment of the Lord allowing Satan to "sift [Peter] like wheat" and Jesus' prayer for him that his faith might not fail in the end (Luke 22:31).

Peter went on to occupy a central role in the early church and in the spread of the gospel, particularly to the Samaritans and other Gentiles. Throughout the rest of Acts, Peter is far from the tempestuous character seen in the Gospels, though he's still far from perfect. Both Peter's own epistles and Paul's letter to the Galatians depict a chastened Peter—someone with greater depth as a result of adversity.

We don't know much about Peter's later life, except that he apparently traveled and ministered with his believing wife (1 Corinthians 9:5), and there is good historical evidence of his crucifixion under Nero. Tradition has it that, when he was on his way to be executed, Peter requested to be crucified upside down, since he didn't feel worthy to be crucified in the same manner as the Lord.

TWO CRITICAL TRUTHS

If the book of 1 Peter has a thesis, verse 10 of chapter five is it: "The God of all grace, who called you to his eternal glory in Christ, after you have suffered a little while, will himself restore you and make you strong, firm and steadfast."

Besides encapsulating the hope of our salvation and the surety of future glory, this verse communicates two key truths about suffering.

First, suffering is a given for every believer; it's a required course in the university of life. Notice Peter does not say *"if* you suffer," but *"after* you have suffered." Jesus communicated this reality in John 16:33: "In this world you *will* have trouble." Paul, too, reiterates the inevitability of believers' suffering in his second letter to Timothy: "In fact, everyone who wants to live a godly life in Christ Jesus will be persecuted" (2 Timothy 3:12). Pain and adversity are not optional—they *will* come.

The idea that our sufferings will decrease when we place our faith in Jesus is a false gospel. The philosophy that Jesus just wants us to be happy, healthy, safe, and materially blessed is a far cry from the picture Jesus presented for his disciples about what to expect when we follow him:

> Remember what I told you: "A servant is not greater than his master." If they persecuted me, they will persecute you also. . . . They will treat you this way because of my name, for they do not know the one who sent me. . . . [T]hey have seen [my miraculous works], and yet they have hated both me and my Father. But this is to fulfill what is written in their Law: "They hated me without reason." . . .
>
> They will put you out of the synagogue; in fact, the time is coming when anyone who kills you will think they are offering a service to God. They will do such things because they have not known the Father or me. I have told you this, so that when their time comes you will remember that I warned you about them. (John 15:20-21, 24-25; 16:2-4)

Too many of us have failed to remember Jesus' warnings, favoring more palatable verses instead—often taken out of context (for example, his promise of peace [John 14:27], of rest [Matthew 11:28-30], and of comfort [Matthew 5:4]). Without the full counsel of Scripture, a prosperity gospel can easily take root—and it has. Today, that gospel is preached in both blatant and subtle forms from many pulpits. This is one reason I believe 1 Peter is so pertinent to us in the twenty-first century: it provides a godly perspective on suffering so desperately missing in churches today.

While the first critical truth is that suffering is guaranteed, the second is that it is brief. It only lasts for "a little while," comparatively, as 1 Peter 5:10 says. In relation to eternity, even our worst and longest-lasting pain on earth—regardless of how unending it feels—is a mere blip on the time line of history (in reality, it's not even a blip!). Peter emphasizes this truth in another verse as well: "In all this you greatly rejoice, though now for a little while you may have had to suffer grief in all kinds of trials" (1 Peter 1:6).

These two truths—the inevitability of suffering and the relative brevity of suffering compared to eternity—undergird Peter's message. And the crux of 1 Peter's message is this: our own sufferings allow us to share in the sufferings of our Savior—tasting just a little of what he tasted during his time on earth and ultimately on the cross. Not only is Jesus our ultimate example for how to suffer righteously, but he himself was made perfect through suffering (Hebrews 2:10). God used his sufferings for a greater purpose, as he will use ours. If the One we're called to follow and imitate suffered, then surely we are not exempt, nor should we be surprised when troubles come our way.

A WITNESS TO CHRIST'S SUFFERINGS

In the final chapter of his first epistle, Peter refers to himself as a "fellow elder and witness of Christ's sufferings" (1 Peter 5:1). He could have called himself a "witness of the resurrection" or of the transfiguration or countless other miracles of Jesus; instead, he specifically references Jesus' sufferings (the ultimate of which was his death on a cross and all the pain entailed in that event—physically, emotionally, mentally, and spiritually). Peter is summoning up the most painful, shame-filled moment of his life—a time that undoubtedly evoked the greatest sense of failure and regret in him as he recalled his three denials—and reminding his readers that no adversity in our lives is wasted or without purpose; he can use our worst failures and pains to teach us the most. Peter was a living testimony to the fact that our God is the God of second chances.

Peter's words aren't shallow; they stem from an intimate knowledge of despair and disappointment, which led to a matured, eternal perspective. At one time, he was the one who, upon hearing the Lord's predictions of his own coming sufferings and death, had the gall to rebuke Jesus, saying, "Never, Lord! This shall never happen to you!" (Matthew 16:22). At that point in his life experience, Peter simply couldn't believe such bad things would happen to the Son of God. Jesus had some harsh words for Peter in return: "Get behind me, Satan! You are a stumbling block to me; you do not have in mind the concerns of God, but merely human concerns" (Matthew 16:23). How many of us, like Peter prior to the resurrection of Christ, look at our own sufferings with merely human concerns?

Peter had learned a key lesson by the time he wrote his first epistle, and it's a lesson we all need to learn. He had *watched* God incarnate suffer during his final years on earth. The apostle came to understand that the way of glory and grace goes through the cross—that the brutality of the crucifixion was, somehow, not only necessary but "fitting" (as Hebrews 2:10 puts it). Furthermore, Peter knew that the hard goodbye he said to the Lord at his ascension was the only path to receiving his Spirit at Pentecost and to Jesus one day coming back a second time as the reigning King of kings. Peter wanted his readers to see that suffering—though not a good thing in and of itself, but a result of the fall of humankind recorded in Genesis 3—often becomes an instrument of change, "a grace disguised," just as it did for my friend Barry Morrow as he was dying of cancer.[9]

God doesn't abandon us in our suffering. Moreover, he doesn't look at our suffering from afar but as one who also suffered. *He understands.* He sympathizes. He walks with us in our adversities. And as he does, he will (if we let him) transform us into someone more beautiful than if everything went our way.

Jesus as our exemplar and fellow sufferer is a major motif throughout 1 Peter. As we continually return to this theme, keep in mind that Peter did not speak of Jesus' sufferings from second-hand knowledge. Unlike Paul, who never met Jesus prior to the resurrection, Peter wrote from the perspective of being one of Jesus' closest friends on earth—someone who watched Jesus' ministry and sufferings unfold, and who saw him up close immediately prior to (if not at) his death. Here was a man who understood what it feels like when God's timeline isn't ours, the agony of waiting, and the crushing disappointment when all hope appears lost.

Moreover, Peter wrote from the context of intensifying persecution of Jesus' followers in an increasingly pagan world not unlike ours today. The rejoicing and praising he encouraged in the midst of difficulties (see 1 Peter 1:3, 6) didn't come from an untested or ignorant heart. He knew deep pain personally; indeed, many of his original readers knew it—and had been forced to flee their homes as a result of persecution. But Peter clung to the promise that the story of our lives as believers really *will* end well. The day will come when our God "will wipe every tear from [our] eyes," and "there will be no more death or mourning or crying or pain" (Revelation 21:4).

Until God makes everything new, he calls us to fix our eyes on the One who both suffered *and* who conquered suffering once and for all.

THE ALCHEMY
OF GRACE

These [trials] have come so that the proven genuineness
of your faith—of greater worth than gold, which perishes
even though refined by fire—may result in praise,
glory and honor when Jesus Christ is revealed.

1 PETER 1:7

A FORERUNNER TO MODERN CHEMISTRY, the idea of alchemy was introduced in Europe by Arabs around the eighth
century and spread across the continent and beyond. Even before
that, many historians believe an early concept of alchemy existed
among the ancient Egyptians. Once the idea came to the West, the
process was best known for its claims of turning base metals (most
notably lead) into gold, though it was related to other fields too,
such as medicine.

No one ever succeeded in actually turning lead into gold, so alchemy is now recognized as a pseudoscience, but the process

became a metaphor for the soul's search for immortality (the "philosopher's stone" or "sorcerer's stone" as it's better known by today's Harry Potter fans).

The process of alchemy, as proposed, was a laborious one. With each step in the purification process, the heat intensified until, supposedly, the lead—one of the densest elements, yet also highly malleable—would be changed into the lighter, more beautiful substance of gold (which is, incidentally, directly adjacent to lead in the periodic table of elements). The process required an agent strong enough to promote such dramatic change, and the outcome was known as the *magnum opus* or "great work."

FROM LEAD TO GOLD

Writing long before modern alchemy was proposed, the apostle Peter was probably not thinking of alchemy but of the process of refining or purifying gold in the following two verses of his first epistle; nevertheless, alchemy is a powerful metaphor to keep in mind as you read his words:

> In all this you greatly rejoice, though now for a little while you may have had to suffer grief in all kinds of trials. These have come so that the proven genuineness of your faith—of greater worth than gold, which perishes even though refined by fire—may result in praise, glory and honor when Jesus Christ is revealed. (1 Peter 1:6-7)

Peter was addressing readers undergoing *many types* of suffering: perhaps natural ailments and sicknesses, anxieties and discouragements, relational or business struggles, and even direct persecution for their faith. Whatever their individual circumstances, Peter's message is that these difficulties were serving a purpose. They weren't going to be wasted. God was taking their trials and using them to change the sufferers for the better: into people whose lives would more clearly reflect God's glory.

God is still using trials of all kinds to change his followers today. In story after story of believers past and present, we see God's grace transmuting the lead of suffering into the gold of glory so his followers become his *magnum opuses*—his great works, whose quality of character can only be explained one way: by God's power and grace. Our Lord will go through unending effort and diligence to recommence this work of transforming a fallen sinner into a saint who reflects his own glory and beauty. In this process he leads us to Christ himself, the one and only "philosopher's stone" on earth capable of turning the lead of suffering into the gold of glory.

THE AWFUL GRACE OF GOD

Joni Eareckson Tada is well known among American Christians as a paragon of virtue in the midst of suffering. But this was not always the case. Reflecting in 2017, the fiftieth anniversary year of her handicapping diving accident, she wrote:

> I was once the 17-year-old who retched at the thought of living life without a working body. I hated my paralysis so much I would drive my power wheelchair into walls, re-peatedly banging them until they cracked. Early on, I found dark companions who helped me numb my depression with scotch-and-cola. I just wanted to disappear. I wanted to die.[1]

Tada can still taste that "hot anguish" decades later, but it no longer marks her. What took such an angry woman, who desired nothing more than to escape her suffering even if it meant ending it all, and made her into the woman of God she is today? The answer is time and grace. The divine alchemy has done (and continues to do) its work: "Grace softens the edges of past pains, helping to highlight the eternal," Tada writes. "What you are left with is peace that's profound, joy that's unshakable, faith that's ironclad."[2] This powerful grace of God isn't just "grace over the long haul," she adds, but "grace in tiny moments . . . until one July morning, you look back and see five decades of God working in a mighty way."[3]

Today, the same woman who once shook her fists in God's face and used her wheelchair as a vehicle for venting her anger can honestly write, "I really would rather be in this wheelchair knowing Jesus as I do than be on my feet without him."[4] The impurities—the anger, the indignation, the hopelessness—have been skimmed away; the face of Christ is now clearly visible.

The Greek playwright and father of tragedy Aeschylus described this process, probably without even realizing it (he lived half a millennium before Jesus), in these memorable lines:

He who learns must suffer.
And even in our sleep
pain that cannot forget,
falls drop by drop upon the heart,
and in our own despair, against our will,
comes wisdom to us by the awful grace of God.[5]

Tada knows this "awful grace of God" firsthand and recognizes its simultaneous agony and sweetness. No sane person would choose to learn and grow in God's grace by means of pain and suffering; we'd much rather that there be an easier, more comfortable way. But for reasons we'll never fully understand, we often require the refining nature of trials and hardships to learn to truly trust God and rely on his grace.

THE PURIFICATION PROCESS

Lois, too, is no stranger to this refining grace. A believer who has loved Jesus since she was seven, now in her eighties, she found herself experiencing intense, intolerable sciatic pain, worse than she had ever suffered. She knew, and her doctor confirmed, that her response to pain was exaggerated by her state of stress: she was losing her husband of fifty-five years to dementia. Days meant heartbreak and frustration; nights meant pain that made sleep impossible. Desperate, she wrote in her journal:

> The problem with pain is, obviously, that it hurts. But that is not the real problem, given that we are not merely animals, but spiritual beings. The problem with my pain is that it dominates. It shuts out God. It hides His face. It robs me of the sense of His presence—which alone gives meaning to life . . . my only joy. With that incalculable loss, comes fear. Fear replaces faith. Fear now controls. . . . It seems impossible to pray when pain and fear have me in their grip; the focus that prayer requires is not possible.
>
> But surrender is. Behind all fear is self-regard: *what will happen to me?* I don't want to feel pain, I don't want to have an unknown future, I don't want to be helpless. I trust God, but there are limits! Some things are not to be endured. Or even contemplated. None of this is expressed, or even thought, but it is the mute dynamic behind all fear.
>
> Yet I can come and lay down my will, a will that was freed by the mighty work of God's redemption. That surrender robs fear of its power. And pain: even in pain, there is victory . . . the victory of praising Him, of being thankful, of trusting His perfect will for me.[6]

Surgery to relieve the pain did not go well, and infection set in. The surgery was repeated a month later. Still, the incision would not close, and the infection continued. At home instead of in a nursing home because her husband needed her, Lois gave herself medicine intravenously and tended her own wound, changing bandages at all hours of the day and night, at the same time that she continued to care for a husband whose memory had largely declined. It seemed a nightmare with no end in sight. The doctors were discouraged and said so. She wrote again in her journal:

> Waking one morning in August, I hear a voice in my head, "Don't bother to pray. God isn't there or if He is, He isn't listening." Satan overplays his hand. Everything in me recoils, all but shouting, "Not true!" My faith is pitiful, wobbly, and weak, but God is mighty. He is the Covenant-God, a covenant sealed with the blood of his loved Son, and He will not let go. There are abundant tears shed during this trial, often the tears of despair, but at times, the tears of a soul that weeps with wonder and joy in the faithfulness of God, who wraps us in His tender love.

Her letter went on to record the blessing of having so many who were praying for her:

> Friends are praying for healing of the body. (So am I!) God hears those prayers, but He has a prior concern—the healing, even the correcting, of my spirit, that I may share his holiness (Hebrews 12:10). Job affirms, "When He has tried me, I shall come forth as gold" (23:10).

Lois's trial isn't over. The battle for faith, hope, and joy amid trial is a daily struggle for her, as it is for every believer. God is never done working on us, even when we're octogenarians! Lead is becoming gold.

THE SUPREME VALUE OF FAITH

Think of the prayers we so often pray regarding our sufferings; these were the kinds of prayers Lois's friends prayed for her—and that Tada initially prayed: Lord, heal me [or my loved one] instantly and miraculously! Bring me relief! Lord, give me a spouse! Provide the finances I need! Send this good gift into my life, or arrange my circumstances just so!

These aren't bad prayers on their own; God wants his children to ask him for things, to rely on him for our every need and desire. But our prayers can't stop there. God is not our personal genie in a bottle or a cosmic vending machine into which we insert one thing in exchange for another. A god we can manipulate and comprehend is not a god worthy of our worship.

The God of the Bible is, rather, a loving Father who desires a relationship with us. He is not just taking us somewhere but is making us someone in the process. More than anything else in the world, he wants to make us like Christ. As Lois recognized, nothing else takes priority over that. Knowing him and becoming like him is the blessing that trumps all other blessings. And if there's something we need to have, or that he needs to withhold, to achieve that goal, he will do it—not out of cruelty but out of love, the love of an all-wise Dad who knows exactly what's best for his kids even when they cannot comprehend the reasons.

You see, faith is more precious than the finest metal on earth. What's more, the divine Alchemist never wastes any of the original substance; he heats the ores until all the impurities are removed. The hotter the temperature, the more dross rises to the surface. Our Father skims these impurities off the top so that ultimately the only thing that remains is his own image in us. It's a process that begins on earth and is not complete until we get to heaven.

God himself is the only one who knows best how to drive this process. He sovereignly times each of our trials, orchestrating them in just the right intensity and combination. They're not uniform but various (1 Peter 1:6), uniquely formulated and timed for each person. God wanted first-century believers to understand this, and he wants us to understand it today.

Comparison is the enemy of contentment, and it's never wise to compare one person's trials to another's. Just as in nature growth is uneven, and one plant may shoot up fast while another struggles to send out even one branch, every person's growth course is different. We have seasons of tremendous development and seasons when the new growth is hardening, as in a tree ring. We're to fix our eyes not on other people but on Jesus (Hebrews 12:2).

PRODUCING WHAT'S PRICELESS

In this transformation process the impurities that rise to the surface and are skimmed off include those things Jesus mentioned that "defile" a person: "sexual immorality, theft, murder, adultery, greed, malice, deceit, lewdness, envy, slander, arrogance and folly" (Mark 7:20-22). Of course, this is a partial list, not a comprehensive one, and we could add many other sinful behaviors and attitudes to it. The pure gold of faith that results from the purifying effects of suffering creates a character in us that is more like Jesus Christ's: "Consider it pure joy, my brothers and sisters, whenever you face trials of many kinds, because you know that the testing of your faith produces perseverance. Let perseverance finish its work so that you may be mature and complete, not lacking anything" (James 1:2-4).

God's desire for us is nothing less than best. He won't settle on silver when he can produce gold. If this process of change were left to us, we'd likely reach a certain point where the temperature of the furnace of affliction is still just bearable enough and say, "No more; this is good enough!" God, by contrast, wants us to be mature and complete, not lacking *anything*. He wants us to be perfect in every respect, not "good enough" but his *magnum opus*. He, like the good goldsmith, wants to see his own reflection in that molten metal. That reflection includes character traits like integrity, honesty, and selflessness—attributes that can't be cultivated through shortcuts.

WHAT HOLDS US BACK

At this point let's be brutally honest. All of what I'm saying may make complete sense to you; you may even grasp these truths clearly for the first time. But make no mistake: no matter how convinced you are of the truth of what I'm saying, *you will resist this process*. The redemptive process of suffering is painful by definition, and humans, by our very nature, shrink back from pain. We don't enjoy pain no matter how great the outcome may be on the other side. Knowing the outcome and fixing our eyes on the end goal *help* but never completely eradicate the discomfort of the moment.

Imagine an athlete who perseveres through pain and sprints to the finish line in a race. Or think of a mother giving birth to a child and the joy that overtakes her at sight of her newborn—practically erasing the memory of the pain of labor (John 16:21). And yet for us the race isn't over; the labor pains of this life won't end completely until we depart to be with the Lord. In the here and now, which seems far from fleeting as it's happening (Job 7:9; James 4:14), pain is real, and our natural instinct is to look for an escape.

Why do we resist even when we know in our heads that the process of suffering is redemptive? There are a couple of key reasons. First, many of us fear that if we finally turn our lives over to God, he'll make our situation worse instead of better. This fear relates to our innate disposition toward autonomy, inherited from Adam, which is ultimately traced back to a lack of trust (that is, unbelief). We're always seeking to control and orchestrate our own lives. We think *we* know what's best for us. Our self-protective instinct impels us to avoid pain, to seek an escape route. This instinct can be compounded by experiences of broken trust in our earthly relationships (for example, a parent who repeatedly broke promises). When it comes to God, this instinct doesn't magically disappear even if we know in our heads that God is working out the best for our lives. The process of trusting him is gradual, not automatic.

Second, we may resist God's transformative work simply because of the inertia of the flesh. Again, our fleshly natures don't disappear as soon as we come to faith; Paul makes clear in Galatians 5 that we can choose to walk by the flesh or by the Spirit (vv. 16, 25). Daily (hourly!) practicing his presence is critical to overcoming the rebelliousness still present in our hearts as long as we're on this earth.[7]

To be clear, then, just because you understand the truths in this book doesn't mean you will apply them. This book is designed to show you how pain can be redemptive, but (as with any book) it can't produce change in your life on its own. There's a spiritual battle in your life and mine, and to grow better and not bitter through suffering requires far more than a mental shift. We need the power of Christ living and working in us every day.

The forming of Christ in us is no easy matter, then. This shouldn't surprise us, as Christ's own journey on earth encompassed trials of many kinds. Surrendering to what, in his power, he has allowed and willed for us is hard. But it's even harder to fight circumstances on our own. I often cannot see the purpose of a particular struggle or obstacle in my own life. Even after decades of growing in faith and trust, my initial reaction is still, more often than I'd like to admit, one of resistance and frustration instead of surrender. The allure of relief or resolution can be much greater than that of developing character traits like patience and courage. But while we all resist God's purifying work in our lives, I can tell you I have never once *regretted* an act of obedience to him in that process. I have only regretted disobedience. This is because, in the end, disobedience always brings about more pain than obedience.

God really does know best. He wants better for us than we would even choose for ourselves. The question is, will we trust him?

A LIVING HOPE

He has given us new birth into a living hope through
the resurrection of Jesus Christ from the dead.

1 PETER 1:3

J ERRY SITTSER LOST THREE GENERATIONS in a matter of
seconds. His mother, wife, and daughter were all killed in the
same DUI automobile accident on a Native American reservation
where they were doing mission work as a family. He describes the
pain of the tragedy in his book *A Grace Disguised*:

> Darkness descended on me shortly after the accident. . . .
>
> I lost all hope, collapsed to the ground, and fell into de-
> spair. I thought at that moment that I would live in darkness
> forever. I felt absolute terror in my soul. . . .
>
> The accident set off a silent scream of pain inside my soul.
> That scream was so loud that I could hardly hear another
> sound, not for a long time, and I could not imagine that I would
> hear any sound but that scream of pain for the rest of my life.[1]

Sittser observes that just one piece of music or one day on the calendar (one of their birthdays) could set off a fresh wave of grief over one of the three losses. The memories of each person were painful, and simultaneously, he says, he could live neither *with* nor *without* these "vestiges of a past [he would] never again possess."[2]

Perhaps hardest of all was the thought of what was still to come: "Much of what I had imagined for my future became impossible after the accident." The losses created a "barren present" in which he was suspended between the past he longed to return to and a future he once hoped for that could never be. At the center of his grief was this question: "Can life be good again?" In other words, could he still have hope for the future?[3]

While exiled in Babylon, the Israelites wondered the same thing. So God made this promise through the prophet Jeremiah to reassure them that, yes, life could and would be good again: "I know the plans that I have for you . . . plans for welfare and not for calamity to give you a future and a hope" (Jeremiah 29:11 NASB).

The Israelites' hope of returning to the Promised Land would be fulfilled, geographically, in seventy years. But not all of them lived to see that day, and I bet every one of those seven decades seemed to drag on for an eternity, as is often the case in the middle of suffering.

THE NECESSITY OF HOPE

Perhaps one of the most difficult aspects of suffering is not the pain of the moment but the prospect of the pain continuing into the future. Oftentimes, if we know some bout of pain or suffering will be short-lived, that better days are soon to come, we can push through—we just keep our eyes fixed on the light at the end of the tunnel, at the moment of relief that we can see coming.

But what if that moment isn't known, and the light past the present darkness isn't visible? "It is hopelessness even more than pain that crushes the soul," notes author William Styron, whose book *Darkness Visible* chronicles his journey with severe depression.[4]

A friend going through a hard time in her career recently expressed a similar sentiment, declaring, "If only I knew when and how this ends; it's not the pain of the situation so much as the *not knowing* that is hardest—when will this be over?" Her options going forward are unclear, and she's in a long and indefinite holding pattern. She often expresses the need for hope in order to hang on at the moment—and yet hope, for the moment, remains elusive from an earthly standpoint. She feels as though she's in an indefinite fog that will never lift.

Secular scientists and philosophers recognize the necessity of hope even from a biological point of view. One psychologist from Johns Hopkins University, the late Curt Richter, is renowned for his research using rats in the 1950s. In one of his perverse experiments he put wild rats in a tank of water and watched to see how long they'd swim before going down. (Wild rats are known to be good swimmers.) These recently captured rats succumbed within minutes. Dr. Richter repeated the experiment with one notable distinction: when the rats seemed on the brink of death, he picked them up and held them awhile first, then put them back in the tank. With this one tweak, the rats survived much longer. "After elimination of hopelessness, the rats do not die," Richter wrote. As an article in *Psychology Today* summarized, "There are obviously many differences between humans and rats. But one similarity stands out: We all need a reason to keep swimming."[5]

As believers, we've been given ample reason—the *ultimate* reason—to keep swimming. We have the transcendent hope of an unbounded future. We can be fully confident that there's "life after the water tank." As humans, with an innate longing for eternity built into our hearts by God (Ecclesiastes 3:11), we need this hope; it's requisite for life. But that doesn't mean we won't struggle for air from time to time or sometimes feel tempted to give up.

WHEN HOPE FEELS ELUSIVE

I certainly have been in places that seemed intractably hopeless. Even as I write, there's one dear relationship in my life that remains a tangled web of difficulty and pain; I have done what I can do; still, a resolution is elusive. A feeling of hopelessness about the situation can easily overtake me if I allow it.

We've all been in places where we struggled to gain or maintain a sense of hope, but some of us struggle more than others. We often chalk this up to personality differences, but there's more to the hope puzzle. Even the most optimistic among us may know, cognitively, that we *should* be hopeful as believers, but hopeful feelings do not automatically follow when the going gets tough. It's in those times that the scriptural view of hope is different than the hope found in any other world philosophy or religious system. Hope in the Bible rests on its object, not on us and certainly not on our feelings. Biblical hope is rooted in reality: the reality of Christ's work on the cross, his victory over sin and death, and his promise to be with us until (and, of course, forever after) this world is over. The strength of the *object of our hope* is much more important than the strength of our own *feelings of hopefulness*. Praise God that his Word urges us to hope in him, not to *feel* hope in him (see, for example, Psalm 33:18; 42:5, 11; Ephesians 4:4).

When a sense of foreboding about the future seems crippling and you simply cannot gain a sense of hope, a good strategy is to fix your eyes on the God of hope, not on your situation or the feelings it evokes in you. My coauthor, Jenny, reflects on how the Lord used

Psalm 77 at a hopeless point in her life to bring her to a place of
contentment with God, even though her circumstances hadn't
changed at all. In this passage, the psalmist, too, felt a sense of
hopelessness and even abandonment by God:

> My heart meditated and my spirit asked:
>
> "Will the Lord reject forever?
>> Will he never show his favor again?
> Has his unfailing love vanished forever?
>> Has his promise failed for all time?
> Has God forgotten to be merciful?
>> Has he in anger withheld his compassion?" (Psalm 77:6-9)

Yes, Jenny thought to herself, *that is how I feel—like God is silent
and inactive, like this protracted difficulty with no end in sight is a
rejection from above!* But then what? The psalmist didn't stop at his
feelings. He vented, but then he looked up, turning his gaze to the
providential dealings of God in the past—a pattern seen repeatedly
in other parts of the Psalms and Scripture:

> Then I thought, "To this I will appeal:
>> the years when the Most High stretched out his right hand.
> I will remember the deeds of the Lord;
>> yes, I will remember your miracles of long ago.
> I will consider all your works
>> and meditate on all your mighty deeds."
>
> Your ways, God, are holy.
>> What god is as great as our God?
> You are the God who performs miracles;
>> you display your power among the peoples. (Psalm 77:10-14)

As these words jumped out at Jenny for the first time, she recalled
the profundity of pondering God's work over many centuries and

how the wideness of that perspective encouraged her to "hang on" and trust God even when he didn't seem to be acting in her own situation at that moment. It took a long time for Israel to finally make it to the Promised Land. It took many years for Sarah and Abraham to conceive and welcome the promised offspring of Isaac. It took years for Joseph to be raised from the depths of society to its highest ranks. None of these events happened overnight or even in short time periods. God's people are often waiting on him—sometimes not very patiently—for a long time (from our perspective). The mental review of God's works and faithfulness brought to Jenny a sense of hopefulness that came from a source outside of herself, even as her feelings of sorrow and hopelessness persisted.

HOPING *FOR* VERSUS *IN*

Often, hopelessness arises because we've been hinging our life outlook not on a "living hope" (1 Peter 1:3) but on a dead hope—hope in something that will not last beyond this lifetime. Many earthly hopes are not bad in and of themselves, but there's a critical distinction we need to make: wishing or hoping *for* something is different than hoping *in* it.

Wishing for success in school, career, relationships, wealth building, and so on is completely normal. Who doesn't want a fulfilling family life, a productive job, and pleasurable experiences? The problem is that these things have a way of slipping through our fingers even when they *are* fulfilled (and often they aren't, at least in the way we imagined). Maybe you've noticed that the moment you finally acquired something you'd wanted for a long time—that one thing you thought, *I've just got to have that, and then I'll be happy*—and you realize it's not all it was cracked up to be. Within a matter of seconds, your elation fades, and you move on to the next thing.

As Ravi Zacharias says, "The loneliest moment in life is when you have just experienced that which you thought would deliver the ultimate and it has just let you down."[6] Our hope has to be in something better, more sure, longer lasting than these temporal goals—it has to rest in something (or, rather, Someone) *eternal*—or it will always eventually let us down. No earthbound felicity will ever satisfy the deepest human aspiration or hope. We're meant for more than anything the world can provide. No person, no possession, no position, no performance, no popularity can ever sustain our hopes and longings over the long term (and sometimes not even in the short term). We can hope *for* earthly comforts and gifts, but we should never hope *in* them such that they end up consuming us.

God knows often only adversity will reveal to us how dead and shallow our hopes really are. Like nothing else, the pain of suffering calls us to seek a permanent source of hope—one that's certain and can't elude us; a hope that abides.

Jerry Sittser understood this. Grappling for hope in the wake of his three tragic losses, his grief led him to realize that even getting one or all three—his mother, wife, and daughter—back again wouldn't be enough. "Eventually," he says, "I would have lost my loved ones again."[7] Each of his loved ones would've died some other way. He had to find hope *beyond* the grave, on the other side of this life—for all other hope would eventually die or evaporate like mist: "I [came] to realize that the greatest enemy we face is death itself, which claims everyone and everything. No miracle can ultimately save us from it. . . . We really need more than a miracle—we need a resurrection to make life eternally new."[8]

LIVING HOPE

Sittser's words echo the message of 1 Peter. The apostle called his first readers, just as he calls us still today, to praise God for the hope he's given us on the basis of the one source of hope that nothing on earth, not even the severest suffering, can ever kill, the resurrection of Jesus Christ and the eternal life it secures for us: "Praise be to the God and Father of our Lord Jesus Christ! In his great mercy he has given us new birth into a living hope through the resurrection of Jesus Christ from the dead" (1 Peter 1:3).

Peter understood that hope placed in anything else would always be in danger of fading or being defeated. We can put our hopes in a lot of other things besides eternal life in Christ, but every single one of those things will eventually die. Only hope in Christ will never die. In fact, our hope in Christ will actually *grow*, not diminish, with the passing of time.

This hope that Jesus' resurrection secures is not wishful thinking; it's a firm and certain hope that we need not worry will be stolen away or dashed. It's based on reality: the historical fact that Christ rose from the dead and the promise that we too will rise from the dead. It's a dependable hope because it's in an "inheritance which is imperishable and undefiled and will not fade away, reserved in heaven for you" (1 Peter 1:4 NASB). The author of Hebrews compares this hope to an "anchor for our souls" (Hebrews 6:19 NASB) because it steadies us and holds us fast whether our lives are peaceful or stormy.

Peter's words about this "undefiled" or incorruptible hope are reminiscent of the words of Jesus in the Sermon on the Mount:

> Do not store up for yourselves treasures on earth, where moth and rust destroy, and where thieves break in and steal. But store up for yourselves treasures in heaven, where neither moth nor rust destroys, and where thieves do not break in or steal; for where your treasure is, there your heart will be also. (Matthew 6:19-21 NASB)

THE FULL WEIGHT OF HOPE

The question of hope, especially hope amidst suffering, is one of ultimacy. If our hope is ultimately getting temporal relief, we'll be disappointed, which can lead to bitterness. If our hope is in something immoveable (God himself), then our adversities can't destroy us. They might knock us around temporarily, but they can't crush us completely; they can perplex us without driving us to total despair (2 Corinthians 4:8-9).

This type of hope is the only explanation for why a man like the Old Testament character of Job didn't turn to suicide. He lost everything temporal, even cursed the day he was born, but he never cursed God. Though in physical and mental torment, forsaken by his own friends and relatives (Job 19:2, 14), he still knew deep down that the greatest thing in his life hadn't been and couldn't be taken away:

> I know that my redeemer lives,
>> and that in the end he will stand on the earth.
> And after my skin has been destroyed,
>> yet in my flesh I will see God;
> I myself will see him
>> with my own eyes—I, and not another.
>> How my heart yearns within me! (Job 19:25-27)

In his affliction, Job could cling to nothing but the hope of his Redeemer. His "faith and hope [were] in God" alone (1 Peter 1:21). When God returned to him double his possessions from before his testing, Job no doubt welcomed the temporal blessings, but by then his hope had transferred to another place. In all likelihood he clung to his riches more loosely than before. The alchemy of grace had done its work.

In 1 Peter 1:13, the apostle advised his readers, who would soon suffer a great deal, some even to the point of death: "Set your hope fully on the grace that will be brought to you at the revelation of Jesus Christ" (ESV). Some versions simply say "Set your hope on" without the word *fully*. But the original Greek contains the word *teleiōs*, meaning "completely." In other words, the weight of our hope must lean entirely on the grace and eternal life God brings us through Christ. If even an ounce of our hope is leaning elsewhere—whether it's on healing from a disease, the provision of a spouse or child, deliverance from a particular hardship, or any number of things—we're going to be let down in the end. That doesn't mean we don't hope *for* those things, but we don't *count on* them for our sense of fulfillment and worth in life.

PRAYING AND LIVING IN HOPE

So is it wrong to hope (and pray) for healing or relief from suffering in this life? I think Scripture is clear that the answer is no—as long as our ultimate hope isn't resting there. When my friend Al's thirty-eight-year-old daughter Erin, a mother of three young children, was handed a death sentence in 2017 due to an inoperable tumor in her brain, her family and close friends began praying earnestly for a *physical* solution to the problem—a healing miracle. Erin even began special treatment as part of a clinical trial in hopes of extending her life. (She has already surpassed the original lifespan predicted by the doctors.) Through the ordeal, her hope has remained strong and secure.

"Erin remains in perfect peace about all of this," Al reflected in a message to me. "To her, time here and in eternity seems almost seamless for someone who is a believer in Jesus."

Even as Erin and her family cling loosely to the hope for healing and look instead to "the life that is truly life" (1 Timothy 6:19), their simultaneous desire and prayers for healing are not wrong, especially in light of James 5:14: "Is anyone among you sick? Let them call the elders of the church to pray over them and anoint them with oil in the name of the Lord." The key is the heart attitude. Even in a situation this tragic from a human point of view, we are never in a position to demand that God fulfill our request in our own way and timing. Our prayer must always be accompanied by a heart that says, "Your will be done" (Matthew 6:10), with the recognition that his plan is always better than ours—indeed, it's always *the best* plan.

A missionary in China told a story of a friend whose church building was raided and closed amid tightening security in the country. Rather than ask for prayer for safety or the return of the church structure (or some similar request), the friend praised God and asked for peace and wisdom to welcome the opportunity to bear witness to the gospel during this wave of persecution. The missionary added, "Nothing can stop God." What a difference in mentality from those of us in the West who are often more inclined to run to the courthouse instead of our prayer closet!

Persecution, and any kind of suffering, isn't fun or easy; Jesus doesn't invite us to *seek it* out, nor does he dissuade us from praying for God's protection and deliverance. The question is whether or not we'll accept the answer God gives. If we *expect* or feel entitled to see our prayers fulfilled in our own way and timing, we're in danger of grave disillusionment. Instead, our prayers should be infused with the spirit of Jesus' Gethsemane prayer: "Yet not as I will, but as you will" (Matthew 26:39).

ONE FAITH, SAME OUTCOME . . . EVENTUALLY

The ancients of Scripture were commended for the way they hoped. They are chronicled in the famous faith chapter of Hebrews 11. Notice the two groups that emerge in this chapter. "Group A" (as I'll call them) is described in verses 32-35. These were people who through faith conquered kingdoms, administered justice, and gained what was promised; who shut the mouths of lions, quenched the fury of the flames, and escaped the edge of the sword; whose weakness was turned to strength; and who became powerful in battle and routed foreign armies. Women received back their dead, raised to life again. (Hebrews 11:33-35)

But the passage takes a sharp turn in the middle of verse 35, where the author describes what I call "Group B":

There were others who were tortured, refusing to be released so that they might gain an even better resurrection. Some faced jeers and flogging, and even chains and imprisonment. They were put to death by stoning; they were sawed in two; they were killed by the sword. They went about in sheepskins and goatskins, destitute, persecuted and mistreated— the world was not worthy of them. They wandered in deserts and mountains, living in caves and in holes in the ground. (Hebrews 11:35-38)

What differentiated these two groups? Group A was delivered from their adversities in *this* life (as well as the next), while Group B was not delivered from their adversities until the next life (Hebrews 11:39). Why? The text makes it clear that one group didn't act better than the other or have more faith than the other; *both* groups were commended equally for their faith (Hebrews 11:13). The only difference was the outcomes of their hardships on earth.

Contrary to the prosperity gospel peddled by false teachers, having more faith doesn't mean we'll enjoy earthly success or healing. As already discussed, Jesus promised our troubles would actually increase rather than decrease when we decide to follow him. Any believer can land in Group A or Group B. There's no guarantee! We may be delivered in this life from a certain trial, but we may not, and the same goes for our loved ones.

As we grapple with accepting God's will in our earthly circumstances, it can be helpful to realize that ultimately all of us are "terminal." We're all going to die eventually, somehow. By the same token, anyone who is a follower of Jesus will also be healed eventually. It's only a question of time, from the human point of view (from God's point of view, the healing is already complete, since he sees all of human history at once, from beginning to end).

Thus, my prayer for my friend Al's sick daughter, Erin, goes something like this: "Lord, you know my hope, the desire of all of us, that this dear woman would be healed miraculously. But you also know what's best for her, and I entrust her and the outcome to you." Without such a prayer and mindset, we can easily succumb to anger, resentment, and bitterness if the circumstances don't go our way, and to pride if they do go our way (as though we had something to do with determining the final outcome!). Cries of anguish or shouts of victory and joy are still wholly appropriate— we're not called to callous indifference, but we should seek to accompany these emotional responses with godly patience and hope.

NOT FAINTING

The late John R. Claypool—author, pastor, and theologian— counseled many people toward real, living hope. His sermons collected in *Tracks of a Fellow Struggler* reveal his honest struggles when, two years into his pastoral ministry, his ten-year-old daughter, Laura Lue, was diagnosed with acute leukemia. During her first remission period, Claypool conceded, "certain distant hopes [for healing] developed" in his and his family's minds. But when the cancer relapsed nine months later, their lives were once again enveloped in the darkness of an uncertain future. At that time he found companionship with the Jews exiled to Babylon: "They, too, had fallen on hard times and were separated from all their hopes and dreams," he wrote.[9] Into a mood of cutoff hope, Claypool noted, the prophet Isaiah spoke these words:

> Why do you complain, Jacob?
> Why do you say, Israel,
> "My way is hidden from the LORD;
> my cause is disregarded by my God"?
> Do you not know?
> Have you not heard?
> The LORD is the everlasting God,
> the Creator of the ends of the earth.
> He will not grow tired or weary,
> and his understanding no one can fathom.
> He gives strength to the weary
> and increases the power of the weak.
> Even youths grow tired and weary,
> and young men stumble and fall;
> but those who hope in the LORD
> will renew their strength.
> They will soar on wings like eagles;
> they will run and not grow weary,
> they will walk and not be faint. (Isaiah 40:27-31)

Claypool saw parallels in his own situation:

> Joseph Pieper has observed that the two classic forms that temptation takes are presumption and despair. . . . I experienced both of these forms of temptation in a most acute way. . . . As I watched my little daughter suffer, I could see no reason or purpose in what was happening to her. . . . At times I was not far from looking up and shouting: "Just what on

earth do You think that You are doing in all of this anyway?"
At other times the temptation to despair was very strong,
when I felt like saying: "I quit. I give up. I can't stand it any
longer. Stop the world. I want to get off." Yes, both of these
temptations loomed large on the horizon as I stood there
helpless in the darkness, but I am here to report that I did not
succumb to either one. Why? Because down there at the
bottom—[the] promise of Isaiah came true![10]

In the midst of this trial—indeed, one can only surmise, *because*
of this trial—Claypool learned to truly hope in the Lord. It was a
living hope, securely anchored in the unchanging promises and
character of God, ultimately fulfilled in Jesus Christ. His hope, like
those of others who have suffered deeply, didn't necessarily look
like triumphant soaring or running, but it was a hope that *lived*
nonetheless and could not die.

> If I had said: "It has got to be ecstasy or some solution of ac-
> tivism if it is God's help," then I would have been sorely dis-
> appointed, for all I got at the bottom there was strength to
> walk and not faint, just enough power "to hang in there" and
> not give up. . . . I confess to you honestly that I have no wings
> with which to fly or even any legs on which to run—but listen,
> by the grace of God, *I am still on my feet!* I have not fainted
> yet. I have not exploded in the anger of presumption, nor
> have I keeled over into the paralysis of despair. . . . This may
> not sound like much to you, but to me it is the most appro-
> priate and most needful of all the gifts.[11]

The gift of a living hope that will never, ever die is the best
comfort for someone in the midst of suffering. Without an enduring sense of hope, we will faint from the pain and ultimately
die. Without hope, we can't do as Claypool did: keep on keeping

on, no matter what events are happening in our lives or the lives of our loved ones.[12] This hope only comes to us once we've experienced salvation through Christ. And as the rest of this book seeks to clarify, this living hope stems from a greater purpose and destiny beyond this life; it comes from the knowledge that we're heading somewhere glorious—we're not going in circles. As a result, our hope will always stay alive and will allow us to rejoice even in the midst of deep sorrow and pain. It's to that very present joy that we turn next.

A PRESENT JOY

Though you have not seen him, you love him;
and even though you do not see him now, you believe in him
and are filled with an inexpressible and glorious joy.

1 PETER 1:8

PRIDE AND JOY FILLED PAUL, now on his second missionary journey, as he, Silas, and Luke entered the Roman colony of Philippi—the site of Paul's first church plant in Europe.[1] As the men walked along, they became aware of someone following them. The young girl was crying out, "These men are bond-servants of the Most High God, who are proclaiming to you the way of salvation" (Acts 16:17 NASB). She would not leave them alone. Discerning that she was possessed by a demon, a perturbed Paul finally turned around and spoke directly to the demonic spirit: "I command you in the name of Jesus Christ to come out of her!" (Acts 16:18 NASB). Immediately, the girl stopped wailing. The spirit was gone.

Just as the apostle and his companions were starting on their way again, some men came up and grabbed them, shaking them and asking if they understood what they'd done. Paul, Silas, and Luke soon realized these were the masters of the healed girl, whose fortune-telling skills (enabled by the demonic spirit) had brought them a good profit. When the evil spirit left the girl, she could no longer tell people secrets about their lives and futures. The masters' source of income was gone, and they were furious.

Before they could realize what was happening, Paul and Silas found themselves being dragged to the authorities, where they were falsely accused of stirring up trouble in the city. Canvassing the crowd, the slave masters soon won over the local people, and together they pressured the magistrates to punish Paul and Silas. Afraid, and seeing no other choice, the magistrates ordered Paul and Silas beaten with the bundled wooden rods they carried around as a visual reminder of the power of Rome. Bruised and battered from many blows, the accused men were taken to prison. Assumed to be normal inmates, Paul and Silas were led to the "inner prison," where they would not only be securely guarded but tortured and possibly forgotten and left for dead.

Later that night, their feet fastened to the stocks and unable to move, Paul and Silas lay silently near each other, knowing there was no guarantee of release anytime soon—or ever. Uncertain of the future and not a little anxious, they decided to pray. As they did, Paul couldn't help but remember the words God had spoken to Ananias shortly after Paul's conversion on the road to Damascus: "I will show him how much he must suffer for my name's sake."[2]

Even as darkness enveloped Paul and Silas and pain shot through their bodies, the men sensed the presence of God—and joy inexpressible filled them. So they began to sing, quietly at first and then louder: a hymn of praise to God for rescuing them out of the domain of darkness, for the sacrifice of his Son Jesus, for the privilege of suffering for his name.

They were unaware that nearly every person in that prison had sat up and begun listening to the beautiful sound coming out of the most dreaded room in the building.

JOY IN SUFFERING

It's easy for us today to keep reading to the end of the story, where we learn that God caused an earthquake to shake the prison's foundation, which eventually led to Paul and Silas's release (in addition to the salvation of the jailer and his household). The men of God won; the money-making machine of Rome lost. Praise God!

But at the moment they began singing, these men didn't have a clue what their future held. For all they knew, they'd spend the rest of their lives—or lose their lives—in jail. The injustice of their situation could've enraged them, leading them to stew in anger and indignation. Who could've blamed them? What Paul and Silas did made zero sense from the world's standpoint. When they sang, they weren't singing *over* their circumstances but *in* their circumstances. Their response reminds us again of James's words urging believers to "consider it all joy" when encountering "various trials" (James 1:2).

Paul and Silas weren't the first or the last to make joyful noise in the face of unjust suffering and even possible death. Holocaust survivor Corrie ten Boom once taught from the Bible and led fellow prisoners in hymns of praise right in front of executioners at a World War II concentration camp. "I knew that every word I said could mean death," she later reflected. "Yet never before had I felt such peace and joy in my heart as while I was giving the Bible message in the presence of mine enemy."[3]

Similar accounts of God's people, from both the recent and distant past, abound. In more recent history, joy visibly radiated from members of Emanuel AME Church in Charleston, South Carolina, in the days after a gunman opened fire and killed nine people meeting for Bible study in the American South's oldest black church in June 2015. The victims' families responded by extending forgiveness to the shooter and by gathering together not just to mourn but to worship and rejoice together. In an interview following the tragedy, a news commentator remarked regarding the service televised after the shooting, "This is joy. People at home watching may not understand, 'How can they be dancing? How can they be singing? How can there be this spirit of enthusiasm in the wake of this horror?' . . . There's a distinction between happiness . . . and joy. . . . We say, 'Hallelujah anyhow.'"[4]

The commentator was referencing a refrain that is common and important among African American believers in particular—primarily as a response to the reality of discrimination and injustice that they as a people have endured through the course of history. The refrain encapsulates a thoroughly Christian view of joy in general. Any believer can rejoice and sing "Hallelujah anyhow"—pressing into joy amid tragedy and suffering and even death—because we know from Scripture that these do not have the final word.

FROM FUTURE HOPE TO PRESENT JOY

Peter knew it wasn't enough to comfort his readers with good news only about what was to come, as glorious as their future hope and inheritance were. These people needed the presence of God *now*. They needed to know he was close in the middle of their suffering. They needed to know their suffering would not be wasted, that it would serve a purpose.

In the opening of his first epistle, then, Peter moves from a focus on the living hope and glorious future of followers of Christ (1 Peter 1:3-5) to a focus on the present (vv. 6-9). His words demonstrate that rejoicing is not postponed to a time after we suffer but, instead, can come even now *while* we're suffering:

> In this you greatly rejoice, though now for a little while you may have had to suffer grief in all kinds of trials. (1 Peter 1:6)

> Though you have not seen him, you love him; and even though you do not see him now, you believe in him and are filled with an inexpressible and glorious joy, for you are receiving the end result of your faith, the salvation of your souls. (1 Peter 1:8-9)

This theme of joy amid suffering recurs in chapter four of the epistle:

> Rejoice inasmuch as you participate in the sufferings of Christ, so that you may be overjoyed when his glory is revealed. (1 Peter 4:13)

REJOICING *IN*, NOT *OVER*

Peter's enjoinment to rejoice in our sufferings and Paul's similar urging to "rejoice always" (1 Thessalonians 5:16; Philippians 4:4) only make sense when we view joy from a biblical perspective: as something that supersedes our current situation and cannot fade or diminish based on circumstances. Biblical joy flows from an eternal spring, not an external source. An inner feeling of well-being and delight, joy is a gift of God rooted in our salvation and coming glory. Martyn Lloyd-Jones summarizes joy as "a quality which belongs to the Christian life in its essence."[5] He goes on to explain,

> Joy . . . affects the whole and entire personality. . . . There is only one thing that can give true joy and that is a contemplation of the Lord Jesus Christ. He satisfies my mind; He satisfies my emotions; He satisfies my every desire. He and His great salvation include the whole personality and nothing less, and in

Him I am complete. Joy, in other words, is the response and the reaction of the soul to a knowledge of the Lord Jesus Christ.[6]

Both Lloyd-Jones and the apostle Peter emphasize not only the feeling of exultation but perhaps even more, the action (rejoicing) that can lead to that feeling. Rejoicing is the proper response to our experience of God's grace. Three times in his epistle Peter tells readers to "rejoice," and each is in the context of delighting in what God has done *for us*, not in what happens *to us*.

Remember Lois—our eighty-plus-year-old friend experiencing daily physical pain and a postsurgical infection while serving as a caregiver to her dementia-stricken husband? It's no coincidence that the annual Christmas letter in which she documented the trials of a year both began and ended on notes of joy:

> We revel in singing our Glorias and "Joy to the World." And yet, how could it be joy for the One all Heaven worships to leave all that glory and splendor for a bestially-dark earth, filled with his children who will hate, despise, mock, torture, and finally kill him? Or, for his Father, looking on? Yet the angels announce "Good tidings of great joy!" For us, yes, the joy of peace with God that is now possible! And for the Father and the Son, the joy of getting back the children who have rebelled, no matter the cost! Does it not make us weep with wonder?

Her letter concluded:

> So light the Christmas tree, and sing the carols, and have fun getting and giving gifts, because underneath all the merriment is the everlasting, incomprehensible, redemptive, peace-with-God accomplishing, soul-filling Joy of the Incarnation!

Lois's joy was distinct from her circumstances, different from merriment. It was a soul-filling reality that came from gratitude and wonder at Christ's life and sacrifice. This joy has a way of bubbling over and superseding restlessness and impatience, allowing us to consciously, in any given moment, rejoice in the knowledge that *Christ died for me* and he's reigning today at the Father's right hand.

PURER AND DEEPER

Adversity can have the same effect in real life as it does in several of the fictional plots we love. Some difficult event happens, disillusionment and despair threaten, but then adversity deepens us and gives us more substance than before the adversity began. Shakespeare's *Much Ado About Nothing* is a great example.

The comedy begins well: the young lovers Hero and Claudio are set to be married. But nefarious actions and deceit of others lead to misunderstandings, chiefly Claudio's false belief that Hero has been unfaithful; he therefore rejects her at the altar, bringing public shame upon her (even though, in reality, her unfaithfulness was faked by others), and she faints (though all think she has actually died). As the plot worsens, Claudio ultimately learns the truth that Hero is innocent. With a heavy heart, he stands before her family tomb and reads her epitaph, mourning her death and his own error of accusing her of infidelity. All hope appears to be lost until the very last scene. At that time Claudio is set to be married again, but he doesn't realize it's to Hero, who he still thinks is dead. When it's revealed that *she* is the bride he'll soon wed, their joy reaches an obvious climax—and we gain further satisfaction knowing the villain and architect of the deception is brought to justice.

Whether you've seen or read the play, you can imagine how profound Claudio and Hero's joy is in this final act, when Claudio has received Hero back from a symbolic death and Hero's innocence and faithfulness are proved genuine. Their deeper quality of joy is not unlike that which can emerge from a Christian who has gone through intense suffering: the God-rooted joy both on the other side of the trial *and* even in the midst of the difficulty can be far deeper and more profound than joy accompanied by a life of easier circumstances. That was the kind of joy Lois wrote about in her Christmas letter. It's also the quality of joy my friend Barry Morrow and his family experienced in his final days on earth; in a sense, only when he was stripped of all his earthly hopes and belongings, and faced certain death, was he able to have joy and love in a purer sense.

This same joy visited Jerry Sittser, whose trio of losses in an instant exposed for him—as it does for so many who lose loved ones—"the dominant role our environment plays in determining our happiness."[7] With the "props we rely on for our well-being" stripped away, we're better able to separate the positive feelings that are the byproduct of favorable circumstances from the much deeper joy that comes from God through his spiritual blessings.[8] Sittser writes,

> If this world were the only one there is, then suffering has the final say and all of us are a sorry lot. But generations of faithful Christians have gone before and will come after, and they have believed or will believe what I believe in the depths of my soul. Jesus is at the center of it all. He defeated sin and death through his crucifixion and resurrection. Then light gradually dawns once again in my heart . . . [and] I end up believing with greater depth and joy than I had before, even in my sorrow.[9]

Such is the testimony of many a saint who has suffered: joy in sorrow, joy in pain, joy in suffering.

Sittser's words touch on an important truth about joy: its presence in our lives does not mean the absence or disappearance of grief and sorrow. Because Christian joy is divorced from our circumstances, in fact, it can (and often does) coexist simultaneously with sadness, grief, and even distress (as some of Peter's readers were experiencing, according to 1 Peter 1:6). Jesus himself was characterized by deep joy (John 17:13), despite being called a "man of sorrows . . . acquainted with grief" (Isaiah 53:3 NASB).

In a sense, all joy on earth is tinged with some level of sorrow. Henri Nouwen put it this way,

> Our life is a short time . . . in which sadness and joy kiss each other at every moment. There is a quality of sadness that pervades all the moments of our life. It seems that there is no such thing as clear-cut pure joy, but that, even in the most happy moments of our existence, we sense a tinge of sadness. . . . But this intimate experience in which every bit of life is touched by a bit of death can point us beyond the limits of our existence. It can do so by making us look forward in expectation to the day when our hearts will be filled with perfect joy, a joy that no one shall take away from us.[10]

Nouwen isn't suggesting there's no true joy on earth, but our joy here, in a sense, is always incomplete. It's real but imperfect. Even when all our circumstances are just as we'd like them (this being a very rare thing indeed), we're never totally joy-filled so long as we're absent from the Lord and not with him face to face.

Perhaps this is why C. S. Lewis wrote so often about joy using the language of longing and desire. In *Surprised by Joy* (the account of his conversion from atheism to Christianity), Lewis referred to joy as "an unsatisfied desire which is itself more desirable than any other satisfaction."[11] Joy, he continues, "must be sharply distinguished both from Happiness and from Pleasure," sharing just one commonality: "the fact that anyone who has experienced it will want it again."[12] Furthermore, he explained, he didn't desire joy so much as the object of his joy: "Joy itself, considered simply as an event in my own mind, turned out to be of no value at all. All the value lay in that of which Joy was the desiring. And that object, quite clearly, was no state of my own mind or body at all."[13]

In other words, Christian joy is defined by its object, God himself—the One of supreme and infinite value, who loves us with an everlasting love. Because we do not now see him, our joy in him is linked to our desire to be with him. And that desire is, if anything, intensified when this life is difficult.

DISTINCTIVELY CHRISTIAN

Not all religions see joy, hope, desire, and suffering this way. Buddhists, for example, view suffering (along with the rest of the world) as basically an illusion. The first noble truth in Buddhism is that life (as we experience it) is suffering, and the second noble truth is that suffering is caused by illegitimate desires. Third, Buddhism says, you can eliminate suffering by eliminating ignoble desires. Fourth, an eightfold path proposes a way to accomplish this. The upshot of Buddhism is that what you see and feel is not really real— suffering and pain are only illusions caused by wrong desires.

Denial of reality and rationality may seem like a nice idea, particularly when you're surrounded by harsh realities, but you'll notice those who hold to these views still look both ways before they cross the street. They can't live consistently with their own view. Getting hit by a bus is painful and life-altering, if not life-ending, and declaring it an illusion does not work in the real world.

But Easterners aren't the only ones seeking to avoid the reality of suffering. The West is full of similar philosophies. The common slogans "Don't worry, be happy" and "Keep calm and carry on" reveal the tendency among humans to try to ignore or escape difficulties. Live the best life you can, while you can; get while the getting is good; maximize your pleasure, minimize your pain: all of these are messages we often send our kids, and sometimes we even hear them in church. But suffering is unpleasant, plain and simple. It's also very real. Positive thinking isn't a magic pill we can take to make adversity disappear. There's something wrong, within and without, and the mantra that "happiness comes from within" doesn't provide the robust philosophy we need to support the full weight of life's realities. Even an op-ed writer for the *New York Times* acknowledged this in a 2017 column railing against the isolationist, emotionally detached attitude many have taken toward the pursuit of a fulfilling and happy life.[14]

Christianity takes an approach exactly opposite those just discussed. Not only does the Bible acknowledge the full gamut of human suffering in all its brutality, but it acknowledges the deep yearnings of the human heart for eternal significance and happiness. In Christianity the need and the desire of the human heart truly meet as God himself stepped into a broken world and endured it himself, securing ultimate hope and lasting joy for all who believe in him (see John 16:22). There's truly no other religion like ours. Only Christianity offers suffering as a means for bringing us closer to God through unity with the sufferings of Christ. Only the biblical vision shows us the way to the fulfillment of our very real, God-given longings and desires.

CHRISTIAN HAPPINESS

The salvation we have in Christ has secured our destiny, giving us hope for the future that will never die as well as joy in the present that will only enlarge with time. These realities grow in our minds and hearts when circumstances and people on earth let us down or even inflict pain on us. Adversities, then, have a way of sifting out the best goals and priorities in our life from the merely good and ultimately result in praise and glory to God, as he works in and through us (1 Peter 1:7).

One of the best outlines I've ever seen of this biblical view of suffering is found in a sermon by Jonathan Edwards. Incidentally, it's the first sermon ever preached by the famous Puritan preacher (he was eighteen at the time). Titled "Christian Happiness," Edwards's message laid out three truths in answer to the question, Why should Christians be happy? By *happy*, he was speaking of deep happiness—that is, joy. Here were his three points and supporting Scriptures:

1. Our bad things will turn out for good (Romans 8:28).

2. Our good things can never be taken away from us (Psalm 4:6-7; also Romans 8:28-29).

3. The best things are yet to come (1 Corinthians 2:9; see also Revelation 22:1).

These three points are also found in 1 Peter. In addition to looking to our living hope in Christ, Edwards, like Peter, indicates that a Christian can and should be happy (joyful) *right now*—not in a glib sense but in the deep-down sense. Why? Because the sovereignty and goodness of God, as well as anticipation for the greater future he has for us, are all causes for present joy. No matter what happens to and around us, the Rock of our salvation still stands, and we can rejoice even through tears and even if feelings of merriment are absent. As a well-known hymn puts is, "When all around my soul gives way, He then is all my hope and stay."[15]

These foundational truths are critical as soon as we face suffering, whether for his name or simply as a result of the brokenness of this world. It's wise to learn them in advance so when suffering comes, the test it poses to our faith and character does not take us by surprise.

5

PREPARING TO SUFFER

Dear friends, do not be surprised at the fiery ordeal
that has come on you to test you, as though something
strange were happening to you.

1 PETER 4:12

I N TWO SEPARATE INCIDENTS five days apart—the first, December 29, 2014, the second, January 3, 2015—Islamic militants captured twenty-one men in upper Egypt's rural province of Minya. A graphic video released publicly a month and a half later put persecution on display for the whole internet world to see. (The events were too gruesome even for mainstream media to ignore). Members of the Islamic State mass-beheaded twenty-one Christians onscreen. Twenty of the martyrs were from Egypt, one from Ghana, and all were killed while chanting the name of the Lord Jesus Christ. Thirteen came from a single village.[1]

The families of the men had to wait three years to receive their loved ones' remains, which were found in October 2017, apparently near where they were executed in Libya.[2] One widow remarked, "I'm very proud of my husband Samuel because he was martyred on the name of Jesus Christ and he didn't renounce the faith. . . . He honored me, his sons, and Christianity."[3] Her comments echo those of other family members whose husbands, fathers, or brothers died proclaiming Jesus.

In America, many of us watched this video in shock and disbelief (if we could stand to watch it at all). The experience was so distant from our own, the hostage takers like something out of a Hollywood horror movie to most of us. *This really happened*, we had to remind ourselves.

ISOLATION FROM PAIN

In the United States as well as in other countries today, the most visible forms of pain and suffering are not as present in our day-to-day experiences as they once were. With the ubiquity of painkilling substances, we numb ourselves at the first hint of discomfort. With the increase in material wealth, we surround ourselves with more comfort and options than ever. Let's face it: we're able to protect ourselves, physically, in ways unprecedented in history. Whether it's during and after routine surgery, on our deathbed, while enduring an illness, or when undergoing a stressful event, we simply don't have to *feel* pain (physically) as much as prior generations did. We can just pop a pill.

Interestingly, even as physical pain has dissipated from daily life, psychological pain seems to have grown.[4] In the past two decades major depression has especially been on the rise among young people.[5] We have pills for these problems, too, along with a thousand techniques for ignoring, escaping, avoiding, and denying emotional pain. For example, more than one-third of young adults ages eighteen to twenty-five and nearly one-quarter of adults twenty-six and older reported being binge alcohol users—a frequent escape from and perpetuator of depression and anxiety—in the month prior to a major national survey in 2016.[6]

Peddlers of the prosperity gospel tap into the appetite for a more enjoyable, pain-free life. The result: adversity has become an outrage to many modern Christians. We not only avoid pain, but we simply do not expect it, and we feel indignant when we *can't* escape it. We may then pray (unfortunately, often as our last resort rather than our first), hoping for a quick fix. If and when God does not provide the remedy, we shake our fists and wonder why he's let us down.

While this description does not fit every Christian, it's more common than it should be, and we're all guilty of this demanding, self-focused attitude at times, to some degree. As a result, many of us are in danger of grave disillusionment and discouragement, if not a renunciation of our faith altogether, as the prospect of real persecution grows and looms on the horizon. Will we be ready for it? I have a real concern that many believers aren't ready and that our perspective is all wrong, which is one reason for this book.

EXPECTING TO SUFFER

In countries where persecution is common, Christians aren't surprised or shocked when suffering comes their way. Many, in fact, are surprised if it doesn't come. They understand suffering to be a natural consequence of the fallen human condition and, in cases of persecution, of being a Christian. They know Jesus' words and realize none of us is exempt from them:

> Remember what I told you: "A servant is not greater than his master." If they persecuted me, they will persecute you also. (John 15:20)

In the world you will have trouble. But take heart; I have overcome the world. (John 16:33)

Similar warnings pervade the Gospels, speaking to the inevitability of persecution and hatred Jesus' followers will experience on account of him. Jesus pointed to the track record of the past, indicating that such suffering on his account is not a sign of a curse but of blessing:

Blessed are you when people insult you, persecute you and falsely say all kinds of evil against you because of me. Rejoice and be glad, because great is your reward in heaven, for in the same way they persecuted the prophets who were before you. (Matthew 5:11-12)

Later, he warned his disciples that this pattern would continue and even intensify:

You will be handed over to be persecuted and put to death, and you will be hated by all nations because of me. (Matthew 24:9)

His followers' response, today as it was then, is to be one of prayer and rejoicing that we're counted worthy of suffering for his sake (Matthew 5:44).

The martyrs (and their families) killed in Libya in 2015 understood this. Many Christians suffering today all across the globe get this. But many of us who grew up in cushier environments have a harder time with it. Even if we understand it on a mental level, we don't accept it at the level of our hearts and wills. We've come to associate, perhaps unconsciously, health, wealth, and happiness with divine blessing, and we view pain and suffering not only as something disagreeable and to be avoided at all costs, but as something wholly negative, a sign that we're *not* blessed, that maybe we're even doing something wrong to "deserve" our circumstances. If we're serious about what the Bible says, though, we'll see that Scripture clearly indicates we should expect suffering and persecution; Jesus himself told us to "take heart" in the midst of it (John 16:33).

Now, we shouldn't go to the other extreme and actually seek out pain and suffering. Actively inviting suffering is not the same as anticipating and viewing it as a potentially redemptive force in our lives. We can expect to suffer and be willing to endure it without actually enjoying the process.

In addition, Peter is clear (as is the rest of Scripture) that we should never expect to be exempt from consequences that come from sin; this type of suffering is shooting ourselves in the foot. Even from this type of pain, we can learn and grow, though standing up under it isn't admirable in the same way that it is to stand up under undeserved pain that we didn't bring on ourselves.

TYPES OF SUFFERING

I want to say a brief word about types of suffering and persecution. Libraries are devoted to various forms of suffering and those who have endured it. Both Peter's letter and this book address all forms of suffering. In the West, when we hear about suffering for the name of Christ, we often think of tortures, beatings, and even hangings or crucifixion like those the early apostles (and others throughout history) endured. We think of countries where external authorities and laws try to restrict how and where Christians worship and practice their faith, with the threat of physical punishment for those who don't comply. This is often called "hard persecution" (or "bloody persecution").

There's another form of persecution, called "soft persecution," that is more commonly experienced in the West. This type involves mockery and ridicule, social and professional pressure, and marginalization in daily life. This kind of persecution hurts us, but it's not painful in the same way that being imprisoned or lashed on our backs for our beliefs is. But here's the thing: soft persecution may seem easier and, well, *softer*; however, history tells us it is often a forerunner to hard persecution. Moreover, the small compromises during soft persecution make it less likely we'll stand firm when the big tests of faith hit. Those who are faithful in little will be faithful in much. Thus, we shouldn't downplay soft persecution as though it's less important.

Dietrich Bonhoeffer, a pastor in Germany under Adolf Hitler, wrestled with where and when to draw the line. It's easy to forget that the true colors of Nazi Germany weren't initially obvious. Little by little the government broke new ground. The clues were there, but few saw the outcome they were leading to. It was easy for church leaders to rationalize small concessions. An exception was Bonhoeffer, who saw the danger before most. He eventually paid the ultimate price for his resistance, but it all started with a willingness to resist before things got bad. Some have compared his situation, and the line he had to draw in the sand, to the current environment in the United States in which Christians are being asked not only to tolerate but also to support and even promote activities and policies that run blatantly counter to Scripture, from abortion to infanticide to homosexual behavior.[7] Russell Shaw, a Catholic journalist writing in 2015, summarized, "The persecution . . . isn't—thank God—bloody persecution like the persecution of Christians in many countries. But it's real persecution and it's likely to get worse." He divides this "soft persecution" into two prongs, one of the state "pressuring individual religious believers to cooperate with public policies inimical to faith" and the other "targeted at religious groups and institutions to adapt their programs to the promotion of values hostile to the sponsors' moral convictions."[8]

While we often think in these big-picture terms about persecution in the United States (as a phenomenon playing out in the public square), persecution can also occur on an individual basis, for example, due to pressures within a family, workplace, school, or circle of friends. A father subtly and repeatedly pokes fun at his son for committing his life to Jesus, saying religion is only for "weak people." A young professional is mocked by her colleagues for her faith and church attendance. An atheist teacher publicly humiliates a Christian in the classroom who speaks up about belief in the biblical account of creation. Or a student is harassed on a college campus for taking a stand for her Christian beliefs.[9] Jenny and I both have firsthand knowledge of each of these scenarios (and others like them) that have played out in various locales inside as well as outside the United States; you likely know of similar scenarios yourself.

The lesson is clear: staying vigilant for signs of coming and intensifying persecution is a major component of preparation for suffering.

READYING A RESPONSE

Our response to suffering is far more important than the nature of our suffering in determining its effect on us and on those around us. The same event or malady can afflict two people, and whereas one grows bitter and angry, the other opens up to how God wants to use that adversity to bring growth and glory. Persecution in one believer's life may result in compromise, while another believer facing the same threat stands firm and even grows in character. What is the distinction in these situations? Why does one believer hold up while another folds up?

Though not the full answer, one reason is preparation. Peter wrote that we should always be "prepared to make a defense to anyone who asks [us] for a reason for the hope that is in [us]" (1 Peter 3:15 ESV). Paul made a similar admonition in 2 Timothy, urging alertness and readiness in view of coming persecution (2 Timothy 3:10–4:5). When we cultivate an eternal perspective that anticipates suffering before it arrives on our doorstep, we tend to respond better than when adversity takes us by surprise. We will still need the all-sufficient grace and strength of God at the moment, but like a ship that has readied its sails before the storm hits, we can position ourselves in advance so that we're braced and prepared rather than unsteady and vulnerable to being capsized.

We see this type of preparation in the story of Lysa TerKeurst, author, speaker, and president of Proverbs 31 Ministries. In January 2016, TerKeurst fasted for twenty-eight days. During the last seven days of her fast, she felt specially led to pray for her marriage. She also sensed God impressing on her the need to trust his timing and to love her husband in the days ahead (though she didn't know why at the time). Less than three weeks later, the bombshell of her husband's infidelity was dropped on her. She says if she hadn't prepared for that moment, she likely would have reacted more in the flesh than in the Spirit. Resisting the temptation to lash out with angry words, she looked at her husband and simply said, "This isn't who you are." The response disarmed him.

We don't necessarily need to fast to prepare to suffer; however, as TerKeurst reflected in the light of her own experience, it *is* important for all believers to cultivate an ongoing relationship with the Lord, spending daily time with him and incorporating disciplines into our life. Only he knows exactly what's coming in the future *and* how to prepare us for it. TerKeurst's relationship with God anchored her at a time of deep pain, helping her to combat temptations toward disappointment and discouragement.[10]

Esther Ahn Kim also understood the need to prepare for suffering ahead of time. Her adversity came in a completely different context, and her preparation was much more intentional in focus (as opposed to being primarily a result of her normal rhythm of spending time with God). Imprisoned during World War II because of her refusal to bow to the Japanese shrines in her native Korea, Kim went to extreme lengths to prepare for difficulties in her life. Sensing her coming arrest, she fasted, prayed, and—knowing she might not have access to a Bible in jail—memorized loads of Scripture. In one incident during her imprisonment, she tells how God brought his Word to mind to strengthen her when she needed it most.

"Go to sleep!" a female jailer who had just come on duty ordered huskily. At the same time a distant sound of a trumpet was heard. The sound seemed to declare something very grave. Just then a soft voice came to me, as if whispering that the heavy iron gate of the prison was shut forever.

"O Lord," I prayed, "lend me Thy hand."

The extended, faraway sound of the trumpet sounded as if Satan were laughing and glaring proudly at me. I felt as though my chest had been pressed with a heavy stone, and my hands and legs were bound tightly.

I began to recite Bible verses, one after another. Gradually I regained calmness and strength. I found myself becoming light and full of Spirit, as if I had found light in the darkness. I kept reciting Scripture until I came to the book of Isaiah. "Fear thou not, for I am with thee; be not dismayed, for I am thy God; I will strengthen thee; yea, I will help thee; yea, I will uphold thee with the right hand of my righteousness. Behold, all they that were incensed against thee shall be put to shame and confounded" (Isaiah 41:10-11).

I felt as if a trumpet had been sounding forth loudly and strongly from my mouth and as though the sounds had been ringing in every corner of the prison. Because of this trumpet of triumph, the other trumpet ordering us to sleep seemed to be fleeing farther and farther in search of a place to hide itself.[11]

In a short biography of Kim's life, Noël Piper speaks to the important role memorizing Scripture played in Kim's life in enabling her to fight fear and stay true to Christ:

We mustn't overlook the amazing weapon she wielded in this battle for faith, the amount of Scripture she obviously already had memorized. She didn't need the time or resources to hunt up a concordance or Bible or find an appropriate word from God. The Word was on the tip of her tongue exactly when she needed to preach to herself and when she needed to hear God speaking.[12]

Indeed, Scripture played a huge role in TerKeurst's life as well, as it has in the lives of so many other Christians persevering under trial.

NOT FEARING

Piper, in her profile of Kim, notes the frequent fluctuation in Kim's state of mind amid her persecution and time in jail. The pattern may be familiar to you, too, even if your suffering hasn't been as severe in form: "We are afraid. We pray. God gives us confidence. But we don't stay confident. We fall again into fear. And again he rescues us, giving us courage to carry through with the fearful thing that awaits us."[13]

The fear that suffering invokes, in fact, can sometimes feel worse than the suffering itself. Fear as a purely chemical reaction to the threat of harm is not necessarily wrong. It's our natural, most immediate response to something that we think is about to hurt us. (Without fear, we'll stand still rather than run when legitimate danger comes our way.) However, fear quickly becomes sinful when it lingers. At root, it signals a lack of trust in God.

The antidote to fear is a mindset of confidence in God and his promises. This mindset is one that leads us to look ahead with faith, not "anxiously about us," as Isaiah put it in the verse Kim called to mind:

> Do not fear, for I am with you;
> *Do not anxiously look about you*, for I am your God.
> I will strengthen you, surely I will help you,
> Surely I will uphold you with My righteous right hand.
> (Isaiah 41:10 NASB, emphasis added)

Two chapters later, Isaiah reiterated this same message:

> Do not fear, for I have redeemed you;
>   I have summoned you by name; you are mine.
> When you pass through the waters,
>   I will be with you;
> and when you pass through the rivers,
>   they will not sweep over you.
> When you walk through the fire,
>   you will not be burned;
>   the flames will not set you ablaze. (Isaiah 43:1-2)

God understands how easily the *what ifs* start to overwhelm us. Through Isaiah he reinforces a message that appears throughout the Bible: *do not be afraid!* We need not fear. Our future is secure; the end of the story is certain. The crucible of adversity may be hot, but we need not doubt its final outcome. Whether we're delivered in this life or not until the next, we *will be delivered*. This is a truth we have to cling to in suffering.

Advance preparation is important because without it fear will overtake us at the moment. The fight-or-flight response will activate, and we'll react out of emotion rather than respond out of conviction. No one modeled this better than three men of Israel whose story is told in the book of Daniel. Incidentally, it's the story that came to Esther Ahn Kim's mind and gave her courage at a crucial moment in her own persecution.

THE FAITHFUL THREE

Most of us who grew up in church know the story of Shadrach, Meshach, and Abednego. These three refused to bow to the gods of King Nebuchadnezzar of Babylon. When the king got wind of their rebellion, he summoned the trio and gave them one more chance. If they still didn't bow, he said, they would be thrown into a blazing furnace. And then, one can almost picture the king's smug sneer as he asks, "Then what god will be able to rescue you from my hand?" (Daniel 3:15). The faithful threesome stood firm, declaring,

King Nebuchadnezzar, we do not need to defend ourselves before you in this matter. If we are thrown into the blazing furnace, the God we serve is able to deliver us from it, and he will deliver us from Your Majesty's hand. But even if he does not, we want you to know, Your Majesty, that we will not serve your gods or worship the image of gold you have set up. (vv. 16-18)

An infuriated Nebuchadnezzar made good on his promise, throwing the three men into the fire, tied together fully clothed, at a temperature seven times hotter than usual. Then the king witnessed a scene he didn't anticipate.

King Nebuchadnezzar, astounded, jumped to his feet and asked his officials, "Weren't there three men that we tied up and threw into the fire?" (v. 24). When they nodded in affirmation, the king replied, "Look! I see four men loosed and walking about in the midst of the fire without harm" (v. 25 NASB). One can almost picture it: four men walking freely, enjoying a time of lovely fellowship in the fire! The ropes that bound the three men had come off. We later learn that the men and their clothes came out unsinged—without even the *smell* of fire on them (v. 27).

The fourth man in the fire was likely a preincarnate theophany (a manifestation of Jesus before the incarnation). The second person of the Trinity, "like a son of the gods" (v. 25), was making Isaiah 43:2 come true in a literal way for these exiles in Babylon. Notice, God allowed the flames. He didn't take away the fire, and he didn't zap King Nebuchadnezzar on the spot, though he could have. Instead, the God-man showed up in the furnace. The flames did not set them ablaze; instead, their suffering was replaced with glory.

Here's my point: Those three men did not stand firm against idolatry and resist the temptation to compromise for the sake of their own safety without *preparing* for that moment in advance. Their decision didn't come out of the blue. Their answer to the king was born out of a prior understanding of what *could* and very likely *would* happen to them under a pagan king. Like Bonhoeffer in Nazi Germany, they had made a prior commitment to stand firm in their convictions. They knew where they'd draw the line, and they were ready for this test of their faith. They weren't surprised or taken aback by it, just as Peter advises his readers not to be: "Dear friends, do not be surprised at the fiery ordeal that has come on you to test you, as though something strange were happening to you" (1 Peter 4:12).

ARMING YOURSELF WITH CHRIST'S ATTITUDE

None of us knows the exact form or timing of our adversities. Will we be called to testify to our faith before a king or ruler, as Kim bravely did in 1939 (before the Japanese Imperial Diet)? Will we be thrown in jail for our beliefs? Will we be mocked or ignored by family and friends? Will we endure unexplained suffering, such as a chronic disease, the sudden death of a loved one, or an unfulfilled longing?

God in his perfect wisdom allows a different combination of difficulties in each of our lives, and they're never too many or too few. He knows just how hot to heat the furnace of affliction. Despite the unexpected nature of suffering, we can and should anticipate adversity.

Besides committing ahead of time to stand firm and not give way to fear, how else do we prepare for the uncertain? Peter's epistle suggests several more ways. One is to "arm ourselves" with the same attitude toward suffering that Christ had (1 Peter 4:1). We'll discuss Christ's attitude in much greater detail in chapter six, but I will say a few words about it here.

First, a Christlike attitude toward adversity is not developed by accident, and it's not our natural instinct. As we saw in Kim's life, a major way we develop this attitude is by knowing the Word of God and how to apply it. Another key aspect of Christ's attitude toward suffering was his humility—and Peter says we're to "clothe ourselves" with this posture (1 Peter 5:5). The need for humility about our own ability to withstand tests of faith was a lesson Peter learned on the worst day of his life. Hours before he denied the Lord three times, Peter had confidently asserted that he would "never disown" the Lord (Matthew 26:35). That confidence was soon shaken when he denied Jesus three times. Humility in suffering means, in part, acknowledging that we never know exactly which trials will come to us *and never overestimating our own ability to stand firm* during these tests. Rather than being cocky, we should put our confidence and faith squarely in Christ, relying on *his* grace and strength to hold us up.

Just as none of us knows the types of suffering we'll face, none of us knows for certain *how we will respond* to a given type of suffering until the moment arrives. An example from church history offers keen insight in this regard. Under the Roman Empire, in North Africa in the fourth century a group of professing Christians who came to be known as *traditores* failed to stand up under threat of martyrdom, choosing instead to avoid suffering and accede to the governor's demands. Specifically, they agreed to hand over copies of Scripture to appear to be repudiating their faith, in exchange for leniency by the local officials. Some also betrayed fellow Christians, reporting them to the government.

Later, a group called the Donatists refused to allow these *traditores* back into the life of the church, especially its leadership, due to their failure to stand strong under persecution. Much more could be said on this situation and on the identity of each group, but in short, the Donatists considered themselves to be the "true" or "pure" church, in contrast to what they viewed to be the "corrupted church." The Donatists are regarded as heretical due to their departure from the message of grace and of the full definition of sin Jesus gave (relating to the heart and not just external conformity to the law), leading to an unbiblical insistence that priests be pure and blameless (that is, already fully sanctified) in order to take part in the corporate gathering of the body of Christ and the administration of the sacraments (such as baptism).

The Donatists' self-righteous attitude is instructive to us today because any one of us could fail a test of faith and lapse under persecution. God's grace alone sustains us, and we should be careful not to fall into the temptation to harshly and smugly judge those in difficult circumstances. If we see fellow believers struggling in the midst of suffering—maybe they're mired in relationship problems such as a messy divorce or they've become withdrawn and aloof since they lost their job—Scripture indicates that our instinct should be to carry that person's burdens along with them; see how you can ease the load (Galatians 6:2). If the person is falling into a sinful attitude or behavior pattern, seek to put yourself in that person's shoes and be honest with yourself as to how your own reaction might be in a similar situation; if rebuke is appropriate, "restore that person *gently*" while mindful of your own weakness (Galatians 6:1, emphasis added).

Preparation for suffering is important, but it's not foolproof; a humble estimation of oneself and of one's own spiritual mettle will ensure we don't underestimate the very real pull of our sinful nature and of the enemy of our souls. "Therefore let him who thinks he stands take heed that he does not fall," as Paul admonishes (1 Corinthians 10:12 NASB). Realization of our need to depend on God and not on ourselves is a major way God uses our suffering to shape our character to be more like his Son's.

STAYING ALERT

Remaining alert is another way we prepare for suffering. Peter explicitly advises alertness three times in his first epistle:

Therefore, with minds that are alert and fully sober . . . (1 Peter 1:13)

Therefore be alert and of sober mind so that you may pray. (1 Peter 4:7)

Be of sober spirit, be on the alert. Your adversary, the devil, prowls around like a roaring lion, seeking someone to devour. (1 Peter 5:8 NASB)

It's hard to imagine Peter could write these words without remembering one of the most painful periods of his own life when he failed to stay alert. The night of Jesus' betrayal by Judas—the night when Peter also denied the Lord three times—Peter was among the three disciples Jesus beckoned to come closest to him as he prayed in the Garden of Gethsemane. There, Jesus fought the very real temptation to take the easier, less painful path and not "drink the cup" of suffering. As he prayed and surrendered his will to the Father, a parallel plot was taking place: Peter, James, and John were nearby, repeatedly falling asleep at a moment when Jesus most needed their prayer support.

> [Jesus] said to them, "My soul is overwhelmed with sorrow to the point of death. Stay here and keep watch with me."
>
> Going a little farther, he fell with his face to the ground and prayed, "My Father, if it is possible, may this cup be taken from me. Yet not as I will, but as you will."
>
> Then he returned to his disciples and found them sleeping. "Couldn't you men keep watch with me for one hour?" he asked Peter. "Watch and pray so that you will not fall into temptation. The spirit is willing, but the flesh is weak." (Matthew 26:38-41)

This scene repeated itself again—and again! Still, the disciples couldn't stay alert or awake. After the third time, Judas arrived, and Jesus was betrayed "into the hands of sinners" (Matthew 26:45). Not long after the betrayal, every one of the disciples deserted Jesus, abandoning him in his final hours before going to the cross. If anyone understood the danger of a lack of alertness and of falling asleep (literally or figuratively) at the most critical hour, it was Peter.

BUILDING ON A SOLID FOUNDATION

Peter, at the end of his letter, urges readers to "stand fast" in the "true grace of God" (1 Peter 5:12). His admonition is a reminder of the single most important way that we can prepare for suffering: building our lives on that which is solid. Jesus urged the same:

> Everyone who hears these words of mine and puts them into practice is like a wise man who built his house on the rock. The rain came down, the streams rose, and the winds blew and beat against that house; yet it did not fall, because it had its foundation on the rock. But everyone who hears these words of mine and does not put them into practice is like a foolish man who built his house on sand. The rain came down, the streams rose, and the winds blew and beat against that house, and it fell with a great crash. (Matthew 7:24-27)

How do we build our house on rock instead of sand? Most fundamentally, we get to know the unchanging character of God. We study his mercy and grace, his love and forgiveness, his justice and holiness. We ponder his works. The more we know of his character, the less we'll be tempted to think he's carrying out his plans for the world at our expense, and the more we'll see his absolute goodness in his intentions toward us.[14] Of course, as we saw in Esther Kim's life, the Bible is one of the best places to gain this foundation. In addition, getting the perspective of mature believers (whether alive and in person or from books they've written) can be helpful. In any study and reading, we need a heart attitude of prayer and dependence on God—asking him, through his Spirit, to help us not only know more *about* him but to know and rely more on him. The goal isn't knowledge for knowledge's sake but knowledge that breeds trust.

The hymn "The Solid Rock" offers a clear picture of this unchanging character of God amid an ever-changing world:

When darkness veils His lovely face,

I rest on His unchanging grace;

In every high and stormy gale,

My anchor holds within the veil.

On Christ, the solid Rock, I stand;

All other ground is sinking sand.[15]

Standing fast or firm on the foundation of God and his character doesn't mean we always *feel* strong in the trial. We may at times look quizzically toward heaven and wonder, *What are you doing, Lord?* We may feel weak and wobbly like Jerry Sittser did after his catastrophic loss: "I was overwhelmed with depression. The foundation of my life was close to caving in."[16] But by God's grace, Sittser didn't cave. The frame above ground may have almost completely eroded, but the foundation beneath remained rock solid, because it was not built on the sand of his feelings and circumstances.

If you and I, like Sittser, build our foundation on the Rock of our salvation, we too will come out on the other side, changed and weathered, but still firmly attached to Christ and his love.

PREPARATION ON THE CHURCH LEVEL

Not only individuals but also churches (local bodies of believers) need to prepare for suffering.

A report by Advancing Native Missions on the new wave of persecution sweeping across China in 2018 tells of several categories of responses by churches in that country. The pattern is instructive for us. The churches that are responding well to the persecution are distinguished by (1) excitement that God is working amid and sometimes even because of persecution, and (2) their focus over the past few years to "build life rather than build buildings." Although these churches were not "specifically preparing for persecution," the report suggests these churches kept "the main thing the main thing" by focusing on the biblical calling to love God and each other—not simply to create programs or accumulate possessions (even though those aren't bad in and of themselves).

Having property to build a church structure on and meet regularly in is a nice amenity that we often take for granted in the West, but it's not by any means necessary, and sometimes it can even be a hindrance to church life. Because some churches in China have been shut down due to government restrictions, there's been an Acts-like scattering of believers and pastors, who now meet in smaller groups, often in homes. One familiar with the situation says the churches who have been focused on "building people rather than just expanding programs" are now seeing leaders emerge and the body of Christ come to life: "When we just had the big Sunday meetings, we only had 20 leaders functioning each week. Now that we have been officially closed down, we have completely shifted to meetings in homes and now we have more than 200 leaders functioning each week. It is great! We don't want to go back to the old way!"[17]

Of course, not all local congregations will face the same kind of persecution as those in China. Even churches in China widely differ in their experiences from province to province. Our trials on a corporate level are just as varied as those on the individual level. Anchoring our churches in the one sure foundation, staying tethered to God's Word, and keeping alert and humble are all vital for us to stand firm and to serve as effective corporate witnesses no matter what troubles come to our communities.

◈   ◈   ◈

The great nineteenth-century English preacher Charles Spurgeon was plagued by suffering, especially depression and anxiety, as well as direct persecution and criticism of his ministry throughout his life. Words he spoke following a hurricane that struck London in 1878 comforted the nation. They encompass our need as individuals and as local bodies of believers to be simultaneously confident in Christ and humble in our estimation of ourselves because we never know what the future holds: "Do not be happy, dear friend, till you are moored to the Rock of Ages."[18]

In large part, our mooring occurs when we keep our eyes fixed on Jesus, the author and perfecter of our faith who for "the joy set before him . . . endured the cross, scorning its shame, and sat down at the right hand of the throne of God" (Hebrews 12:2). As we consider the example of Christ in chapter six, may his response to sinful people and earthly difficulties encourage you to prepare for and persevere in your own troubles.

IMITATING CHRIST

To this you were called, because Christ suffered for you,
leaving you an example, that you should follow in his steps.

1 PETER 2:21

THE WORD *DISCIPLE* TODAY doesn't have the same rich context of meaning it had in the Judaic tradition of Jesus' day. Today, we think more in terms of interns or trainees, though the scope of those terms is typically narrower, focused on preparation for a paid profession. But discipleship in Jesus' time was life-encompassing. Disciples would follow and imitate their teacher or rabbi, doing exactly as the teacher did. It was a relationship of learning by both listening and watching—with the teacher teaching and modeling what he taught. Disciples would spend time with the teacher, who would invite the disciples into his daily routines. As the disciples observed the teacher, they would mimic his moves, even his attitudes.

Dallas Willard spoke of this master-disciple relationship in terms of the three stages of apprenticeship: apprentice, journeyman, and master. Apprentices learned the skills and secrets of their trade, whether it was silversmithing or wheel-making, which were then passed down through the generations in a way that we've largely lost in today's world.[1] (The remnants of the system remain in last names like Cartwright and Smith.)

Followers of Jesus are apprentices of the heavenly King, disciples who seek to imitate Christ in all areas of their lives—including the area of suffering. We're to observe how Jesus suffered along with the attitude he maintained, and then mimic his response with the help of his enabling grace. He's our Master Teacher in the university of life, in which suffering is a required course. He has the trade secrets to suffer well, and there are also many "journeymen" in his kingdom from whom we can learn much about suffering. And when we don't understand God's guidance and working in our lives, we're still to trust and follow him. This is part of why Jesus reminded us that a servant is not greater than his master (John 3:16; 15:20); if he suffered, then we too should expect to suffer—even if we don't always understand why.

Christ's own suffering can be characterized in three ways: sinless, silent, and substitutionary. We'll look at each of these in a moment. But first, it's important to remember we cannot be *exactly* like Jesus in any of these attributes, especially the first and third. Unlike Jesus, we are *not* sinless as long as we're on this earth. Neither are we the once-for-all sacrifice sent as a substitute for people's sins. However, we can still look to each of these attributes as aspects of his example to imitate. We can strive for righteousness even when we're suffering unjustly. We can hold our tongue when our human instinct would lead us to "revile in return" or issue in-kind threats. We can lay down our lives for others through our suffering, entrusting ourselves and our situations to him, allowing him to use our adversities to form his character in us and help others (in this way, our suffering assumes a substitutionary nature). Overall, the pattern of our response to suffering can emulate our Savior's, imperfectly but in a way that produces the fruit of righteousness.

SUFFERING SINLESSLY

"He committed no sin, and no deceit was found in his mouth" (1 Peter 2:22). In this verse Peter quotes Isaiah 53:9, written seven hundred years before Jesus was born. The verse makes an astounding statement: the sinless One suffered at the hands of sinful humanity. Let that sink in for a moment.

When you and I suffer, we always suffer as fallen humans (albeit, redeemed ones, if we're believers), and sometimes we even suffer as a direct result of sin (ours or others'). Yet, even when our suffering is innocent per se, we are still enduring the domino effects of human sinfulness, of which we're a guilty party. Christ, though, never once sinned in thought, word, or deed. But he still suffered. Not only that but his suffering kept getting worse until finally his enemies put him to death (while his closest friends fled the scene).

The fact that Christ, who was without sin, suffered should remove any doubt in our mind that we, too, as his followers, should also expect to suffer. A demanding spirit that consistently cries out, "Unfair!" or "Why me?" fails to recognize the completely undeserved suffering of the sinless Savior who was blameless in every respect his *entire* life.

Scripture tells us, in fact, that Jesus not only stood up under suffering without sinning but he was actually *perfected* by suffering: "In bringing many sons and daughters to glory, it was fitting that God, for whom and through whom everything exists, should make the pioneer of their salvation perfect through what he suffered" (Hebrews 2:10). This verse isn't saying that Jesus was imperfect and that suffering somehow made him sinless instead of sinful;

rather, as John Piper explains, Christ *learned obedience* to the Father, going from a state of "untested obedience into suffering and then through suffering into tested and proven obedience."[2] This process could be compared to a friendship or other relationship that is tested through adversity; the friendship existed before, but suffering tested its genuineness.

Jesus was a forerunner in this process that we go through as his brothers and sisters (Hebrews 12:7). When we view adverse circumstances in this way, as instruments of God used to accomplish and display his great work in us, we're apprenticing ourselves to the world's greatest Master in the arena of suffering.

When my wife, Karen, was driving along the highway many years ago and her car slammed into a truck that inexplicably had come to a dead stop in her lane, she had done nothing wrong to deserve that particular incident. She was driving along at a normal speed, but this driver's carelessness caused a dramatic shift in her life—from a normal twentysomething to someone regularly plagued with physical pain. However, when her body miraculously survived the impact of slamming into both a windshield and a steering wheel, she got more than two broken legs. That was the day Karen called out to Jesus for the first time. In the moment of the crash, she realized she was not going to heaven, and disaster turned to salvation.

The fact is that God often uses suffering, whether it's instantaneous or long and slow, to draw us to himself. Many of us wouldn't come—and keep coming—any other way.

"INNOCENT" SUFFERING VERSUS SUFFERING FOR WRONGDOING

We're called to imitate Christ by suffering *sinlessly*, not by suffering because we've shot ourselves in the foot with disobedience:

"It is better, if it is God's will, to suffer for doing good than for doing evil" (1 Peter 3:17; see also 1 Peter 2:20). Let's face it, though: often the cause of our suffering isn't clear-cut. We're not sure *why* we're undergoing a particular trial. Much adversity appears to come out of nowhere (for reasons we can't directly pinpoint) or to be caused by a complex combination of factors: an accident happens that is beyond our control, or we contract cancer or some other incurable disease. Superstitious people will try to associate sin with every instance of suffering in a person's life (whether or not the two have any logical connection), but this is simply not biblical. So what *is* biblical?

Jesus addressed this question in a couple of instances. On one occasion his disciples brought to him a man blind from birth and asked, "Rabbi, who sinned, this man or his parents, that he was born blind?" (John 9:2). Jesus rejected the two options presented to him, responding instead that "neither this man nor his parents sinned, but this happened so that the works of God might be displayed in him" (v. 3). From this account we see that the purposes of God go much deeper than human judgments and plans. It's baffling to us how he can use the weak and painful things of this world to bring glory to his name. But he does—all the time. This was the lesson of Job, who never got an answer to the *why* of his suffering; instead he received an answer of *who* was in control of it. Some reasons are only for God to know. Sometimes (in fact, often) only he gets the full script, and we follow him one line at a time.

In another place, Jesus responded to questions about seemingly random mass suffering, as we witness in natural disasters. A tower in Siloam (part of Jerusalem) had toppled and killed eighteen people (Luke 13:4). Jesus rhetorically asked, "Do you think they [who were killed] were more guilty than all the others living in

Jerusalem?" (v. 4). In other words, do natural disasters happen to people who are "worse sinners," who deserve to suffer more than others? Jesus never explained why *those* eighteen died and not *another* eighteen. He simply indicated that such events serve as warnings to those still alive not to let another day go by without getting right with God: "I tell you, no! But unless you repent, you too will all perish" (v. 5).

To be sure, some suffering *does* have a one-to-one correspondence to sin. Those who shoplift, for example, have no room to gripe when they wind up in jail. The man who cheats on his wife can't complain when his familial relationships deteriorate. If God grants a reprieve in these instances, it's only because of his mercy and grace, not because the guilty party deserves to be let off the hook. In terms of biblical examples, the people of Israel suffered as a direct consequence of their sinful disobedience. (The first thirty-nine chapters of Isaiah document the reasons for their condemnation.) While God can and often does still teach us through these situations, our suffering cannot be said to be Christlike in these cases. But so long as our suffering does not entail consequences that are clearly and logically tied to wrongdoing, we can (and should) follow in the footsteps of Jesus in our suffering.

SUFFERING SILENTLY

Jesus was not only sinless in his suffering, but he was silent. He did not lash out and defend himself even when he had every right to do so. First Peter 2:21-25 makes this point by alluding to several verses from the following passage in Isaiah:

> We all, like sheep, have gone astray,
>   each of us has turned to our own way,
> and the Lord has laid on him
>   the iniquity of us all.

He was oppressed and afflicted,

    yet he did not open his mouth;

he was led like a lamb to the slaughter,

    and as a sheep before its shearers is silent,

    so he did not open his mouth.

By oppression and judgment he was taken away.

    Yet who of his generation protested?

For he was cut off from the land of the living;

    for the transgression of my people he was punished.

He was assigned a grave with the wicked,

    and with the rich in his death,

though he had done no violence,

    nor was any deceit in his mouth. (Isaiah 53:6-9)

In keeping quiet during his suffering, Jesus was no passive victim; he actively submitted to God. He was entrusting himself to him who judges righteously: "While being reviled, He did not revile in return; while suffering, He uttered no threats, but kept entrusting *Himself* to Him who judges righteously" (1 Peter 2:23 NASB).

When we also hold back our own assessment of the situation and entrust ourselves to God in the middle of (undeserved) suffering, we imitate Christ. This doesn't mean we never make a peep, or that we become doormats. I would certainly never advocate that people hold back from reporting (especially when mandated by law) situations of abuse or violence. But we should accept that there are some circumstances we can't control or change, and God knows best whether (and how long) to allow suffering to continue. Any defense we offer should be done out of love for God and others, not out of a selfish desire for personal vindication. We can still pray that we're vindicated and that justice is served—King David *often* prayed that God would vindicate him and deliver justice to his enemies; but we ultimately leave that task to God, making sure we're ready to forgive and bless those who hurt us: "Bless those who persecute you; bless and do not curse," as Paul said (Romans 12:14).

Jesus' silence before his mockers is astonishing. The one with all knowledge and who always had the right words to say could've given a rock-solid defense on his own behalf from the cross. Don't underestimate the temptation it must've been for Jesus' humanity when people mocked and hurled insults at him: "'He saved others,' they said, 'but he can't save himself! . . . Let him come down now from the cross, and we will believe in him. He trusts in God. Let God rescue him now if he wants him, for he said, "I am the Son of God"'" (Matthew 27:42-43).

Most of us look at this scene and wonder, *How could he remain quiet?! Maybe he didn't have to come down from the cross, but couldn't he at least have explained himself just a little?* What amazing self-control it took for Jesus not to respond to their mockery! Rather than stoop to their level by replying to their foolish ridicule, he asked for the Father's forgiveness of his perpetrators, knowing they didn't understand the gravity or reality of what they were saying or doing (Luke 23:34).

LISTENING IN SUFFERING

Compare Jesus' silent suffering to the case of Job. His response is admirable at first. For two whole chapters he's largely silent despite losing everything—his possessions, his children, and his health. So far, so good. We even see him bowing in worship: "The LORD gave and the LORD has taken away. May the name of the LORD be praised" (Job 1:21). In Job 2, he maintains composure even after his wife questions him, suggesting he's crazy for continuing to hold fast to his faith: "Do you still hold fast your integrity? Curse God and die!" she says (Job 2:9 NASB). Even still, the text says Job did not

respond sinfully but said to his wife, "Shall we indeed accept good
from God, and not trouble?" (Job 2:10).

Then Job's friends enter the picture. Job's silence is broken at
that point, as he gives full vent to his distress: he "opened his
mouth and cursed the day of his birth" (Job 3:1), and "complain[ed]
in the bitterness of [his] soul" (Job 7:11).

The situation goes downhill from there as his friends seek an
explanation—and tacitly accuse Job of being an agent in the situation. "Fess up, Job," his friends effectively say at first. In the face of
ongoing, unexplained, severe suffering, these "friends"—perhaps
out of discomfort or a desire for a quick answer—suggest Job must
have done something wrong to deserve his predicament: "According
to what I have seen, those who plow iniquity and those who sow
trouble harvest it," one friend (Eliphaz) says (Job 4:8 NASB). The
friends continue in this speculative, self-righteous vein for some
time, with Job growing increasingly self-defensive in response.

Job keeps muddling through, though it's notable that he never
curses God (in fact, he makes a beautiful testimony to his still-
intact faith right in the middle of his complaints [Job 19:25-27]). But
he's impatient for a divine reply; he doesn't understand his pain,
but even worse he doesn't understand God's silence toward his
pain (Job 23:8-9). Certain he'll be vindicated before God if only he
can gain a hearing, Job declares,

> Oh that I knew where I might find Him,
> That I might come to His seat!
> I would present my case before Him
> And fill my mouth with arguments. . . .
> Surely He would pay attention to me.
> There the upright would reason with Him.
>   (Job 23:3-4, 6-7 NASB)

When Job finally gets a response from God, notice the Lord's first words to him:

> Pay attention, Job, and listen to me;
>> be silent, and I will speak. . . .
>> be silent, and I will teach you wisdom. (Job 33:31, 33)

Job needed to shut his mouth in order to hear the divine perspective. He had to stop talking and listen.

Job's previous insistence on understanding the cause or purpose behind his suffering evaporates as the Creator and Sustainer of the universe speaks:

> Listen to this, Job;
>> stop and consider God's wonders.
> Do you know how God controls the clouds
>> and makes his lightning flash?
> Do you know how the clouds hang poised,
>> those wonders of him who has perfect knowledge? . . .
>
> Have you ever given orders to the morning,
>> or shown the dawn its place? . . .
>
> Will the one who contends with the Almighty correct him?
>> Let him who accuses God answer him!
>>> (Job 37:14-16; 38:12; 40:2)

After a long monologue from God, Job's response signals the start of his humbling—he realizes he's out of court to try to understand the all-wise God of the universe. *Who am I to question God?* he effectively asks:

> I am unworthy—how can I reply to you?
>> I put my hand over my mouth.

I spoke once, but I have no answer—
> twice, but I will say no more. (Job 40:4-5)

But God isn't done yet. Job understands he spoke out of place, but he hasn't yet repented. More than fifty verses later, that repentance finally comes as a silenced Job comes to the end of himself and his accusations against God:

I know that you can do all things;
> no purpose of yours can be thwarted.
You asked, "Who is this that obscures my plans
>> without knowledge?"
> Surely I spoke of things I did not understand,
> things too wonderful for me to know. . . .
My ears had heard of you
> but now my eyes have seen you.
Therefore I despise myself
> and repent in dust and ashes. (Job 42:2-3, 5-6)

God's silencing of Job is not out of harshness but out of love. He never tells Job why he suffered, because that's not what Job really needed. Job was in greater need of trusting God than of understanding the exact reasons for the circumstances of his life. He needed to understand that some knowledge is for God alone to possess. He needed to see that as long as we're talking and coming up with our own narrative for our lives, we can't hear God's narrative.

We must face the same question in our own pains: If we keep complaining and uttering our ingratitude while we're suffering, how can we hear the voice of truth? It will be drowned out. And if Jesus himself suffered silently, how much more should we, who are not perfect in wisdom and understanding, keep quiet and listen?

Os Guinness speaks of the need to "suspend judgment" about our own lives, especially with respect to seasons of darkness when our circumstances don't make sense to us; as fallible humans with limited understanding, we simply don't know all that God is doing or how he is working.[3] We can't see how all the threads of the tapestry are being woven together because we can't see all of time in a single moment as God can. We're always missing critical facts. Instead of complaining and defending ourselves, a better response is to ask, What do you want to teach me in this, Lord? and to pray, Lord, please change me for the better in this, even if I can't see the reasons you're allowing this suffering.

The great theologian and thinker Blaise Pascal modeled this attitude well. Famous for his French prose and contributions to mathematics, Pascal's lifelong suffering (both inward and outward) is known to fewer people. The last two years, particularly the final six months, of his life were filled with intense physical suffering—a time when "he lived deeply in the Scriptures, especially in Psalm 119."[4] On the heels of years of suffering of various kinds, Pascal's renewed bouts of sickness led him to pen a long and beautiful prayer, asking God to use his suffering for good. In this prayer, we glimpse a soul purified by past suffering, expressing a Christlike desire for his "Sovereign Master" to use his ongoing adversity to conform his will more to the divine will.

> Grant me, O Lord, grace to join Your consolations to my sufferings, that I may suffer like a Christian. I pray not to be exempted from pain, for this is the recompense of saints. But I pray that I may not be abandoned to the pain of nature without the comforts of Your Spirit. . . . I pray that You will dispose of my health, my sickness, my life, and my death, as for Your glory, for my salvation, for the usefulness to Your church and Your saints, among whom I hope to be numbered. You alone know what is expedient for me. . . . Being as sick as I am now, may I glorify You in my suffering.[5]

SUFFERING AS A SUBSTITUTE

In addition to suffering sinlessly and silently, Jesus, in suffering and dying for our sins, became a substitute for us. "'He himself bore our sins' in his body on the cross, so that we might die to sins and live for righteousness; 'by his wounds you have been healed'" (1 Peter 2:24). Again, Peter is referencing Isaiah:

He was pierced for our transgressions,
    he was crushed for our iniquities;
the punishment that brought us peace was on him,
    and by his wounds we are healed. (Isaiah 53:5)

While hanging on the cross for our sins, Jesus could have called up legions of angels, any one of whom could have destroyed everything around him. Instead, he chose to drink the cup of suffering, and so it was not really the nails that held him to the cross but his love for us. He easily could have gotten down from the cross if he had wanted to do so.

Amazingly, the Son of God suffered a punishment he did not deserve, enduring not only physical suffering but also the much worse spiritual and mental anguish that came from alienation from his Father because of becoming the sin bearer for the world (Matthew 27:46; 2 Corinthians 5:21); he did this so you and I do not have to endure the same isolation from God and eternal suffering in hell. His decision to suffer in our place shows a love greater than we can comprehend. His substitutionary death on the cross was the most undeserved suffering ever experienced by a human, and his resurrection—the final triumph over death and suffering—is the greatest picture of the redemptive purpose of adversity.

As believers, suffering can be substitutionary as well by giving us a ministry to others. As we suffer, God uses our own suffering to allow us to comfort and assist others who are suffering. Paul puts it this way:

> Blessed be the God and Father of our Lord Jesus Christ, the Father of mercies and God of all comfort, who comforts us in all our affliction so that we will be able to comfort those who are in any affliction with the comfort with which we ourselves are comforted by God. For just as the sufferings of Christ are ours in abundance, so also our comfort is abundant through Christ. But if we are afflicted, it is for your comfort and salvation; or if we are comforted, it is for your comfort, which is effective in the patient enduring of the same sufferings which we also suffer; and our hope for you is firmly grounded, knowing that as you are sharers of our sufferings, so also you are sharers of our comfort. (2 Corinthians 1:3-7 NASB)

God not only uses the comfort we ourselves have received from Christ in our suffering in order to provide comfort to others, but he can even use it for the salvation of others (2 Corinthians 1:6). In other words, our suffering can contribute to others coming to and growing in Christ. As George Eliot summarized the impact of the main character in the novel *Middlemarch*, our effect on others can be "incalculably diffusive," though our faithfulness may have been largely hidden to the vast majority of people, and we may one day "rest in unvisited tombs."[6]

IMITATING CHRIST TODAY

Believers through history have imitated Christ in their suffering in various ways, extending Christ's grace and forgiveness to their persecutors and enemies. One such believer was Louie Zamperini, whose story is told in Laura Hillenbrand's bestselling book *Unbroken* (as well as in two films based on the book).

Zamperini miraculously survived two plane crashes, forty-seven days on a raft in the middle of the ocean, and two years in a brutal Japanese POW camp during World War II. During his time on the raft, he promised to seek and serve God if God allowed him to survive. After returning to his country, though, he—like many war veterans—spiraled into a battle with mental illness (depression) as well as addiction to alcohol. This struggle reached fever pitch before God grabbed his attention during a Billy Graham crusade in 1949. For the first time, Zamperini recognized the depth of his hatred toward his primary torturer, Mutsuhiro "the Bird" Watanabe.

Zamperini's conversion softened his heart and led him to realize the need to forgive his archenemy. He returned to Japan not only to find Watanabe and extend forgiveness but also to share the gospel with the very people who once imprisoned and tortured him and his comrades. Many of these Japanese soldiers placed their faith in Christ as a result.

A more recent example of a Christlike response to suffering is former American gymnast Rachael Denhollander. Starting at age fifteen, Denhollander was sexually abused at the hands of Larry Nassar, a former physician for Michigan State University and the USA Gymnastics team. She was not alone; hundreds of other young women and girls also suffered from his unspeakable cruelty over many years. A devoted follower of Christ and the first to speak out against her abuser, Denhollander did so at great risk to her own reputation and privacy. The provost at the school where Nassar then worked even mocked her, and her church family and closest friends at the time distanced themselves from her. Denhollander spoke out not so much for her own sake but for the sake of others who had been abused and who could be abused if she remained silent. Her words in court, directed toward Nassar, captured the attention of a nation—and spoke the gospel loud and clear.

> Larry . . . you chose to pursue your wicked desires, no matter what it cost others. The opposite of what you have done, therefore, is choosing to love sacrificially, no matter what it costs me. . . . If you have read the Bible you carry, you know that the definition of sacrificial love portrayed in it, is of God Himself loving so sacrificially that He gave up everything to pay the penalty for sin He did not commit. By His grace, I too, choose to love, no matter what it costs. . . . The Bible you carry speaks of a final judgment where all of God's wrath, in all its eternal terror, is poured out on men like you. Should you ever reach the point of truly facing what you have done, the weight of guilt in the face of the horrific evil you committed, will be crushing. And that is what makes the Gospel of Christ so sweet. Because it gives hope and grace where none should be found. And I pray you experience the soul-crushing weight of guilt someday, so that it can be followed by true repentance and forgiveness from God.[7]

Following in the footsteps of her Lord, Denhollander chose to extend both forgiveness and truth to her abuser. She spoke out not from some desire for personal vengeance but out of the love of Christ. And she stood ready to forgive, although her enemy did not yet comprehend the depth of his wickedness. She followed Jesus' pattern of suffering in that she was motivated to report her story to the police largely by her desire to save others from experiencing the same abuse. Her substitutionary act reflects her understanding of the call to lay down her life for others (John 15:13) and to do what's right no matter the cost to her.

Although Denhollander was not sexually abused because of being a Christian, her story illustrates a Christlike response to innocent, undeserved suffering. It, and the story of Zamperini, are just two of the great many that could be told.

There's another important way we imitate Christ in our suffering—it's a response that encompasses the three responses discussed in this chapter (sinlessly, silently, and as a substitute): by submitting to God's authority over our lives. This response is so important that we will devote chapter seven to it.

SUBMITTING TO GOD

Humble yourselves, therefore, under God's mighty hand,
that he may lift you up in due time.

1 PETER 5:6

A YOUNG CHRISTIAN NAMED LING (a pseudonym) began distributing Bibles in China, against government law, while Chairman Mao was still in power.[1] Somehow she eluded the authorities until the mid-1990s, when officials tracking her evangelistic efforts finally found her and threw her into prison. After being tortured and questioned, she was released months later only to be recaptured and sentenced to three years in a "labor reformation camp."[2] At the camp, Ling and all the other prisoners were under orders not to talk about their faith or God or even to pray. If they did, they risked severe punishment.

Although Ling displayed exemplary behavior in every other respect at the camp, she was disobedient to the camp authorities in one area: practicing her faith. She would not keep quiet about the message of Jesus, and at great risk to herself she shared the gospel with fellow prisoners. One day, Ling also shared the gospel with a prison official. Here's an abbreviated version of the exchange recorded in a Voice of the Martyrs publication:

Ling's supervisor, Ms. Tao, stopped her in the factory hallway. "Ling, I saw your file," she said. "I know about your activities and the fact that you were an influential Christian leader. And now that you've been here for eleven months, I've also seen your work and your behavior with the other prisoners, especially those coarse and perpetually angry ones who so easily cause trouble. You seem to have great affection for these prisoners, yet you don't act like them. Why?"

Ling felt a nervous excitement as she told her boss, "I don't act like them because I'm a Christian, and I've surrendered my whole life to Jesus Christ. He's the reason I live. He's the reason I can love all these unlovely people."

Ling held her breath, waiting for Ms. Tao's reaction. The mere mention of religion could add more time to her sentence or get her locked in "the box," a solitary confinement cell. She never knew if any inquirer might be trying to trap her. But to Ling's surprise, her boss blurted out, "Can a person like me believe in Jesus?"

"Of course!" Ling replied. "But aren't you afraid of losing your position? Aren't you afraid the government will drive you out of the army?"

"Aren't *you* afraid I might punish you by adding time to your sentence for talking such nonsense?" Ms. Tao shot back . . .

Ms. Tao was interested, but she wasn't easily convinced, and they continued their clandestine conversations over many months.[3]

One day, Ms. Tao indicated that *if* she did believe, she would have to do so secretly because of her job. Ling never knew whether her boss came to Christ, but she continued to pray for her. Ling calls her time in prison and the labor camp a "school of suffering" through which she learned "complete dependence on God."[4]

A continent away an American teenager was a brand-new Christian around the time Ling was slaving away in a Chinese labor camp. The daughter of a loving Christian couple, her vision for her future was to finish college, get married, and raise a family of her own. She could imagine no future more fulfilling.

Fast forward more than two decades, and this young woman—the coauthor of this book—was indeed married, but at age thirty-seven, she still had no children. Jenny's vision of a full home had evaporated. A canopy of disappointment and despair fell over her life as the silent grieving process over infertility took its toll. Even as the reality of barrenness sank in on the outside, the terrain of her heart was anything but barren. A fierce, silent battle raged as she grappled with the lack of a child—something God himself calls a blessing and a reward (Psalm 127:3, 5). She delved deep in Scripture and other books, reading and meditating as much as she could on the absolute goodness, love, and wisdom of the Lord.

As time went on, Jenny sensed the Father asking her, *Do you trust me—I mean really trust me? Do you believe I'm good and that I know what's best for you, even better than you know yourself?* Then came the kicker, *Will you submit this whole situation to me, surrendering to my plans and purposes instead of insisting on your own vision for your life, even if that means you never become a mother?*

Slowly, Jenny's decision from her early twenties to "give [her] life to the Potter's hand" was being tested and proven, but not without a daily struggle of her will, layered with grief, as she sought to truly surrender control and loosen her grip on her own life.[5]

SUBMITTING TO GOD'S AUTHORITY

These two sisters in Christ, Jenny and Ling, may seem worlds apart in terms of their experiences. But there's an important commonality in their stories: the realization that God has the ultimate authority over our lives, and he, not we (nor other people), has the best vision for our lives—as well as the power to bring that vision about. In other words, each of these women learned submission through suffering.

The close connection between suffering and submission explains why submission takes a close second place to suffering as a major theme of 1 Peter. Indeed, adversity is often the means by which God teaches us to recognize his authority over our lives. Though they're not the *only* way he teaches us, difficulties are a primary means by which he leads us to acknowledge a fact we might otherwise fail to grasp: God is God, and we are not (a great one-sentence summary of the entire Bible).

Our suffering may be for the sake of Christ like Ling's or for some unexplained reason like Jenny's, but whatever the cause, we're all, at some point, thrust headlong into the crucible—faced with this critical question: Will we submit to our Father's will (as Jesus did) or insist on our own way? Will we trust him no matter the outcome or shrink back and try to maintain a grasp on our own lives?

First Peter mentions submission explicitly in five verses, though many more verses in the epistle are infused with the concept, such as 1 Peter 5:6: "Humble yourselves, therefore, under God's mighty hand, that he may lift you up in due time." Even amid undeserved suffering, we're to humble ourselves under the One who is not only Savior but also Lord, trusting that he has a better vision for our lives than we have for ourselves. We're to pursue godly lives, holiness, and service to others "for the Lord's sake" (1 Peter 2:13).

The main Greek word for submission is *hypotassō*, which refers to placing, ranking, or arranging ourselves under authority, either God's direct authority or his divinely appointed authorities on earth. Another word for this term is "subjection." The word is closely related to obedience. Peter uses the term *hypotassō* primarily in the context of four spheres of our lives on earth: the political realm (1 Peter 2:13), marriage and home life (1 Peter 3:1, 5), the servant-master relationship (1 Peter 2:18), and the church (1 Peter 5:5). (The only other usage is in 1 Peter 3:22, where he uses the term to speak of the subjection of "angels and authorities and powers" to Jesus.) Paul uses the same word in Ephesians, where he too addresses submission to divinely appointed authorities in spheres such as marriage and the workplace—and in all our relationships with fellow believers: "Submit to one another out of reverence for Christ" (Ephesians 5:21). In chapter eight we'll look at the four spheres of human authority Peter mentions, but this chapter will stay focused more broadly on our submission to God and his intentions and purposes for our lives—the driving force behind our submission in any other area.

DISTINGUISHING SUBMISSION FROM FATALISM

Weeks before being diagnosed with acute myelogenous leukemia, Brad was a vibrant, energetic young man—one known to eat healthily and go on long runs. A successful student about to enter his senior year of college, he seemed to have a promising future ahead. He was also a committed Christian, best known to others for his deep, uncompromising faith and servant's heart. As leukemia suddenly and with little warning took over his once-strong body, friends and family prayed fervently for a healing miracle. Many of them (my coauthor among them) had a hard time believing God would allow Brad to be taken away so soon from this earth—there was so much this young man could still accomplish for God's kingdom!

And yet God did take Brad home shortly after his twenty-second birthday (about three months after he learned he was sick). The impact of this young man's life became quickly evident. Person after person, nonbelievers and believers alike, came forward and spoke of Brad's Christlike example, shown to them in big and small ways: eagerly washing their dishes when he came to their home, giving them rides to meetings, always being willing to drop everything to help or listen, never failing to show love and grace even toward those he disagreed with.

From the time he first learned of his disease, Jenny recalls Brad expressing his reaction with surprising lightheartedness, his big, signature smile spread across his face: "If God wants to heal me, great; if not, that's up to him. He knows best." This attitude became Brad's unwavering stance during his final days on earth. His response puzzled some and amazed others. How *normal* it would have been for him to think, *But there's so much more I could do for the Lord here!* And many of us in his shoes would've been asking, *But why me? I've done everything right!* Yet Brad showed little sign of any attitude but acceptance of his disease.

A question worth asking is, Was this fatalism, or was it simply a remarkably mature trust in and submission to the One who does all things well (Mark 7:37)? The two can indeed appear similar from the outside, but they differ in a significant way: while fatalism (or determinism) generally views God as all-powerful but not all-good, the Christian view is that God is both all-powerful and all-good. Charles Spurgeon offers this helpful explanation: "Fate says the thing is and must be; so it is decreed. But the true doctrine is—God has appointed this and that, not because it must be, but because it is best that it should be. Fate is blind, but the destiny of the Scripture is full of eyes."[6]

In other words, God always acts and allows circumstances and events for a purpose. His purposes, though they may seem harsh and even cruel from our finite perspective, are always generous and good *in the end*. He is both good and all-powerful, and his will is done from the perspective of eternity.

This can be a hard pill to swallow, but it's not quite as hard to swallow when we remember that our God is utterly unique in that *he himself suffered*. As Malcolm Muggeridge once put it in an interview with William F. Buckley Jr., the cross as a symbol of both suffering *and* salvation is "the heart of the thing" (that is, the heart of the Christian faith). The cross reminds us that God does indeed use evil and suffering for good, and that he doesn't underwrite it, but neither does he stand far off from evil and suffering—he takes it upon himself and ultimately defeats it on our behalf. This view is "freedom within the context of God's will, which is not the same as determinism," Muggeridge explained. Thus, in this grand drama of human history, a man like Stalin isn't "God's prophet" but "God's instrument." Why? "Because in history, it's impossible for anybody to function except as God's instrument because history is the scenario that God has written," Muggeridge continued. "And the part, all the parts, are necessary, just as Judas was necessary."[7]

SUBMISSION AS A LIFESTYLE

If we surrender ourselves to God's purposes, we can be sure that the alchemy of grace will do its work, slowly but surely changing us—hewing the edges of our character, growing our love and compassion for others, and exposing our self-centeredness and desire for control over our own lives. He'll also use us powerfully to minister to others.

Submission to God's authority over our lives almost always appears easier from the outside looking in. Submission is typically grueling, and it's also a process—a daily, moment-by-moment choice; a lifestyle, not a once-and-done action. We can easily take up our own plans and desires again, sometimes without even realizing it. Jesus himself actively submitted to his Father's purposes to the very end of his life, as seen in that powerful scene in Gethsemane (see Matthew 26:36-46; Luke 22:39-46). In this lifestyle of submission, we arrange ourselves under his authority, trusting that the all-knowing, all-good Father knows what's best for us. Of course, this process isn't just for times of hardship, but submission becomes much harder when we're "in the dark," experiencing difficulties for which we can't see a reason.

Amy Carmichael, a missionary in India from the turn of the twentieth century, led a lifestyle of submission to God's will for her life. Yet, even as a mature believer late in her life, this submission was put to the test when she found herself in a new difficulty she had not yet known. One morning she wrote this prayer: "Do with me as Thou wilt. Do anything that will fit me to serve Thee and help my beloveds."[8] Little did she know what would befall her that very day:

> She went the five or six miles to a Muslim and Hindu town where they were preparing facilities for a medical dispensary. As she examined building work which was being done, she entered a half-finished hut in the twilight and fell into a pit which was being dug for a toilet in the wrong place. She broke her leg, dislocated an ankle, and twisted her spine.[9]

Initially, she hoped to recover, but over time it became clear that the sixty-three-year-old would never be the same again:

> The toll of uninterrupted years in India had weakened her constitution. Neuritis and arthritis set in and she could rarely sleep without medication. There would be no more "whizzing"

about the compound [of her Dohnavur Fellowship], or climbing in the forests and mountains. . . . Life would now be spent very largely in her room.[10]

The active, energetic missionary who had previously viewed indoor life as "anathema" struggled, but she resubmitted herself to the Lord's purposes. Biographer Iain Murray writes, "When the dramatic change came she knew the lessons to be practiced: 'You must never ask God why?' 'To will what God wills brings peace.' The school of suffering became the richest school of her life."[11]

Carmichael's accident may have halted her physical activity, but it didn't halt her mental activity or her ministry to others. She wrote thirteen books after that, several of which are counted among favorites on the topic of suffering. The title of her book *Gold by Moonlight* (1935) comes from a line by Samuel Rutherford that speaks to the spiritual treasures we can find even in the darkest moments of our lives: "It is possible to gather gold, where it may be had, with moonlight."[12]

For all of Carmichael's impact prior to the accident, biographer Frank Houghton notes that her impact through her pen after the accident allowed her to bless hundreds of thousands for decades, including us today. We would do well to heed the advice she gave one of her nurses before her death, knowing it was the last time she'd see her: "When you hear I have gone, jump for joy."[13] Carmichael's lifelong submission to the Lord was complete—she was prepared to meet the loving Father she had served tirelessly for so long.

It's easy to think, *But I'm no saint. I'm no Amy Carmichael.* And yet submission to God's authority in our lives is never easy; it wasn't easy for Amy Carmichael! It only *looks* easy from the outside and in hindsight. In the middle of very difficult circumstances, this woman served—faithfully, joyfully. But she wasn't without her faults; in fact, relational conflicts posed a major threat at points in her ministry.

Humility and repentance always accompany a lifestyle of submission to God. Humility helps us recognize that God has the best plan for our lives—and the power to bring it about; we do not. Humility before others helps us recognize that we're flawed and sinful, like all people, and unworthy of God's grace and blessing. Thus, we do not actually merit *any* good gift from him.

AGENTS OF THE KING

In submitting to God, we're making an important acknowledgment: not only do we not know what's best for ourselves or have the power to bring it about, but we don't even really own our lives. Our lives are God's. We're his agents in the world—subversive agents, in fact, since we are agents in an alternate kingdom that is not of this world. You and I are ambassadors representing the affairs of our God, and we're stewards of his possessions. Hence, Peter writes, "Since Christ suffered in his body, arm yourselves also with the same attitude, because whoever suffers in the body is done with sin. As a result, they do not live the rest of their earthly lives for evil human desires, but rather *for the will of God*" (1 Peter 4:1-2, emphasis added).

As believers, our lives are not about being self-actualized or meeting a certain ideal for ourselves. Our lives are not our own, and they're not to be lived as if they are (1 Corinthians 7:23; Romans 14:7). We're bought and owned by the one who gives us life and breath—both biological life (*bios*) and eternal, spiritual life (*zoē*).[14] Our purpose is to live for God's will, and we have the capacity to do this (because of his Spirit dwelling in us) now that we're no longer in bondage to sin. This is the eternal perspective God wants us to have.

How does this relate to suffering? In suffering there's a temptation to see oneself not as an agent but as a victim. If we play this card too strongly, there are a couple of dangers. First, we can overlook any responsibility that we have in our own adversities. Sometimes, we're blind to our own failings. To see the reality of our own culpabilities, we need to open ourselves to God and allow him to search our hearts and show us the truth (this again requires humility). A second reason we should be careful about overplaying the victim card is that even if we are innocent in a situation, as believers we're *also* agents of the King who has complete authority over all things.

"All authority in heaven and on earth has been given to me," Jesus said (Matthew 28:18). These were among his last words before ascending to heaven, so we should assume they're important. Jesus is declaring that he has been given *all* authority in heaven *and* on earth. The implications of this statement are staggering. We're all both agents and victims at various points in our lives, but even when we're victims, we're never *solely* victims. God is always in ultimate control and can stop or allow any hardship at any point. Thus, we can and should have a steadfast commitment to God's sovereignty even though we can't fully understand how it operates vis-à-vis human free will.[15]

As a side note, refusing to assume an overdone victim mentality does not mean we take a passive stance toward wrongdoing, especially abuse from another. There are legitimate bullies, abusers, and predators who not only victimize others but are highly skilled in shifting blame and avoiding accountability. We should be aware of these individuals who have established a life pattern of denying culpability and always seeing others as the problem (often lying or distorting the truth to spin the situation in a certain way); this pattern epitomizes human frailty at its worst. Victims of these individuals do not face their suffering alone, and seeing oneself as an agent or subject of the King of heaven (versus only as a victim of bad behavior) can in fact be empowering.[16]

THE CENTURION AND AUTHORITY

There was a man who understood well the concept of God's authority and our need to place ourselves under it. He was one of the few Jesus commended for having "great faith." In Matthew 8, this unnamed Roman centurion comes to Jesus and asks him to help his servant who is "at home paralyzed and in terrible suffering" (v. 6). When Jesus says he will go heal him, the man responds: "Lord, I do not deserve to have you come under my roof. But just say the word, and my servant will be healed. For I myself am a man under authority, with soldiers under me. I tell this one, 'Go,' and he goes; and that one, 'Come,' and he comes. I say to my servant, 'Do this,' and he does it" (Matthew 8:8-9).

Perhaps the reason this story can seem so unimpressive to us is that our view is tainted by our environment in which questioning authority has become commonplace. We fail to grasp and appreciate the importance of submitting not only to our earthly authorities but most importantly to our heavenly Authority. We may resonate strongly with the image of being beloved children of God—and "that is what we are!" (1 John 3:1)—but we bristle at the idea of being subjects in a kingdom, even the heavenly one. *Yet that too is what we are.* If we only embrace God as our good, loving Father who promises to give us what we need, we run the risk of disillusionment when we encounter the reality of God's authority: he and he alone determines exactly what is best for us and exactly what we need. None of us deserves to have him come under our roof, just as the centurion realized—but come he does when we open the door to him.

God's character doesn't change. He's perfect, loving, and good. Our perspective has to change to encompass all of God's character so we can see our changing circumstances through the filter of his unchanging character. This is what submitting to God's authority is all about: seeing our trials as being allowed by God through his love and care for us.

ALL THINGS WORK *TOGETHER*

In recognizing the authority of God in our lives, I've said we need to recognize his sovereignty. Earlier, I also warned against dropping Romans 8:28 bombs on those who are suffering. But there is a place for this important Scripture: "We know that God causes all things to work together for good to those who love God, to those who are called according to His purpose" (NASB). Notice, first, that God is the one doing the work in this verse, not us. Second, notice the word *together*. If we look at adversities and other circumstances of our lives in isolation, we may not see the hand of God. Paul urges us toward a perspective that sees the interlocking nature of the details of our lives.

Only when we take this view can we literally "give thanks in *all* circumstances" (1 Thessalonians 5:18, emphasis added), even in the trials. The word Paul uses in this verse for thanksgiving is *eucharisteō* (where we get the word *Eucharist*—one term for the Lord's Supper or Communion). There's a phrase called "the hard thanksgiving" that I discussed in my book *Life in the Presence of God*. This means thanking God, even when our circumstances are undesirable, to confirm and affirm that God works all things *together* for good. When we thank him for the difficulties, we're effectively thanking him that he will use these difficulties to form

Christlike character in us, for our good and the good of others. He won't waste them. We can still tell God in our prayers, "This hurts" or "This is hard." He knows our pain and thoughts anyway before we even have them. We can be assured Jesus weeps and grieves with us, just as he wept at Lazarus's tomb, even when he knew the miracle that was coming.

We can hold to the promise of Romans 8:28 tenaciously, knowing God sees the full picture while we do not (yet!). John Newton, author of the hymn "Amazing Grace," advised a similar perspective to a fellow believer, in a letter he wrote to her.

Your sister is much upon my mind. Her illness grieves me: were it in my power I would quickly remove it: the Lord can, and I hope will, when it has answered the end for which he sent it. . . . All shall work together for good; everything is needful that he sends; nothing can be needful that he withholds. . . . You have need of patience, and if you ask, the Lord will give it. But there can be no settled peace till our will is in a measure subdued. Hide yourself under the shadow of his wings; rely upon his care and power; look upon him as a physician who has graciously undertaken to heal your soul of the worst of sicknesses, sin. Yield to his prescriptions, and fight against every thought that would represent it as desirable to be permitted to choose for yourself.

When you cannot see your way, be satisfied that he is your leader. When your spirit is overwhelmed within you, he knows your path: he will not leave you to sink. He has appointed seasons of refreshment, and you shall find that he does not forget you. Above all, keep close to the throne of grace. If we seem to get no good by attempting to draw near him, we may be sure we shall get none by keeping away from him.[17]

At another point in the letter, Newton reminded this grieving sister that God "has a sovereign right to do with us as he pleases." Our Lord is always crafting a masterpiece painting, a *magnum opus*, where we would be content with only a thumbnail sketch. He may bruise the reed (that is, us), but he will never completely crush it (Isaiah 42:3; Matthew 12:20). And in everything his wisdom and aspirations far surpass our own limited understanding and imaginations. If only we would see that, like those mosaic-tiled puzzles with a thousand pieces that don't appear to fit together in the same composition, we'll one day stand back, look, and stand in awe of God's handiwork. We'll see he does all things well, making everything beautiful in its time (Ecclesiastes 3:11).

THE CONSECRATED LIFE

Submission is closely related to a second aspect of the Christian life: committing ourselves to God in the pursuit of holiness. This transformation process is known as consecration. It begins with a recognition of God's authority in our lives and moves on to obedience to that authority in day-to-day living. Peter emphasizes this aspect from the beginning of his epistle: "As obedient children, do not conform to the evil desires you had when you lived in ignorance. But just as he who called you is holy, so be holy in all you do; for it is written: 'Be holy, because I am holy'" (1 Peter 1:14-16).

Peter isn't giving his readers a pass to wallow in misery or remain spiritually stagnant because of their suffering; there's no hunkering down and waiting until smoother waters come before we pursue the life God calls us to. As Os Guinness says, "The hardest thing to do then is to wait *and work on*. Suspending judgment [about the final outcome] does not mean suspending operations."[18]

We're to work on, to live on in a godly manner no matter what the circumstances of our lives are—and no matter how others treat us. We can do this because we're active agents in the world, not mere victims, and we have a sovereign God who is working all things together for the good of his children (though we may suffer for "a little while" now).

Holiness is often defined as "set-apartness"—that is, set apart *from* the world system. But the term has no single English equivalent (the closest in meaning is *dedicated*). Meaning more than separateness, holiness also carries the idea of being set apart *to* something else—or, rather, to *Someone*, for his service and purposes. Moreover, the way we become holy is not by conforming more and more to a set of rules or regulations, but by looking to the Holy One and following his example: walking as Jesus walked. A holy life involves increasing *shalom*—wholeness or harmony— in our life and relationships.[19] Being holy is not following some code of ethics but fulfilling the law of Christ, which is the law of love: love of God and love of neighbor. Loving our neighbors and giving them a blessing instead of a curse even when they have wronged us is a key way that we pursue holiness amid suffering.

It's painful to turn the other cheek when our flesh cries out for vengeance, but the Holy Spirit dwelling in us enables us to reject the desires of the flesh and instead walk in the way of God. This is the new quality of life he has made possible for followers of Christ, and it's to be lived right in the middle of a secularized, pagan society: "Dear friends, I urge you, as foreigners and exiles, to abstain from sinful desires, which wage war against your soul. Live such good lives among the pagans that, though they accuse you of doing wrong, they may see your good deeds and glorify God on the day he visits us" (1 Peter 2:11-12).

Peter's words echo Paul's in Ephesians: "You were taught, with regard to your former way of life, to put off your old self, which is being corrupted by its deceitful desires" (Ephesians 4:22). In this pursuit of holiness—putting off the old self and putting on the new self—we have to daily remember the cross. Each day, we'll put ourselves either on the altar to God as a living sacrifice in his service (Romans 12:1) or on the altar of self, living for ourselves.

Daily consecration of ourselves to him becomes particularly important in our dealings with others in the various spheres of authority in which God has sovereignly placed us. In these spheres, which are filled with sinful human beings, it's easy to revert to flesh-based living, selfishly insisting on our own rights and desires, especially when we've been wrongfully treated. Submission to God and his authority is the only way we'll be able to submit with a Christlike attitude in each of those spheres.

THE MASTERFUL WORK OF GOD

All believers are called to submit to God and commit to pursuing holiness, whether we're in the middle of a significant bout of adversity or not. Submitting to God in suffering can be especially agonizing because it's then that our spiritual senses are piqued, and we begin to ask questions like, Why hasn't God healed or delivered me from this yet? And if he hasn't, and doesn't, is he still good—does he still love me?

We're never truly in control of our lives, but in the midst of suffering, our decision is forced in a way that we don't usually recognize: we'll either submit our lives to his authority (leading to a better character forged in adversity), or we'll live for ourselves (and grow bitter, perhaps coming up with ever-new ways to mask our pain with temporary solutions). As we make this decision, one thought and one action at a time, we will often feel nothing is really changing, at least not at first. But slowly, as time passes, we'll start to notice a difference in our thought patterns and our responses. God is chipping away at us. Like the statue *David* very gradually emerging from that initial block of stone, one cut at a time, we'll begin to resemble that Christlike saint God intends to make out of us. That saint is how God already sees us, just as Michelangelo is said to have claimed he saw his masterpieces in advance: "In every block of marble I see a statue as plain as though it stood before me, shaped and perfect in attitude and action. I have only to hew away the rough walls that imprison the lovely apparition to reveal it to the other eyes as mine see it."[20]

As a side note, if you ever have a chance to see *David* in person, I recommend standing far back from it at first to get the full effect; then approach it up close and notice the intricacy of detail Michelangelo achieved. It's quite astonishing, with clear analogies to the spiritual life.

Jerry Sittser experienced this slow, gradual change in his character. Facing a life far from how he'd imagined it would look after the accident that killed his three loved ones—without the remote possibility that it could return to that original vision—his grief was compounded by his usual in-charge, impatient tendencies. Writing years later, he notes an inward change in himself as a result of the grief: "The accident . . . transformed me as a person."[21] How and why did that transformation happen? He explains,

> I can think of nothing—no moment in time, event, decision, or effort—that marked a turning point or led to a major breakthrough. . . . God simply used the stuff of ordinary life to expose my weaknesses and to develop my character. The process was so gradual and subtle that I was never conscious of it. It just happened as slowly and surely as a tree grows.[22]

Sittser's change came about through a slow submission of his will to God's will for his life, instead of a demand to see his own desires and plans fulfilled. Previously the type of person who desired control and hated interruptions, he found himself suddenly thrust into the position of primary caretaker of his kids (kids he himself never yearned for as much as his now-deceased wife had). He says, "My life over the past twelve years has been nothing but one long series of interruptions. I can control very little, except my response to my lack of control! ... I have raised Catherine, David, and John [his three surviving children] on my knees."[23]

The depth of tragedy that God chose to use in Sittser's life—or in the life of someone like Job—to achieve his divine purposes can induce a certain amount of fear in us. But remember, God knows each of us perfectly, and he will never send us adversities except those that are in the exact amount, form, and timing he has permitted in advance. Proverbs 3:25 tells us, "Have no fear of sudden disaster or of the ruin that overtakes the wicked." *We need not fear*. Why? Because "the LORD will be at your side and will keep your foot from being snared" (Proverbs 3:26). He is with us in our sufferings; our foot will not be snared, and we will not be set ablaze even if we are thrown into the crucible of affliction. There's truly no greater comfort we can receive—or offer another—in the midst of suffering.

In chapter eight we'll examine the four spheres of human authority ordained by God in which Peter's first epistle emphasizes submission ("for the Lord's sake"), even amid a context of adversity. Incidentally, these spheres are often the very cause and exacerbators of our suffering, yet they're also the places where the believer's response can enable the beauty and message of Christ to shine all the brighter, bringing an eternal perspective to bear on temporary difficulties.

8

SUBMITTING
TO AUTHORITY

Submit yourselves for the Lord's sake to every human
authority. . . . For it is God's will that by doing good
you should silence the ignorant talk of foolish people.

1 PETER 2:13, 15

THE APOSTLES PETER AND JOHN went through a lot together. They stood close by Jesus throughout his time on earth
and were the first disciples to enter the empty tomb. In Acts 3, God
uses them to heal a lame beggar at the temple gate called Beautiful.
Shortly afterward the two are confronted by the religious leaders
following a powerful sermon by Peter. The men were standing
where Jesus once taught, on a porch known as Solomon's Colonnade,
in the outer court of the temple as the Jewish leaders approached
them. Peter's message was still ringing in the audience's ears:

> The God of Abraham, Isaac and Jacob, the God of our fathers,
> has glorified his servant Jesus. You handed him over to be

killed, and you disowned him before Pilate, though he had decided to let him go. . . . You killed the author of life, but God raised him from the dead. We are witnesses of this. . . .

Now, fellow Israelites, I know that you acted in ignorance, as did your leaders. But this is how God fulfilled what he had foretold through all the prophets, saying that his Messiah would suffer. Repent, then, and turn to God, so that your sins may be wiped out. (Acts 3:13, 15, 17-19)

Peter's words incensed the approaching leaders, who Luke tells us "were greatly disturbed" by the apostles' proclamation of the resurrection of Christ (Acts 4:2). But what the authorities really zeroed in on was the incident that had just wowed the crowd: the healing of the lame beggar in Jesus' name. Their action against Peter and John was swift: "They seized Peter and John and, because it was evening, they put them in jail until the next day" (v. 3).

Questioning the apostles the following day, the religious authorities demanded to know, "By what power or what name did you do this [healing]?" (Acts 4:7). Unlike in the hours before the crucifixion, Peter didn't waver this time. Shame and embarrassment were gone in this man who'd seen the risen Savior with his own eyes. "Filled with the Holy Spirit," Peter boldly responded:

Rulers and elders of the people! If we are being called to account today for an act of kindness shown to a man who was lame and are being asked how he was healed, then know this, you and all the people of Israel: It is by the name of Jesus Christ of Nazareth, whom you crucified but whom God raised from the dead, that this man stands before you healed. . . . Salvation is found in no one else, for there is no other name under heaven given to mankind by which we must be saved. (Acts 4:8-10, 12)

The religious leaders were at a loss for words. The text says that because the healed man stood before them, clearly without his former disability, "There was nothing they could say" (Acts 4:14). The astonished leaders conferred, then issued a command that Peter and John not "speak or teach at all in the name of Jesus" (v. 18). In this Shadrach, Meshach, and Abednego moment, Peter and John rose to the occasion, replying to those who wielded both religious and political power: "Which is right in God's eyes: to listen to you, or to him? You be the judges! As for us, we cannot help speaking about what we have seen and heard" (vv. 19-20).

Peter and John were released shortly after that, though not without further attempts by the religious leaders to intimidate the men into keeping quiet about Jesus (Acts 4:21). The men were anything but silent in the days to follow because they had made their choice—when it came to submitting to authority in their lives, if a choice had to be made, God would win the day over people, no matter how powerful those people were.

GOD OR MAN?

Peter, of all people, knew that life as a follower of Christ is fraught with difficulties, risk, and persecution. Thus, in an epistle filled with reminders of our eternal hope and destiny, the apostle also gets very practical about the temporal realm. Peter knew his readers had to learn how to go on living and dealing with adversity in a way that would honor God. They needed not only good theology but also theology-driven practice to employ in all areas of life. So Peter's first epistle helped them, as it helps us today, address real-world questions like, What do I do if the government—or even a religious leader—tells me to do something that contradicts God's commands? and, What if my master is harsh—do I still have to obey him? and, What if my boss threatens to fire me or not promote me if I don't support the company's unbiblical agenda?

Peter covers four main realms in which our faith will be tested and tried, and in which we will sometimes have to endure suffering for the sake of our witness to Christ:

1. Government (civil authority)

2. Household

3. Workplace

4. Church (local)

Submission in these four arenas, Peter contends, is a response of obedience to God himself, who is our ultimate authority. This submission is arranging oneself under another "for the Lord's sake" (1 Peter 2:13).

God is our top authority, trumping all others, and he has created other links in the chain of command to govern various areas of life. However, if a divinely appointed authority contradicts the commands of God, then we should obey God over people. This is the choice Peter and John faced in Acts 4 under the religious authorities of their day. It's the choice Shadrach, Meshach, and Abednego made when faced with the command to bow to the false gods of Babylon. And it's the decision our Lord Jesus often faced (see, for example, Matthew 12:1-14, where Jesus defied human religious traditions that would have prevented him from healing on the Sabbath).

Submitting to God-ordained human authorities, as long as those authorities do not contradict God's laws, is one way we demonstrate our trust in God and offer a Christlike witness to a watching world. Willing submission is, in general, for our good, as God originally set up these authorities for our well-being and protection; placing ourselves under them helps make the authorities' work "a joy, not a burden," which in turn benefits us (Hebrews 13:17).

On the other hand, the sad truth is that God-ordained human authorities do not always follow God, and their leadership often falls short of God's standards. At times their instructions will blatantly contradict his standards. A climax of our submission to God is the joyful choice to obey God rather than people when those human authorities are in violation of God's clear commands. In this process we must be willing to pay the high price of suffering, in some cases even to the point of being willing to die, as a result of our identification with and obedience to Christ. Following the example of our Lord, we are shaped and perfected in this process (Hebrews 2:10), conformed more and more to his image.

TWO DANGEROUS TENDENCIES

Before delving into each of the four spheres, I want to reiterate that in these four areas some of the deepest pain and confusion in our lives can arise. Thus, we should beware of two dangerous tendencies—one in the authorities and one in us.

First, sinful humanity since the dawn of time has tended toward abuse of power and exploitation of others for selfish gain. Mass suffering such as genocide under an authoritarian government comes immediately to mind. But remember, many of the egregious cases emerged out of more benign contexts in which abuses were smaller and more sporadic, part of a slow-growing pattern. This is the reason alertness and preparation are needed so adversity in civil and other spheres doesn't take us by surprise.

A second danger is that we can be tempted to put too much hope or trust in God-ordained human authorities. Human institutions are fallible, and they *always will be*. Since humans are at the helm, no government, marriage, workplace, or local church will ever be perfect. Every human authority will fail us, some more than others. We should never expect perfection in our leaders.

A PILGRIM MINDSET

In all four spheres, and indeed in all of our relationships, tension exists between our call to be grace-filled peacemakers who move through life as pilgrims bound for another land and being bold, unashamed truth-tellers, willing to stand for what's right and just on earth. We can easily fall off one side of the horse or the other—caring either too much or too little about what happens on this side of eternity.

While we shouldn't put too much stock in this world, we also have to realize that *this* world and this cultural moment matter, and in them we're called to be a light in the darkness. Perhaps this is why, just before admonishing his readers toward submission in each realm, Peter is careful to remind them of the mindset they're to have as they enter into those arenas: they are "a chosen people, a royal priesthood, a holy nation, God's special possession, that you may declare the praises of him who called you out of darkness into his wonderful light" (1 Peter 2:9). Peter goes on, urging a pilgrim mindset among his readers: as "foreigners and exiles," they are to "live such good lives among the pagans that, though they accuse you of doing wrong, they may see your good deeds and glorify God on the day he visits us" (vv. 11-12). In other words, our response in this life, even if false accusations (or worse) come against us, should reflect our true identity and home so others will see Christ in us. This is the will of God, and this is our primary purpose in every sphere of our lives.

THE GOVERNMENT

The first sphere of authority that Peter discusses is the civil one. As believers, our permanent citizenship is in heaven, but while we're on earth, we are also temporarily citizens of communities, states, and nations. In these contexts, we're called to submit to the

God-appointed authorities because of their important role in re-
straining evil: they are "sent by [God] to punish those who do
wrong and to commend those who do right" (1 Peter 2:14). Peter
reiterates later in his letter that we're to honor and "show proper
respect to everyone," including "the emperor" (v. 17), the equivalent of a president or monarch today. Paul offers a longer explanation in Romans 13:

> Let everyone be subject to the governing authorities, for
> there is no authority except that which God has established.
> The authorities that exist have been established by God.
> Consequently, whoever rebels against the authority is re-
> belling against what God has instituted, and those who do so
> will bring judgment on themselves. For rulers hold no terror
> for those who do right, but for those who do wrong. Do you
> want to be free from fear of the one in authority? Then do
> what is right and you will be commended. For the one in
> authority is God's servant for your good. But if you do wrong,
> be afraid, for rulers do not bear the sword for no reason.
> They are God's servants, agents of wrath to bring punishment
> on the wrongdoer. Therefore, it is necessary to submit to the
> authorities, not only because of possible punishment but also
> as a matter of conscience. (Romans 13:1-5)

The role of governing authorities as "agents of wrath," that is,
to punish wrongdoing, is vital but easily abused. Examples
abound of a government going beyond its boundaries of authority
and ballooning into an institution with responsibilities it was
never intended to bear. Yet, in spite of their faults and context
within a world of sin and rebellion, human-run governments still
have a purpose, and ultimately God is in control of them: "he de-
poses kings and raises up others" (Daniel 2:21) and "the king's

heart is in the hand of the LORD . . . : he turneth it whithersoever he will" (Proverbs 21:1 KJV).

Although governing authorities serve a necessary purpose, if they ask us to do something flatly wrong and unbiblical, a Christian has a higher obligation to God than to a human. The God-fearing midwives of Israel understood this, and they refused to obey the king of Egypt when he commanded them to kill the baby boys born to Israelite women (Exodus 1:17), a clear violation of God's commandment not to murder. The midwives' resistance pleased God, who protected them.

It's hard to fathom why God allows people like that king of Egypt to come into power, but he does. One need only skim portions of 1–2 Kings, 1–2 Chronicles, and Judges in the Old Testament to see how many evil kings God raised up to rule Israel. He has allowed despot after despot over the past century, some of whom oversaw tens of millions of murders: more than 61 million under the Soviet gulag and over 20 million under the Nazi regime. Peter, for his part, was not ignorant of the extent to which a government may actually inflict evil. Writing in the context of the Roman Empire just before Nero's rise, he had already seen and been an object of serious persecution by the time he wrote his first epistle. Thus, his injunction to believers to submit to the governing authorities, insofar as their consciences allowed, isn't to be taken lightly. At that time a declaration that "Jesus is Lord" was more than a bold statement of faith; it was also a political statement that "Caesar is not Lord."

In America we have been blessed for a long time not to experience such obvious crimes against our citizens, though certain people groups such as African Americans and Native Americans have endured varying levels of discrimination and mistreatment in our national history. Today, many point out that the death of well over 60 million unborn babies by abortion in our country amounts to a veritable genocide on par with (or even larger than) that of the Soviet gulag. Decisions of civil disobedience in America, nonetheless, have been fewer by comparison, in large part because our country was founded on Christian principles. The US Constitution was set up specifically to protect against abuses of the state through a system of checks and balances that respect the conscience and liberties of its citizens. But we are entering a time when that constitution has come under fierce attack, and more and more believers in the United States will have to make decisions about whether to obey certain national and state-sanctioned laws or succumb to political pressures that violate the clear commands of Scripture.

There may come a time when Christians will not be allowed to preach Romans 1 (including its passage on sexuality) with impunity. This is already happening in England, and it's beginning to happen in America. The consequences of such decisions will be painful—from believers' marginalization in their careers to legal action against them to the soft persecution of mockery and ridicule. We've already seen these types of consequences in various places, from a county courthouse in Kentucky to a cake shop in Colorado. But the highly publicized cases aren't the only instances of persecution taking place, and I believe these instances will only escalate in number and severity.

The frequently asked question is, Where do I draw the line? How do I know when a government has overstepped its bounds and civil disobedience is appropriate? While some instances are clear (as in the case of the Hebrew midwives who were commanded to kill innocent babies), others are not as obvious. In these latter cases the decision to disobey civil authority is between a believer and God as a matter of individual conscience or conviction. A conviction is a thought-out resolution between yourself and God that governs your behavior. It deals with something that is not explicitly commanded or commended in Scripture.

The prophet Daniel, we're told, continued to pray toward Jerusalem, kneeling three times a day, while in captivity in Babylon, despite a decree by the king forbidding this kind of prayer (Daniel 6:10). Although prayer itself is obviously a practice all believers should carry out, Daniel's practice of praying three times a day while facing a certain direction was neither commanded nor commended in the Torah; rather, it was something Daniel had resolved between himself and God to do daily. And Daniel accepted the consequences (being thrown into a den of lions) when he was caught. In his case God rescued him from the potentially fatal result of his civil disobedience (v. 16), though such an outcome is not guaranteed to believers in similar situations.

Where does this example leave us? When we face these types of decisions, it's wise for us to seek the whole counsel of Scripture, the guidance of the Holy Spirit through prayer, and the input of like-minded believers. We must realize that Christians can't and shouldn't fight on every issue, as every civil institution will have *some* measure of corruption simply because it's run by humans. Whatever our choice, we must be prepared to accept the consequences of disobedience. God may or may not rescue us in this life; even Shadrach, Meshach, and Abednego said they were prepared to die if God did not deliver them (Daniel 3:18).

It's important, too, to be mindful of Peter's repeated cautions against suffering for wrongdoing. We should be careful not to shoot ourselves in the foot. If civil disobedience truly appears to be the only viable course of action, we must always maintain a Christlike attitude: one of humility and love for God and others, not one of unrighteous anger or smug self-righteousness. When Jesus suffered at the hands of civil authorities, he did so sinlessly. In answering Pilate's questions before going to the cross, he showed freedom, not fear, emphasizing that his allegiance was to another world—a world from which all authority in this world is derived: "My kingdom is not of this world. If it were, my servants would fight to prevent my arrest by the Jewish leaders. But now my kingdom is from another place" (John 18:36). Later he said to Pilate, "You would have no power over me if it were not given to you from above" (John 19:11).

As we discern the best course of action in this sphere, we should be mindful that all human kingdoms will one day be destroyed—they're never intended to last forever.

THE WORKPLACE

The workplace is a second divinely mandated sphere of authority. Peter's words regarding this arena were spoken into a cultural context in which slavery was an assumed reality for many workers: "Slaves, in reverent fear of God submit yourselves to your masters, not only to those who are good and considerate, but also to those who are harsh. For it is commendable if someone bears up under the pain of unjust suffering because they are conscious of God" (1 Peter 2:18-19).

Before we delve into the application of Peter's words, it's important to realize that a sizeable percentage of those living in the Roman Empire were slaves (average estimates put the number at a quarter or more of the total population, depending on time and location). Slavery was considered a norm across the empire. Moreover, the behavior of Christian slaves affected the treatment of Christians (slaves and nonslaves) everywhere in the empire, so the consequences of nonsubmission were far-reaching, affecting not just a single worker.

Slavery in Peter's day was not the oppressive brand once found in the American South and other parts of the New World. One key difference is that both the Old and New Testaments condemn kidnapping and would not have condoned the manner in which slaves were brought over to the Americas. Also, though some masters were harsher than others in the Roman Empire, it was not uncommon for Roman servants and masters to share a filial connection and for slaves even to be viewed as members of the household. Neither was it unusual for children of the household to develop a greater affection for the slaves who cared for them than for their own parents. Roman slaves even faced the prospect of being freed one day (though Rome set a limit on the number and age released each year).

I'm certainly not suggesting that Roman slavery was pleasant. Not only slaves but nearly all workers at that time, in general, enjoyed fewer freedoms and options than we have today. It was much harder to change jobs if one found oneself in a difficult master-slave relationship. And there were fewer outlets or legal remedies people could resort to for resolving disputes and problems between masters-employers and workers.

Despite the differences between the modern workplace and that of the Roman Empire, the two are not as different as the terminology suggests (indeed, many workers today—essentially chained to their desks for eight or more hours on end—often *feel* as stuck in their situations as slaves did back then!). Thus, the principles Peter promotes transfer to today's context.

What are those principles? First, a worker's obligation to work hard, with an attitude of humble submission, is not negated by a master's (employer's, boss's) harshness. Other words for "harsh" in 1 Peter 2:18 are *unreasonable, unfair, crooked, perverse,* or *tortuous.*

Second, our submission is actually to Christ, first and foremost. We're to submit in the workplace "in reverent fear of God," not in fear of the boss. Colossians 3:23 encapsulates this principle well: "Whatever you do, work at it with all your heart, *as working for the Lord*, not for human masters" (emphasis added).

In following these two principles, we're following Jesus' model. And in the remaining six verses of 1 Peter 2, as well as in chapter 3, the apostle points to that example. We're to imitate the One who suffered sinlessly and silently, making no retaliating threats even when they were well warranted from a human perspective (1 Peter 2:23). Moreover, the mercy and grace we have received through Christ's death provide us with reason to treat people well even when they don't deserve it. Peter's words echo those of the Beatitudes in Matthew 5:3-12: let them (harsh masters or anyone who treats you badly) be ashamed of their malicious "slander" because of your "good behavior in Christ" (1 Peter 3:16).

Let me reiterate: this passage does not advocate slavery as an institution, especially the type that occurred in parts of the New World and embraced a treatment of enslaved human beings as chattel. Nor was Peter advocating staying in a dangerously abusive workplace situation if it was possible to escape it. Rather, Peter was imploring believers in the workforce (most of whom at that time had few avenues to pursue to seek an equitable understanding with employers) to have a Christlike response to unjust treatment on an individual level. While some masters were gentle and just in how they treated their slaves, others were not, and Peter was addressing how a person should respond under a harsh master. Do we resist, maybe even try to run away? Or do we quietly obey and endure? (Again, this is about the individual response, not the corporate response—where it would be appropriate to fight for justice on a larger scale, as William Wilberforce and others did to effect the abolition of the slave trade and slavery.)

Submission in today's workplace. Today, our response and example are to be the same. Rather than impulsively fighting back, our first and primary response should be one of submission and grace even in the face of slander or other unjust treatment. Justice should not be what we give others, because when it comes down to it, justice is not what we would want for ourselves; if we received what we really deserved, we would be bound for an eternity of torment. Instead, Jesus secured for us eternity and a quality of life we do not deserve, and he wants us to follow his example by showing others his graciousness and forgiveness even when they don't deserve it. This applies in our offices and jobs, with bosses and colleagues, as well as in our homes and communities.

Now, when a boss or coworker treats us unfairly, there's certainly a time and a place to speak up or perhaps even leave the situation entirely (that is, quit and find another job); overlooking repeated wrongdoing is not necessarily virtuous, and respectful confrontation, as well as formal actions in extreme cases (for example, abuse and bullying), may be wholly appropriate. But in general, humans tend to be too quick to resist or fight back (or even become a little conniving) and too slow to extend forgiveness and grace. As a rule, as Jesus taught in his Sermon on the Mount, we're not to repay evil for evil on the individual level, but rather to leave justice up to God. Turning the other cheek is one way we imitate Jesus (Matthew 5:39).

Dan is a good example. A young professional, he came under the supervision of a boss whose bullying tactics had become well known in his immediate office (though not throughout his company). This boss, Amanda, alternated between fronts of charm and irrational outbursts of anger, such that her employees never knew which side of her would show up on a given workday. Systematically, she began to eliminate direct reports she didn't like, usually demoralizing them to the point of being so miserable they would quit before she could fire them. Amanda always put on her nice front in the presence of upper-level management, though, so only those in her inner office knew the truth of what was going on.

Dan, as a highly competent worker who quietly did above and beyond all that he was asked, was occasionally targeted by Amanda, but since she needed his talent to successfully do her own job, she was careful with him—seeking to instill just enough fear that kept him from getting comfortable, but also turning on the charm frequently to give him a sense of being "on his side" so he would remain in his job.

Dan was a committed Christian, and his faith very much affected how he went about his work. As he suffered under Amanda and witnessed others suffering even more severely under her, he grew concerned. Still, most of her bad behavior happened behind closed doors or could simply be categorized as "mean." Sometimes, she had valid criticisms, too, and it was more the tone in which they were communicated that was the problem. He didn't know what to do. His instinct was to hunker down and keep to himself, but as the environment grew more toxic, he increasingly considered searching for a new job. At the same time, he wondered if God had a role for him to play in the situation (besides escaping it).

Dan began to pray for Amanda and for how he viewed her. He read through verses such as 1 Peter 2:11-12 and 1 Peter 3:16, which prompted him to enter his workday determined to treat his boss with a grace that, based on her behavior, she didn't deserve. He also began to recognize that Amanda's angry disposition came from somewhere—a place of deep pain and difficulties in her life, of which he only saw a snippet (he knew she was recently divorced and raising a teenage son as a single mom). Dan asked God to make him a conduit of Christ's unmerited love, and to help him be "as shrewd as a snake and as innocent as a dove" (Matthew 10:16). This attitude gave him a sense of agency instead of victimhood (see chap. 7) and helped him view Amanda through God's eyes instead of with hatred or dread. Fear began to be replaced with courage in his dealings with Amanda, stemming from his fear of God over this difficult and unpredictable human "master."

Amanda showed growing favor toward Dan, who continued to submit to her leadership; however, her poor treatment of others persisted. Dan began documenting her behavior, just in case he ever needed a record of it. One day, events precipitated his decision to report her pattern of behavior to her supervisor. He did so along with one other colleague (as a fellow witness to the situation), knowing he was risking his job if Amanda found out what they had done. Months earlier Dan might've walked into that appointment with Amanda's boss out of his own anger, hoping Amanda would "get what was coming to her." Now, he did so somewhat reluctantly, knowing it was the right thing to do but also wishing that this boss he'd been praying for would experience the life-changing transformation that God's grace brings about.

Shortly after Dan reported Amanda, she left the company for another job. He never knew whether his example made any difference to her, but his lingering prayer is that she will one day wake up to the reality of her sin (including the hurt she's inflicted on others) *and* to her need for Christ. If God uses a small seed planted by his own behavior toward her, all the better.

A place for workplace resistance. Dan never reached the point of needing to outright resist Amanda's authority, though he was prepared to do so if she had instructed him to do something blatantly wrong—such as join her in berating their colleagues.

Resistance or disobedience has its role in the workplace when we're asked to violate God's commands and when his standards are at stake. Our allegiance is always to God first. In these cases, many of the same principles that applied to the civil sphere apply to our work relationships. Indeed, because many are employed by a civil authority, there is much crossover between these spheres—as was the case for a Japanese man named Chiune Sugihara.

Born in 1900, Sugihara was appointed vice-consul of a Japanese consulate in Lithuania in 1939. There, he was supposed to report back to his government on the movement of Russian troops. But while fulfilling his duties, Sugihara realized the town where he was stationed (Kaunas) was filled with Polish Jewish refugees spilling over from the border as they fled the Nazi regime. These refugees faced an uncertain future. When hundreds of them showed up at the doorstep of his office one day, he asked his boss to issue transit visas to them—which would allow them to pass through Japan to a safe country, and literally save their lives. His boss refused, rejecting Sugihara's request three times. Glenn Sunshine explains the dilemma this civil servant faced:

> Sugihara was in a difficult situation: if he issued the visas, he could be fired and disgraced; if he didn't, the Jews would die. He told his wife, "I may have to disobey my government, but if I do not, I will be disobeying God. I know I should follow my conscience." Yukiko agreed with him, and the two went to work. From July 31 to September 4, Sugihara began writing visas by hand at a rate of 300 per day. He didn't even stop for meals—he ate sandwiches that Yukiko left for him by his desk. He even made arrangements for the Soviets to transport them via the Trans-Siberian Railroad (albeit at five times the normal price). The refugees began to arrive by the thousands

begging for visas. When some began to scale the walls of the consulate, Sugihara came out and promised them he would not abandon them. And he didn't. When he was forced to leave Kaunas before the consulate was closed, Sugihara spent the entire night before writing visas. Eyewitnesses said that he continued to write them on the train, tossing them out of the windows as he completed them.[1]

Sugihara paid a high price for disobeying his boss. After being reassigned to other posts (and imprisoned in Russia during one of them), he was eventually asked to resign from his job. Some believe it's because his superiors had learned of his actions in Lithuania. He worked mundane jobs, selling lightbulbs at one point, and was often separated from his family due to his work for the remainder of his career. But he never regretted his workplace disobedience:

No one knows exactly how many visas Sugihara wrote. . . . The most commonly accepted number is that 6,000-10,000 Jews escaped the Holocaust because of Sugihara's actions. Today, somewhere between 40,000 and 80,000 people are descendants of the Jews saved by Sugihara. . . . After the war, many of the "Sugihara Survivors" tried to locate him, but no one in the Japanese government or the Foreign Ministry seemed to remember him. Finally, in 1968, Joshua Nishri, economic attaché from Israel to Japan and one of the survivors, managed to track him down. All this time Sugihara had no idea whether his actions had saved anyone, and he was surprised and gratified to discover that they had: he felt that if he had saved even one life all his sacrifices would have been worth it. The following year, he and his family were invited to Israel, and in 1985, Israel named Sugihara one of the "Righteous among the Gentiles," the highest honor Israel can grant.[2]

Submission to God rather than the employer, in Sugihara's case, resulted in a measure of earthly honor toward the end of his life, but this will not always happen. Most of his life Sugihara's impact went unrecognized and unknown even to himself. That didn't matter; his conscience before God was clear, and he knew where his reward lay.

THE HOUSEHOLD

The third sphere of authority is the household. The concept of submission in marriage is a controversial one. In 1 Peter 3, we see a command to wives to "submit yourselves to your own husbands" (v. 1) for the reason that their submission may win over their husbands if they're not already believers. The text goes on to cite Sarah as an exemplar, as she "obeyed Abraham," her husband (who, you may recall, made some pretty poor decisions!). Paul offers a similar command in Ephesians 5:22 and 5:24 and in Titus 2:5: wives, be subject (submit) to your husband. Husbands like these verses very much, but I argue that they only represent one side of the coin. These verses hit the nerve of a wife's struggle— submitting to her husband as the God-ordained head of the household. This headship authority is not a dictatorship, by the way, but the loving exercise of divine authority *under the lordship of Jesus Christ*.

But the husband also has a nerve. The other side of the coin is the husband's call to self-sacrificially love his bride, in which he gives up himself to serve his wife and her needs in a lifelong covenant relationship: "Husbands, love your wives, just as Christ loved the church and gave himself up for her" (Ephesians 5:25). (Note that this command comes four verses after Paul's call for mutual submission in all believers' relationships "out of reverence for Christ.") Likewise, in 1 Peter, the author instructs, "Husbands, in the same way be considerate as you live with your wives, and treat them with respect" (1 Peter 3:7).[3] Why? Because they are coheirs in the "gracious gift of life"—in other words, they're coequal in God's eyes.

Just as wives are to respect and submit to their husbands "as to the Lord," husbands are to nourish and cherish their wives as *their* act of submission to God, building up their wives by *leading in love*—even when there's no reciprocity. This is not a husband's natural bent; believe me, I know, from being married for more than fifty years (and counting). This type of love has to come from a greater source. It's much more than an emotion or a romantic feeling. It's a daily choice.

So, a wife's natural inclination is to resist submitting to and respecting her husband, while a husband is more naturally inclined to take the selfish route and treat his wife harshly and without love. Neither gets a pass—both are to submit to God by submitting to one another, regardless of how the other responds; in a sense, their submission is to the design of marriage, and that submission is easier for both spouses when it's mutual. My pastor friend Steve All often counsels wives by asking them, "What would you do for a husband who was willing to die for you?" Looking at the question that way makes both spouses' calls to submission more straightforward—and challenging. The inevitable response of the wife is, "I'd do anything!" to which Steve responds, "Well, that's submission!"

Pain and suffering pervade this relationship, which is a prime battleground for the devil to gain a foothold. That pain may come from within, due to failures on the part of each spouse, and it may also come from without, as it did for Rick and Polly Rood.

Till death us do part. Though I don't know him personally, Rick is a fellow alumnus of Dallas Theological Seminary. His journey, told in his book *Our Story . . . His Story*, beautifully demonstrates mutual submission in marriage. When his wife of twelve years contracted the neurodegenerative illness known as Huntington's disease at age thirty-four, the couple was initially in disbelief but hopeful (a normal reaction); then reality set in, along with the typical feelings of uncertainty and fear. They decided to still live their lives as best they could, and one particular day Rick (a pastor) says he sat in his office and, after reading Psalm 68:19, consciously placed his trust in God to "daily bear [his] burden," no matter what the days ahead looked like.[4]

As Polly's disease progressed and she could no longer live at home, she entered a nursing home long before most people ever do. Rick easily could've left her to die and moved on with his life. Instead, he allowed the entire pattern of his life to be altered, taking time to care for and visit his dying wife every night as her days on earth dwindled. (Sadly, only one other resident at Polly's nursing home received a nightly visitor.) Polly's suffering was relieved when she went home to the Lord, despite the couple's desire and prayers for a miraculous healing. While Rick sometimes asked God why he was allowing the restricted nature of their lives to be prolonged—Polly in her nursing home, Rick visiting daily as the routine of life carried on—he never imagined abandoning Polly in her final days. He truly led with love, praying as he drove to see her one night: "Lord, I don't understand the reason for our life right now—but if You decide that the best way we can bring glory to You is by our living out the remainder of our days like this, I'm willing. If this means spending the rest of my life at her bedside, until You take her home, then give us the grace to do it one day at a time."[5]

Modeling Christlike love toward one's spouse can be hard because it's in the context of a lifelong bond, where we see the other, warts and all, and are still called to love no matter what life throws our way. While the Roods shared a deep mutual love for each other, this is not the case in every marriage. Our love often goes unappreciated and unacknowledged. Unrequited love, whether in marriage or another relationship, is a form of sharing in the sufferings of Christ, and it's a hard but important way God forms Christlike character in us as he prepares us—and others—for eternity.[6]

THE CHURCH

Local churches (bodies of believers) are the fourth and final sphere of submission Peter discusses in his epistle. Churches were, and still are, to be overseen by elders with the help of deacons, according to the New Testament (see, for example, 1 Timothy 3:1-13; Titus 1:5-9). These church leaders exist to serve members through guidance, teaching, and pastoral care. Peter speaks specifically to church elders in his first epistle, emphasizing how they're to carry out their roles:

> To the elders among you . . . Be shepherds of God's flock that is under your care, watching over them—not because you must, but because you are willing, as God wants you to be; not pursuing dishonest gain, but eager to serve; not lording it over those entrusted to you, but being examples to the flock. And when the Chief Shepherd appears, you will receive the crown of glory that will never fade away.
>
> In the same way, you who are younger, submit yourselves to your elders. (1 Peter 5:1-5)

As in the other three spheres, the pattern is clear: Christ is head of the church, and the elders are to place themselves under God's authority as they carry out the responsibilities God has entrusted to them for the good of the people. The congregants, in turn, are to submit to the elders' authority.

When submission in this sphere works as designed, the results can be beautiful, building up the body of Christ on an individual and corporate level. Linda Graf offers one such example.

Involved in music ministry at her church, she describes in her book *Bitter Truth* how, for years, she led a "lifestyle of self-pity, bitterness, and anger" stemming from emotional wounds and circumstances of her childhood. The deep hurt she felt spilled over into her relationships as an adult, particularly her relationship with her pastor (who was also her boss).[7] Eventually, the situation came to a head. As Linda was beginning to recognize the reality of her own sin, she still found herself at odds with her pastor, and she still thought *he* was in the wrong. So she called an elder in the church to step in and help. The elder listened long and hard to her side of the story. Then he offered his assessment: "Look, he [the pastor] isn't perfect . . . but it's not him. It's you. You're bitter."[8] Though taken aback at first, Linda swallowed this "bitter truth," listening and ultimately submitting to this elder's gentle but firm rebuke. She stopped pointing fingers at her pastor and began working on her bitterness problem.

Over time, by the power of God working in Linda's willing spirit, wounds healed, and love replaced bitterness. Though her suffering as a child initially made her bitter, she has now been made better, by God's power and grace, and her book and openness to sharing her story are ministering to thousands.[9] She remains an integral member of the music ministry team at the same church, under the same pastor she previously couldn't get along with.

Resistance to church authority. When church authority runs amok, resistance is in order. The best example in history is the Protestant Reformation, which emerged at a time when the twin spires of the civil government and the Roman Catholic Church exercised totalitarian power over the people of Europe. The churches were erecting magnificent buildings while the people who met in them were paupers. The abuse of their power, coupled with theological errors within the church, prompted Martin Luther's posting of his Ninety-Five Theses—the inciting event that set the Reformation into motion.

Today, we think of Luther as a bold and fiery man—the one who dared defy the highest authorities of his time. But in his initial presentation to then-emperor Charles V in April 1521, Luther was actually barely audible, humble, and even uncertain of himself. The emperor granted Luther's request to think overnight about whether he really believed what he was saying or wanted to recant his teachings that contradicted church teachings of that time. When Luther came back the next day, he'd apparently found his voice, as he was louder and more confident. Still, his humility and respect were intact as he spoke:

> Unless I am convinced by the testimony of the Scriptures or clear reason, for I do not trust in the Pope or in the councils alone, since it is well known that they often err and contradict themselves, I am bound to the Scriptures I have quoted and my conscience is captive to the Word of God. I cannot and I will not retract anything, since it is neither safe nor right to go against conscience. I cannot do otherwise. Here I stand. God help me. Amen.[10]

Defiance of church authority is rarely so dramatic. Another example in this arena is William Carey, known today as the father of modern missions.

At one time the church was not convinced of the importance of investing in foreign missionary work. But a young schoolmaster and cobbler turned pastor knew it was important, and he was willing to be sent himself. Yet, when Carey first presented the "wider vision" of missions abroad, a church leader at the time apparently told him to "sit down" and, in effect, let God worry about converting the heathens.[11] While the accuracy of this rebuke by his elder is questioned, we do know Carey was met with strong resistance to his (completely biblical) ideas of evangelism and missions.[12] It took great personal devotion to God and his Word to "arouse the apathetic Christians in the churches," starting with the ministers who led them.[13] If he had submitted to the leaders' wishes, he'd have returned to being a pastor and lived a quiet, comfortable life in England. Instead, he became one of the most important missionaries to India in history and laid the groundwork for international missions around the globe.

The question to ask in this sphere is whether the authorities are deviating from the Word of God on *essential doctrines of the faith* and not merely on nonessentials that are a matter of interpretation. This can be a complicated matter, however, since even well-intentioned believers do not always agree on what is and isn't an essential doctrine.[14] Christian charity should always mark these conversations, and in a church where the elders' opinion differs from one's own, it's best for a believer to strive for unity and only make an issue out of a matter that is clearly an essential doctrine of the faith. A few of these essentials include the doctrine of the triune God and of the God-man, as well as the historicity of Jesus' death, burial, and resurrection.

One final note on submission to church authority: as in any of the other three spheres, a command to submit to elders in a church does not give those leaders a blank check to behave however they want. Principles of accountability and church discipline should be followed for leaders, especially since the standards for elders and deacons are laid out so clearly in Scripture.

HUMILITY TOWARD ALL

As Peter wraps up his discussion of the four spheres of submission, he makes a summary statement to cover all arenas involving relationships:

> All of you, clothe yourselves with humility toward one
> another, because,
>> "God opposes the proud
>> but shows favor to the humble." (1 Peter 5:5, quoting
>>> from Proverbs 3:34)

Peter's words ring true with Paul's in Ephesians 5:21: "Submit to one another out of reverence for Christ." They also ring true with James's letter, in which he quotes the same proverb as Peter:

> But he gives us more grace. That is why Scripture says:
>> "God opposes the proud
>> but shows favor to the humble."
> Submit yourselves, then, to God. (James 4:6-7)

Our submission is mutual within the body of Christ: whether we're young or old, an elder or not, married or single, all believers are to submit to each other as members of one body in which no member is more or less important (1 Corinthians 12:12-25). This submission is part of our joint submission to God himself, our Chief Shepherd.

Submission to one another means we love and serve one another not because of what people give us but because Christ loved us first. We'll talk more about the importance of showing Christlike character in chapter nine as we focus on the role suffering plays in equipping us to minister to others.

9

MINISTERING
TO OTHERS

Use whatever gift you have received to serve others,
as faithful stewards of God's grace in its various forms.

1 PETER 4:10

FOUR YEARS AFTER CIVIL WAR broke out in Rwanda, tensions between the majority Hutu population and the Tutsi minority came to a head. The Rwandan genocide of 1994, which occurred over a period of just one hundred days, is one of the most tragic incidents in human history, killing as many as a million Rwandans (an eighth of the population) and displacing many others.[1]

One of the refugees from the genocide was John Rucyahana, a Tutsi. Rucyahana grew up near the border and fled with his parents as a young man to the Congo (as it was known then) and eventually to Uganda, where he met Christ in a refugee camp at age twenty-one. He forewent other professional opportunities, sensing that God was calling him into vocational ministry.[2] He was eventually ordained and became an Anglican bishop.

In 1994, weeks after the genocide ended, he and eleven other pastors traveled to Rwanda to embark on a ministry of reconciliation—reconciling both Rwandans with God and Rwandans with Rwandans, some whose family members and neighbors had slaughtered each other weeks before. Though it was risky to go back so soon (especially since Rucyahana was a Tutsi, the ethnic minority that the majority had vowed to eliminate), he felt it was necessary to be able to minister effectively: "If God is going to use us; we need to go there and see this for ourselves. If we are going to preach God again there, we don't need to be told by anyone what happened. We must see for ourselves."[3]

In his subsequent ministry, he saw God take "the brokenness caused by evil and [use] it for a greater purpose."[4] "Preaching hope, from the top of a pile of bones," Bishop Rucyahana spoke not as an outsider but as one whose own family members were murdered during the genocide, and who also had to forgive.[5] His ministry was further augmented by his own experience as a refugee. In his book *The Bishop of Rwanda*, he writes:

> I am not preaching such things [like forgiveness through Christ] from an isolated altar far away from the conflict and oblivious to the pain. I speak from Rwanda, and I speak through my own pain. My sixteen-year-old niece, whom I dearly loved, was raped and killed in a torturous, horrible way. . . . I know what it is to forgive through the tears.[6]

THE CONTEXT OF ADVERSITY

Examples abound of individual believers, such as Bishop Rucyahana, who have developed vibrant ministries out of the context of their own painful backgrounds. Both Ling and Esther Ahn Kim, mentioned in chapters seven and five, respectively, benefited from the ministry of godly mothers, whose prayers and spiritual support for their daughters grew out of their own suffering and risks they had taken for their faith. Nearly all heroes of the faith experienced major trials or pains in their lives at some point—ranging from the death of a parent while young to poverty, chronic sickness, or some other challenge. The idea that God uses our own difficulties so we can turn around and help others is not surprising, given the universal nature of human suffering. This idea also comes straight from Scripture:

> Praise be to the God and Father of our Lord Jesus Christ, the Father of compassion and the God of all comfort, who comforts us in all our troubles, so that we can comfort those in any trouble with the comfort we ourselves receive from God. For just as we share abundantly in the sufferings of Christ, so also our comfort abounds through Christ. (2 Corinthians 1:3-5)

In some mysterious way the comfort we personally receive from God is given through us to others. The comfort itself is God's, but we're one of the means by which he provides it to a hurting and broken world. As his body we become his channels of comfort, which expand over time. George Müller, a nineteenth-century English pastor, explained the process this way:

> The child of God must be willing to be a channel through which God's bounties flow, both with regard to temporal and spiritual things. This channel is narrow and shallow at first, it may be; yet there is room for some of the waters of God's bounty to pass through. And if we cheerfully yield ourselves as channels for this purpose, then the channel becomes wider and deeper, and the waters of the bounty of God can pass through more abundantly.[7]

In modern times Joni Eareckson Tada is one of these ever-widening channels, as her story and books have ministered to millions (and counting). Her ministry wasn't inevitable, though—remember the anger and bitterness that first marked her after she became a quadriplegic. What's more, her story of suffering continues to add chapters, with a new cancer diagnosis at the end of 2018.[8]

A man who is in a similar situation to Tada became the opposite of a channel: more like a dam or a dead-end pond, with almost no input and no output. Embittered by the disability that put him in a wheelchair, his attitude pushes away everyone who tries to come into his life and show him love. Not only is he a very unhappy man, but he's lonely. His practically nonexistent sphere of influence contrasts sharply with Tada's, whose ministry name, Joni and Friends, signals the vast community that has emerged and continues to expand out of her own adversity.

ROYAL PRIESTS

The ministry of comfort George Müller described and that Paul communicates in 2 Corinthians strikes at the heart of Peter's first epistle. In his letter Peter urges his readers to minister right where they are, in the context of their adversities. To communicate this role, he reminds them (and us, by extension) that believers are not only pilgrims and citizens of another world but priests:

> You also, like living stones, are being built into a spiritual house to be a *holy priesthood*, offering spiritual sacrifices acceptable to God through Jesus Christ. . . .
>
> You are a chosen people, *a royal priesthood*, a holy nation, God's special possession, that you may declare the praises of him who called you out of darkness into his wonderful light. (1 Peter 2:5, 9, emphasis added)

Priesthood is a foreign concept to most of us today. In the Old Testament, the priests of Israel were given specific instructions on making repeated offerings and sacrifices to mediate between God and the people. They had special access to God that the people didn't, and the high priest had even greater access (to the Holy of Holies—the innermost room of the tabernacle). Their how-to handbook, the book of Leviticus, is one of the least-read and least-favorite in the Bible. (I confess to joining the majority on that opinion!) A careful study of the tabernacle, with all its details, however, can be greatly rewarding, as the rich symbolism pointing to Christ is astounding. But for now, all you really need to know is that the priestly role in the Judaic tradition had two basic components: (1) representing God to the people, and (2) representing the people to God.

When Christ came, he fulfilled this mediator role in a permanent sense, becoming our great high priest forever (Hebrews 2:17; 3:1; 4:14-15; 6:20). He is the ultimate priest who "truly meets our need" in a way no other priest ever has or ever will (Hebrews 7:26). As our high priest Jesus mediates God's *saving grace* by sacrificing himself on our behalf to save us from eternal punishment in exchange for eternal glory. He also mediates God's *sustaining grace* by both ministering to us moment by moment through his Spirit (Romans 8:26-27) and interceding (praying) for us at the Father's right hand on an ongoing basis (Romans 8:34).

In saying that believers are members of the royal priesthood, Peter is emphasizing, first, that *all believers* have access to the Father through Christ; we need no other mediator (Hebrews 10:19-22). Second, we serve in priestly roles through ministry to others. We don't mediate between God and people in the same way the Levitical priests did—the days of that institution are over (Hebrews 7:27)—but God uses us to minister to people, and he listens to us when we intercede on behalf of people. In this "priesthood of all believers," we are *all* called to full-time ministry, but in different spheres of influence (from the home to the marketplace to vocational ministry). We're agents of God in the world, manifesting him to others and mediating his grace in a Christlike role.

PRACTICING SYMPATHY

Among the various admonitions Peter gives in his letter is to "be sympathetic" (1 Peter 3:8). This is a critical aspect of our priestly role—and it brings us back again to the example of Jesus. In the Old Testament, God is often called "compassionate," but in the New Testament he sends his Son as the one perfect high priest, whose experience in the flesh means he now identifies and sympathizes fully with humanity. Thus, Hebrews points to Jesus as our *sympathetic* high priest: "We do not have a high priest who cannot sympathize with our weaknesses, but One who has been tempted in all things as *we are, yet* without sin" (Hebrews 4:15 NASB).

Like Bishop Rucyahana ministering on the soil where his own deep pain was inflicted, Jesus ministered on the soil of sinful humanity—becoming one of us, experiencing the same types of challenges and difficulties we face (in fact, much worse than what most of us will face), from physical persecution and slander to exhaustion and betrayal by friends and family. While God is omniscient and thus knows exactly what we're going through at all times, there's something altogether different about the all-knowing God actually coming into the midst of our suffering and experiencing it *with us*. Indeed, the mysterious fellowship of sharing in Christ's sufferings is often the single greatest comfort to a believer during adversity—even greater than the comfort of the promise of future glory (which is, after all, *not yet*, at least not completely).

Just as Jesus' sympathy with us is a vital aspect of our relationship with him, our ability to sympathize or empathize with others is a critical facet of our ministry to them.[9] This was the case for Jerry Sittser, who wrote of the importance both of knowing that Christ himself suffered and also of fellow believers emulating Jesus' example by entering into his suffering with him. As friends came around him to mourn with him the losses of his wife, daughter, and mother, he says the reason community helped instead of hurt him in this process was because they made his suffering their own. They felt his pain (not literally, but on the soul level), living out the words of Paul that "if one part [of the body of Christ] suffers, every part suffers with it" (1 Corinthians 12:26). Sittser writes:

> When people suffering loss do find community, it comes as a result of conscious choices they and other people make. . . . They [others] must be willing to be changed by someone else's loss, though they might not have been directly affected by it. Good comfort requires empathy, forces adjustments, and sometimes mandates huge sacrifices. Comforters must be prepared to let the pain of another become their own and so let it transform them.[10]

In their actions toward Sittser and his family, these brothers and sisters in Christ fulfilled their role as "royal priests." They mourned with the mourning. And they represent a contrast to the largely unsympathetic friends of Job. Job's friends, author John Claypool points out, missed a key point about suffering: "The basic issue of grief is never a rational explanation."[11] Through "misguided intellectualizing," Job's friends wound up causing, or at least speeding the onset of, Job's "seething resentment against God and the whole universe."[12] Granted, they commiserated with him for seven full days without saying a word, but once they opened their mouths, their empathy disappeared as they assumed a punitive rather than a purifying approach to Job's suffering.

With something as complex and mysterious as suffering, we'd do well to learn the negative lessons of Job's friends: don't be prideful, don't speak hastily, don't assume you have the answer to the situation. We can also learn the positive lessons of Sittser's community: be humble, quick to listen, loving, and sympathetic; willing to speak the truth, but in a grace-filled manner (Colossians 4:6). It's trite but true that people don't care how much we know until they know how much we care—and that means, in our priestly role we need to make a conscious effort to feel the other person's pain (sympathy) or at least imagine what they are going through (empathy), and to realize that we cannot fully comprehend what their experience is truly like (even if we have been in a similar situation).

At the same time, we need to be discerning, because in some cases sympathy is not what the other person needs at all—in fact, showing sympathy may enable a victim mentality or false narrative instead of actually helping a person. Remembering we're all both agents and victims will help us determine that fine line between indulging a person's self-pity and ministering at a true point of need.

Our own suffering can have a tenderizing or softening effect on us, enabling us to sympathize and empathize with others in a way we couldn't before. Joni Eareckson Tada can minister to people bound to a wheelchair and others with physical disabilities in a way others cannot do as well; likewise, someone who has experienced persecution, family betrayal, depression, loss of a child, miscarriage, or any number of other specific forms of grief or trouble often are able to minister to people in a similar boat in an especially effective manner. In addition to having an inside view and being able to say, "I've been where you are," a person who's been in a similar situation has insight into the temptations unique to that adversity. The words of someone who can say "I've been there" while also reminding of God's love and sovereignty carry a lot more clout than the words of someone who has never been in your shoes.

REPRESENTING GOD TO PEOPLE

Now that we know more of *how* we're to go about our priestly role—drawing close to God and others with a discerning and sympathetic approach, just as Jesus did—let's turn to *what* a priest does.

The first part of the priestly role is to represent God to people. This role entails both delivering the words of Scripture (speaking or proclaiming) and serving one another in love. These broader categories of speaking and serving that we see in 1 Peter are encompassed in the lists of spiritual gifts detailed elsewhere in Scripture (especially Romans 12 and 1 Corinthians 12). Here are Peter's words: "Each of you should use whatever gift you have received to serve others, as faithful stewards of God's grace in its various forms. If anyone speaks, they should do so as one who speaks the very words of God. If anyone serves, they should do so with the strength God provides, so that in all things God may be praised through Jesus Christ" (1 Peter 4:10-11).

Notice the emphasis on grace, which runs throughout Peter's letter: we're to be "faithful stewards of God's grace in its various forms." When an action is done in service to the King, it becomes an external expression of an inward grace. That communication of his grace, often paired with the fulfillment of a tangible need, is the purpose of service. Likewise, the purpose of the speaking gifts is to communicate God's truth, "as one who speaks the very words of God."[13]

Speaking God's word. A speaking ministry can take an oral or written form. A wonderful example of the latter is Anne Steele, whose hymns once comprised up to a third of songs in hymnbooks for American churches. The daughter of a merchant and pastor in the eighteenth century, Steele was plagued throughout her life by physical ailments, including "symptoms consistent with malaria."[14] Although she led an effective ministry of her own as well as in support of her father's ministry, her writing betrays the context of inner pain and struggle out of which she served and edified others. She was ultimately confined to her bed in the final years of her life.

Despite, or perhaps *because of,* her chronic adversities, Steele penned dozens of hymns and poems in which she poured out her soul to God and sought solace in him alone. These words comforted thousands of believers on both sides of the Atlantic for at least two centuries. Her hymns have enjoyed a recent resurgence, and perhaps her best-known today begins

Dear refuge of my weary soul,
On thee, when sorrows rise;
On thee, when waves of trouble roll,
My fainting hope relies.[15]

Line after line, Steele's words minister to hurting souls, bodies, and hearts, urging people to cast their cares upon the Lord and "wait beneath [His] feet."[16]

Whether through the written or spoken word, or merely our presence, our priestly ministry of representing God to people reflects the pattern of the great high priest himself, who came "full of *grace and truth*" (John 1:14, 17, emphasis added). As we minister through speaking and serving, all is to be done in the control of the Holy Spirit and driven by love.

Loving one another. Peter tells his readers to love other believers deeply or "fervently" (NASB). In fact, he gives this charge three times in the letter:

Above all, love each other deeply, because love covers a multitude of sins. (1 Peter 4:8 NASB)

Since you have in obedience to the truth purified your souls for a sincere love of the brethren, fervently love one another from the heart. (1 Peter 1:22 NASB)

Love the family of believers. (1 Peter 2:17)

Love for other believers (and for nonbelievers) is in fact *God's* love channeled through us. We're agents of his love in the world, just as we're agents of his comfort. Loving people, of course, is the Second Great Commandment, and it's the identifying mark of Jesus' followers (John 13:35).

Suffering has a way of sharpening our focus, helping us see the importance of this crowning commandment. For one thing, we will never suffer greatly for the sake of Christ *merely* out of duty, but we will sacrifice much out of our love for him, which necessarily flows into love for others.

Second, when it comes to loving others, adversity helps us see people more clearly from an eternal standpoint. Our possessions, positions, and pleasures won't last beyond this lifetime, and as they begin to let us down, we start to look for a longer-lasting investment and legacy. People (as immortal souls) and the Word of God are the only two things that fit the bill. Thus, the greatest thing we can do in this life is to invest God's Word into people, both through our lips and through our lives, by loving them for their own sake, just as Christ did. This investment is the only kind that won't slip through our fingers.

Being hospitable. As an extension of our love for those in the family of God, we're to offer hospitality without grumbling or complaining (1 Peter 4:9). Hospitality encompasses an element of care for others, even strangers (including those outside the family of God). Every Christian is called to show hospitality—not only those who consider it their special gifting (see also Romans 12:13). Showing hospitality isn't restricted to those who have a home to open up to others. Hospitality is simply a show of genuine friendly warmth toward others through whatever means are available to us.

My coauthor Jenny told me about an incident during a difficult season of her life. One day she invited a friend over just to talk and enjoy some much-needed company. When the friend showed up at the door, Jenny apologized in advance that she hadn't had time to tidy up her home. The friend looked at her with perplexity, then embraced her in a giant hug as she laughed and said, "I didn't come to see your house; I came to see *you!*" Jenny never forgot her friend's freeing statement. Today, it permanently affects how she hosts: she seeks to focus on preparing for the people who are coming over, not only on preparing the physical appearance of her house.

The purpose of hospitality is not to show off or impress others but to demonstrate authentic care and concern for the needs of another. It will often mean inconveniencing ourselves and sacrificing our own agendas for the sake of others—something those of us in a clock-driven culture may find difficult.

Indeed, with self-absorption rampant, thanks to the ubiquity of personal mobile technology, the art of hospitality has begun to be lost in many places, especially when distraction is layered into an already individualistic society. A missionary in an African country told a story of how a man was several hours late to work one day without alerting his boss ahead of time. Those of us in the West, this missionary noted, would likely exclaim, "How irresponsible!" The missionary went on to explain that one of this man's distant relatives arrived at his house unexpectedly that morning just as he was about to leave for work. In his culture it's customary to drop everything to welcome visitors (no matter how well you know them), even if it means not only being late but losing a half-day's wages. While not a Christian custom, this custom puts many Christians to shame in that it prioritizes immortal souls over productivity and punctuality.

We could take this example to an inappropriate extreme, but the point is that we are called to a fervent love and should freely and often show hospitality toward others. Many of us miss out on incredible blessing by not prioritizing these commands in our walk with God. Some of the people who are the most willing in this area are those who have suffered and know the power of personal contact as a means of mediating God's grace in our lives. Ours is an incarnational faith, and impromptu shows of hospitality among fellow believers can be one of the greatest blessings both to give and to receive. I believe it's an art we need to recover, particularly in a society that is growing increasingly hostile toward the faith. At a time when "the love of most will grow cold" (Matthew 24:12), hospitality spreads the warmth of Christlike love to others—and it also changes us in the process.

REPRESENTING PEOPLE TO GOD

The second component of our priestly roles is representing people to God. This role is most obviously accomplished through intercessory prayer. As I explain in my book *Conformed to His Image*, intercession as a ministry entails more than praying for someone a couple of times; it refers to the ability to pray "for a long period of time on a regular basis for the ministries and needs of others."[17] We're to "pray through," as R. A. Torrey says—not just praying for something or someone once but for years or as long as it takes.[18] He adds, "One of the great needs of the present day is men and women who will not only start out to pray for things but pray on and on and on" until "we get it [whatever we're praying for], or until God makes it very clear and very definite to us that it is not His will to give it."[19]

It's a tremendous blessing to me when friends make a point to tell me that they're praying daily for me and Karen. Some of my friends and relatives have told me on numerous occasions that they remember us every day in their prayers; I know these people are actually doing it—it's not just politeness. To know I'm being held up to God regularly by these individuals is a great encouragement. Their ministry is even more robust than that because they will often share a word of encouragement back from God's Word with me (that first aspect of the priestly role). When someone is going through a dark time, especially a prolonged one, intercessory prayer can be a particularly big blessing, sometimes presenting people to God when they themselves don't have the strength to pray for themselves. In any ministry of intercession we're never alone but are aided by the Spirit:

> In the same way, the Spirit helps us in our weakness. We do not know what we ought to pray for, but the Spirit himself intercedes for us through wordless groans. And he who searches our hearts knows the mind of the Spirit, because the Spirit intercedes for God's people in accordance with the will of God. (Romans 8:26-27)

I've felt the truth of these verses keenly as I've watched Karen undergo the diagnosis of Parkinson's disease and the impact of that news. While my heart keenly desires physical healing for my wife, God does not seem to be giving it. I've had to resist the urge to demand of God and instead ask his help in knowing how best to pray for Karen. I also have to guard my heart against hoping *in* her healing, even though I hope *for* it.

Years ago I developed a little booklet on prayer that I recently republished.[20] While the entire booklet is relevant to intercession, one section that lists ten principles of intercession is especially apropos and can be found in appendix two of this book. When we intercede for others as a ministry, particularly those who are suffering, one important principle is to pray in "the will of God" (Romans 8:27). When we hold up others to our Father, we should always keep in mind that he has a larger plan for that person than the particular need we're aware of. Our prayers for others can easily be small and shortsighted, with only temporal needs and happiness in mind. The greatest way we can intercede for people is to pray for their salvation if they're not yet believers and for their sanctification (growth in Christlikeness, including their ministry to and impact on others) if they're believers. I personally like to use Paul's four life-changing prayers for others, found in three of his letters, and these are in appendix three along with three prayers of hope I adapted out of passages from Peter's first epistle.

The power of intercession. In addition to friends and family who faithfully pray for me (especially when I let them know I'm facing a particular challenge), several people from history come to mind when I think of inspiring examples of intercessors. The first is my former professor, the late Howard Hendricks (better known to students as "Prof"), who taught for sixty years at Dallas Theological Seminary. The story of his persistent prayers for his father is publicly known. He prayed faithfully for his dad to come to Christ for more than four *decades*. Can you imagine praying for someone that long and not giving up? His father did come to Christ late in life (a few months before he died)—responding to the same gospel message his son had taught for years, but using another of God's messengers.

Another exemplar in the area of intercession is George Müller, a German-born English pastor in the 1800s. Müller, remember, spoke of being ever-widening channels of grace used by God. In addition to pastoring the same church for more than six decades in Bristol, England, this humble man built orphan houses—and cared for more than ten thousand orphans in his life—on the foundation of prayer. He never asked people for money but simply prayed God would provide and then waited for God to answer (which he always did, in one way or another). Müller's ministry included regular intercession on behalf of the children he oversaw, but it also extended well beyond the orphans. In his writings, he tells of fervent intercession for five different people in his life starting in 1844. He determined to represent these people to God, one by one, praying for their conversion. All five came to Christ— two after his death; Müller had prayed for over half a century for those two individuals![21]

One final example of an intercessor who not only prayed for someone suffering but did so out of her own adversity is the sister of French pastor Adolphe Monod. Monod is little known to Americans today but was the most prominent Protestant preacher of nineteenth-century France, where he became the voice of a great spiritual awakening. His influence did not come, however, until after he emerged from a deep, personal spiritual crisis.

As a young, ordained pastor, Monod was in a state of spiritual confusion when assigned a pastorate in Naples, Italy. Preaching weekly, his doubt grew and "escalated into a crisis" as he wrestled with whether he really believed what he was speaking from the pulpit.[22] In his inner turmoil he had pleaded for prayer from family and close friends, particularly his older sister, Adèle Babut. Although she had been praying all along for her brother, a breakthrough and resolution to his crisis came shortly after she wrote him, and right on the heels of her loss of a second daughter (this one at six months old). In the pain of her own tragedy, Babut wrote (in part):

Adolphe, in this solemn moment, I thought also of you. No doubt it was God who, in his infinite goodness, said to my torn soul that it could also receive blessing on your behalf and that the anguish of your poor sister could be the source of the Christian peace that we ask for you with such fervor. Dear Adolphe, if I am not mistaken, if my daughter in her death could preach to you with more eloquence and conviction than all those who have been seeking your good . . . I would thank God for all I have suffered. The thought of the happiness of my daughters and of the happy change in my dear Adolphe would . . . give me the strength to resign myself to all that may still await me, convinced that no sorrow would be too much to pay for such a great benefit. . . . Oh, in these days of misery and mourning, what would I become without him [God]! If he is not alive, if his words are not eternally true, where can we draw strength against so many sorrows?[23]

Within months of receiving his sister's letter, Monod's crisis ended and "real peace came into his life."[24] In his reply to Babut, he indicated the central role her ministry of intercession played in his turnaround:

My tender and beloved Adèle, you are a sister who has pushed fraternal love and Christian charity toward me to the point of finding consolation in the death of her only child. If God used the rending of her heart to restore peace to mine, such a sister has first rights to be told immediately of the first steps God has caused me to take in Christian peace.[25]

The letter continues with a detailed description of his inner transformation through the Spirit's power—a transformation that would lead to many other people saved in France and beyond, all because a sister was willing to minister out of her own pain.

Of course, the stories of countless other prayer warriors, both modern-day and from history, could be told—many of whom, like Babut, intercede in the midst of their own weakness and suffering. Indeed, their prayers are often enhanced and uttered with greater urgency because of the mysterious fellowship that comes from suffering. Many a believer will testify to the mutual blessing of praying for others, as God uses such ministry to take our eyes, at least momentarily, off our own pain and onto the needs of others (Philippians 2:4).

A final note about intercession: it's common for a believer to pray for another person in a moment of crisis. But that person often is abandoned in our prayers as the crisis fades into the past. We ought not to give up in prayer so easily, and when we do "pray through," those we lift up to God will be blessed, and so will we, as we become a part of his continued work in that person and the world at large.

THE NEED FOR A SECOND REFORMATION

The Protestant Reformation (with a little aid from the invention of the printing press) successfully put the Scriptures back into the hands of the people in God's family, but we need to put ministry back into the people's hands too. The priesthood of all believers is too often neglected in the full sense of the role. Peter would not be pleased!

Today, there's a prevalent sacerdotal mindset whereby we hold to the notion that the priestly role, which Peter reminds us belongs to every believer, is a role we should leave to the "professionals" (that is, paid clergy). Nowhere in the New Testament, though, do we see this division between a professional priest or pastor and the laity. Elders are appointed to serve in a capacity of authority within local bodies of believers; however, their roles are primarily spoken of in terms of shepherding or overseeing the flock while the flock as a whole (not only the leaders) does the work of ministry.

Without this robust view of ministry encompassing the full body of Christ, it's no wonder so many people find the church to be one of the places they feel least comfortable or welcome during seasons of suffering. We're neglecting our priestly role, and when we do try to embrace it, we're not very skilled in it— we're more apt to seek a quick solution, not one that will require ongoing involvement and investment of time, energy, and patience on our part.

This problem dates back as far as the fourth century, when the waves of persecution under the Roman Empire waned and the church began accumulating power and wealth.[26] A full-blown consumeristic mindset now pervades many churches, although thankfully, there's evidence of a refining process taking place among Christians in the West as a result of an increasingly anti-Christian culture.[27]

EMBRACING OUR PRIESTLY ROLE

As a Christian view of the world is increasingly in the minority in the United States (despite a majority still claiming the Christian label), and as persecution (of various kinds) spreads, it's imperative that true believers take seriously the call to minister to one another as royal priests—through prayer, hospitality, and love, using our God-given gifts of service and proclamation.[28] When we do, God will transmute the lead of suffering into the gold of glory, not only in our lives but in others' lives too.[29]

This is not unlike what happened, and continues to happen, in and through the Amish community of Nickel Mines, Pennsylvania. After a gunman shot and killed five children and seriously wounded five others in a schoolhouse before killing himself, the community was quick to offer forgiveness. Although they hadn't worked through all the emotional difficulties yet (the healing process takes much longer), the victims, their families, and others in the community made an immediate, conscious choice to extend grace to the family of the shooter. Historian and professor Steven Nolt, who coauthored *Amish Grace: How Forgiveness Transcends Tragedy*, noted that the forgiveness extended was not only on an individual level but also collective. Moreover, words of forgiveness were followed by acts of compassion. Stories emerged of quiet hospitality and kindnesses shown between the victims and their families, and the shooter's family. The shooter's parents initially thought they'd have to move far away—the mother, Terri Roberts, recalls thinking initially, "I will never face my Amish neighbors again."[30] But instead of being ostracized as they feared, the Roberts family was shown forgiveness, and even more than that, they were "embraced" by the entire community.[31]

Holt explains, "For [the Amish] this is . . . about following Jesus, about doing what Jesus said, . . . 'Forgive us our debts as we forgive our debtors.' . . . [The Amish] have a 300-, 400-year history of responding to wrong in this way. They have examples, and they also do it as a community."[32] The message is not lost on the Roberts family. Terri was amazed by the love she says "emanated" from the Lancaster County Amish; it even inspired her to return the love with her own gestures of service and compassion (for example, regularly visiting the most traumatically wounded of the survivors).[33]

What a powerful picture of how an entire body of believers can come together and administer grace to the hurting in a priestly role. This tiny town in Pennsylvania is just one example of many where this kind of Christ-centered reconciliation has happened. And in spite of the news headlines, it's clearly not just about Amishness. It's about imitating Jesus in the face of suffering, whether that adversity is inflicted by a violent crime or some other source.

AN ETERNAL GLORY

The God of all grace . . . called you to his eternal glory in Christ.

1 PETER 5:10

WITH HER YOUNG DAUGHTER IN TOW, Elisabeth Elliot chose to live among a South American tribe that, in 1956, speared to death her husband, Jim, and four other missionaries. Jim is the one who once wrote the well-known words, "He is no fool who gives what he cannot keep to gain what he cannot lose."[1] His widow, who shared her martyred husband's passion to tell others about Jesus, shocked the world when she returned to continue the work she and her husband had begun, which would ultimately bring God's Word to the Quichua people and their neighbors (including the Waodoni, then called the Aucas, who had murdered the missionaries) in their own tongue.

Tragedy of another kind struck Elisabeth when, one day, she lost all of her language work down a mountainside; with no file recovery option available at that time, years of work were lost in a moment.

The adversity in this one woman's life seemed never to let up; she remarried after Jim's death, but within a few years she lost her second husband to cancer. Elisabeth went on to write about her suffering (among other topics), becoming one of the most influential Christian women and authors of the twentieth century. The titles of her books about her husband's martyrdom—*Through the Gates of Splendor* and *Shadow of the Almighty*—speak to the great faith this tenacious woman held in a sovereign God in the face of unspeakable tragedy. In one of her books, she expressed God's use of suffering, even to the point of death:

> The death of the seed that falls into the ground produces a new cycle of life—the fresh little shoot, the full stalk, the bud, the flower. . . . The fruit dies to allow the seed to fall once again into the ground. The seed dies and there is a new beginning. Nothing is ever wasted. . . . In God's economy, whether He is making a flower or a human soul, nothing ever comes to nothing.[2]

This attitude comes from one who endured trial after trial, and yet, instead of growing bitter, she let God use her suffering to change her and to minister to others. In one of Elisabeth's regular newsletters later in her ministry, her insights reveal the results of a lifetime of suffering, submission, and relinquishing herself to the alchemy of God's grace:

> Being very much of the earth . . . we always want tangible, visible things: proofs, demonstrations, something to latch on to. If we always had them, of course, faith would be "struck blind." When Jesus hung on a cross, the challenge was flung at Him: Come down! He stayed nailed, not so that spectators would be satisfied (that miracle, His coming down, would have been a great crowd-pleaser), but that the world might

be *saved*. Many of our prayers are directed toward the quick and easy solution. Long-suffering is sometimes the only means by which the greater glory of God will be served, and this is, for the moment, invisible.[3]

In 2015, that greater glory became visible to Elisabeth at last, as she entered the "gates of splendor" following an eighty-eight-year sojourn on earth. After battling dementia and living her final days without fanfare or the ability to communicate, her faith at last became sight.[4] She may rest in an "unvisited tomb," but her influence, without any doubt, has been and continues to be (to borrow George Eliot's phrase again) "incalculably diffusive."[5]

BRIEF VERSUS ETERNAL

Elisabeth Elliot was "all in." She was insistent that God never wastes anything in our lives, including our suffering, and she lived in light of that belief. Her life modeled everything Peter taught his first-century readers—summarized in 1 Peter 5:10: "The God of all grace, who called you to his eternal glory in Christ, after you have suffered a little while, will himself restore you and make you strong, firm and steadfast." In this theme verse, Peter clarifies both our context (adversity) and our ultimate destiny (eternal glory). The one precedes the other: suffering before glory. And no one escapes; Jesus promised we *will* have troubles—suffering is a required course in the university of life, though the syllabus looks different for everyone. But in the end, all our suffering is worth it because compared to the everlasting glory that awaits, it's only brief ("a little while"). Even if we suffer our entire lives, that time will be as nothing compared to eternity.

Imagine a ninety-year-old man who dies and enters God's presence. After just five minutes, if God were to say, "Would you go through those ninety years again, just for these five minutes?"

I claim he would because God's glory is that worthwhile—it would make nine decades of pain seem like nothing. Adversity *feels* like a long time when it's happening, but it's actually not. And although suffering is very real and painful, a life surrendered to Christ will always be more than worth the while.

Remember the thief on the cross, crucified next to Jesus, who made the choice to repent? Matthew's Gospel tells us that criminal initially joined the other criminal, crucified on the other side of Jesus, in heaping insults at Christ (Matthew 27:44). But something changed as that first man hung there dying. God broke through in the context of the most brutal form of capital punishment ever devised. The thief recognized that his own punishment and pain were deserved, while Jesus' were not. To the other crucified criminal, who apparently rejected Jesus to the end, he said, "We are punished justly, for we are getting what our deeds deserve. But this man has done nothing wrong" (Luke 23:41). The God-fearing man then turned to the one in the middle and made a simple request: "Jesus, remember me when you come into your kingdom" (Luke 23:42).

Right then and there, with nail-pierced hands and feet, Jesus transmuted the suffering of that man into the gold of glory in the last hour of his life. Christ's words breathed hope and eternal life into his soul even as the man's body was dying: "Truly I tell you, today you will be with me in paradise" (Luke 23:43). If ever there was a reason for a man to doubt or lose hope, that was the moment, yet even then, redemption was possible. Jesus' words on the cross echo his promise to all his disciples in John 14:3: "If I go and prepare a place for you, I will come back and take you to be with me that you also may be where I am." These words of comfort are a balm to the weary soul: *Don't worry, this won't last forever; I'm coming back—I promise!*

The thief's story differs significantly from that of my friend Barry Morrow, whose story I began this book with; for one, the thief's suffering was deserved, and, second, Barry was already a believer when he was on his deathbed dying of cancer. But both have this in common: their final moments on this earth were marked by deep pain, yet in both cases they surrendered to God in their suffering, which they came to see as nothing compared to the glory promised for all eternity.

LIGHT VERSUS WEIGHTY

In addition to being inevitable and brief, our suffering is *light*, in terms of both duration and intensity, compared to the weight of eternal glory. Paul put it well in some of my favorite verses in the Bible: "Therefore we do not lose heart. Though outwardly we are wasting away, yet inwardly we are being renewed day by day. For our light and momentary troubles are achieving for us an eternal glory that far outweighs them all" (2 Corinthians 4:16-17).[6]

To say that suffering is "light" is not to downplay its felt intensity or difficulty—far from it. Rather, it's a matter of using the correct scale. If our suffering and our future glory are placed on two sides of a scale, the suffering side would immediately zoom up in the air while our future glory would fall with a loud clunk. Paul goes even further in Romans 8:18: "I consider that our present sufferings are *not worth comparing* with the glory that will be revealed in us" (emphasis added).

Any of us can attest to the fact that, at the moment, suffering (sometimes even a smaller-scale kind, like a bad head cold) feels major, not trivial. Often, the picture I just gave of the scale is exactly the opposite in our minds. Our adversities typically feel heavy, burdensome, consequential, as though our world (as we know it) is ending. Sometimes, our suffering is so oppressive or overwhelming that we feel we can't carry on (those who have experienced clinical depression and anxiety know this feeling well).

Paul was no stranger to the all-consuming reality of how suffering can feel. The apostle's résumé of adversities was impressive:

> Five times I received from the Jews the forty lashes minus one. Three times I was beaten with rods, once I was pelted with stones, three times I was shipwrecked, I spent a night and a day in the open sea, I have been constantly on the move. I have been in danger from rivers, in danger from bandits, in danger from my fellow Jews, in danger from Gentiles; in danger in the city, in danger in the country, in danger at sea; and in danger from false believers. I have labored and toiled and have often gone without sleep; I have known hunger and thirst and have often gone without food; I have been cold and naked. Besides everything else, I face daily the pressure of my concern for all the churches. (2 Corinthians 11:24-28)

Yet, even with such an abundance of troubles in his life, much of it for the name of Christ, Paul insisted that *by comparison* the greatness of eternal glory far outweighs the pain of suffering. It's a matter of scale—and of our response.

DESIRE, LONGING, AND GLORY

C. S. Lewis captured this perspective better than anyone in his fittingly titled sermon "The Weight of Glory." Lewis delivered this famous address on June 8, 1942, in a church in Oxford, England, just across the street from where I studied for my doctorate. In the sermon he argued that the problem we humans have is not that our desires are too strong but too weak.[7] We turn down God's offer of "infinite joy," settling instead on lesser and fleeting things that are bound to eventually let us down—wealth, beauty, pleasure, and so on.[8] This is one reason suffering can make someone bitter: if we don't let God use our difficulties to pry our fingers off the tight grip we have on our expectations and turn our attention to a *living* hope (one that won't let us down), then disillusionment can quickly result. If, on the other hand, we go after what God says is valuable, rather than pursuing what's trivial, we won't be disappointed in the end; our treasure will be in its proper place (Matthew 6:19-21).

If the glory God has in store for us is so great, his "unblushing promises of reward" so "staggering" in nature (as Lewis says), then why do we have such a hard time desiring it and letting go of our own puny visions for our lives?[9] Why, in other words, does God's call to eternal glory found in 1 Peter 5:10 fail to motivate so many of us?

I believe we fail to be allured by the right things because the world has switched the price tags on us, and we've fallen for the new pricing scheme. Tony Campolo tells a story of his childhood during a tradition called "Mischief Night" in Philadelphia held the day before Halloween.[10] One year, a friend and he planned to break in to a local department store (then called a five-and-dime) and, when no one was looking, switch the price tags on merchandise throughout the store. It was a scheme far more nefarious than stealing. Mayhem would ensue the next morning as hairpins that once sold for mere cents were found with $5 price tags and expensive items were marked down to a quarter.

This is exactly what has happened in the world today, except it's Mischief Night every day, all day long. The world and the devil have changed the price tags, and many of us, allured by the toys, trinkets, and tinsels offered, have come to treasure the trivial while we eschew the valuable. This isn't new—it was happening in Jesus' day too: "What people value highly is detestable in God's sight," Jesus remarked to a crowd of sneering, money-loving Pharisees (Luke 16:15).

People of all ages are ever "fooling about with drink and sex and ambition when infinite joy is offered us," as Lewis says.[11] The author goes on to say that the problem isn't the existence of longing but the object our longings are placed on: "Now, if we are made for heaven, the desire for our proper place will be already in us, but not yet attached to the true object, and will even appear as the rival of that object."[12] We're desiring and treasuring less-valuable things (in God's economy) more highly than those that he says matter most (starting with the fear of God, leading to wisdom [Proverbs 1:7; 4:7; 16:16]). Even good things such as family, friends, a healthy lifestyle, and ministry work—valuable as they are—aren't ends in themselves and can become idols if not submitted to God. Lewis says, "If a transtemporal, transfinite good is our real destiny, then any other good on which our desire fixes must be in some degree fallacious, must bear at best only a symbolical relation to what will truly satisfy."[13]

Part of the image of God in us (our *imago Dei*) includes a deep longing for God himself, the only one who will fully satisfy us and never let us down (Ecclesiastes 3:11). He is the source of all that is good, our "very great reward" (Genesis 15:1), and one day we will be with him and "drink joy from the fountain of joy," an experience Lewis notes we can't possibly fathom in light of our "present specialised and depraved appetites."[14]

No single image suffices in painting a picture of the future that awaits believers. Scripture uses descriptions of gates of pearls and streets of gold "as transparent as glass" (Revelation 21:21), but these are only analogies—symbols—of a future we cannot lay hold of with our current vocabulary. Our wildest imagination of what our best good looks like will always be deficient. We simply don't have the imaginative capacity to see the vision God actually has for us. But our lack of imagination and understanding doesn't negate the longing. It only points to the fact that we're not God, and we're not home yet.

GLIMPSES OF GLORY

Although Scripture indicates that we can't ever really wrap our minds around how *good* eternal glory really will be (1 Corinthians 2:9; 13:12), we have hints.

Imagine walking into a thick forest on a bright sunny day. As you enter these woods, there's just enough light shining through the thick leaf canopy to illuminate a pathway. You can't see the sun, but you know it's there. Now imagine you were born in those woods. Since your youth you knew there must be something beyond the forest because of the shafts of light coming in, but you've never actually seen the sun directly. The shafts merely give you an idea of what the sun is like, but they're not the source of the light.

Lewis says the Christian life is like this (it's a vision bearing some similarities to the cave of Plato's *Republic*). Lewis compares our lives on earth to living in shadowlands. We do not yet see God face-to-face, but we do see "'patches of Godlight' in the woods of our experience."[15] These patches help us begin to see God and ourselves in light of reality.

Three of the shafts of light streaming through the thick canopy of the forest of life are beauty, intimacy, and adventure. These are the experiences you have that you never want to end, in which you feel an ineffable sense of joy and eternity: that time your breath was taken away by a magnificent painting, or when you stood atop a mountain with a spectacular valley view below, or when you enjoyed a moment of deep connection with a spouse or friend. It's critical that we not mistake these experiences as merely lesser or diminished versions of the good things we'll enjoy in heaven. Scripture offers no support, for instance, of the idea that a great experience with a friend on a golf course means there will be golf with friends in heaven—only better, more glorious golf. Rather, that world transcends this one, and these shafts of light or hints of heaven that we have on earth are pointers to a better good that we can't yet name or comprehend.

We may experience these glimpses of our eternal home individually or with others. The other day I had one such experience that included both—time alone in my home garden and then with my wife, Karen. Let me see if I can put it into words.

It was a Wednesday evening, and I went out to cut some peonies for Karen. The sun hadn't quite set yet; it was just before the blue hour, the sky displaying a magnificent array of pastels. I stood there taking in the beauty with a floribunda on a pole before me. The temperature was perfect, the humidity low. With succulents at my feet, my eyes slowly panned the exquisite view before me: lilies, peonies, roses, delphiniums—myriads of flowers. I reveled at the endless variety and beauty, wondering how the human mind can even process such a scene. I reflected on each flower's distinct appearance, the lilac so different from the rose, for example; not one of these could have emerged out of the other as the evolutionists theorize; each is so unique, so precisely designed.

Suddenly, my other senses were awakened, beginning with smell, then touch (a light breeze began to blow), and finally sound. A symphony of birds was calling all around me, joined by the synchronization of insects. *It's like a symphonic suite with all its counterpoints*, I thought to myself, *or a well-conducted concert. How do they do that?* Then, a third group of sounds emerged out of the distance—voices of people enjoying life together, playing and laughing on a field about a quarter of a mile from my house.

The peonies awaited me, but I stood fixated at the moment, fully immersed. Just then, I looked up and beheld a dragonfly, backlit against the darkening sky, flying backward and forward, over and over, going nowhere in particular. *It's playing in the fields of God,*

I thought, *doing what it's meant to do.* I watched it dart around for a minute or two.

Finally, after about ten minutes had passed, I returned to my original mission: snipping off peonies to form a handsome bouquet. Back inside, I gave Karen the flowers and shared with her about the experience I'd just had. Seizing on the moment, we clasped hands and listened to some music together ("Parce mihi, Domine," composed by Cristóbal de Morales and played by Jan Garbarek, was the selection), allowing the notes of the beautiful soprano saxophone to fill the air. It was a shared moment of heavenly intimation, amplified by my garden experience moments earlier.

And yet that evening—a time when everything on earth seemed to resonate—was still *only a hint.* Even our best moments on earth cannot come close to comparing to the heavenly vision God will one day reveal to us. In those moments it's as though our Father whispers in our ear, "Child, there's still more. What I'm preparing for you will be even better than you can think or imagine."

Maybe you haven't had an immersive experience like mine, or maybe your life is so full of dark shadows right now that it's hard to remember a time such as that one. The places of darkness speak to us too, just as the shafts of light do. The opposites of beauty, intimacy, and adventure can serve as powerful reminders that we're not home yet, much as hunger reminds of food. Beauty contrasts with ugliness (moral, spiritual, and physical); intimacy contrasts with alienation, estrangement, betrayal, and misunderstandings; and adventure contrasts with ennui (or dissatisfaction, boredom, malaise—the feeling that you're spinning your wheels in life). The light may be partially or even totally occluded for a time, but one day the darkness *will* dissipate, and only the Light will remain (Revelation 21:23; 22:5).

When we're young (and even when we're older), it's easy to deny or ignore these realities; it's as though our eyes adjust to the dark, and we think life on earth is pretty good. But as we age, the decrepitude of morbidity begins to creep in. We suddenly realize that the earth suits God gave us aren't going to last forever. (This realization, termed the midlife crisis, hits some people earlier than others but on average it comes between age thirty-eight and forty-five.) At that moment we realize our bodies fit the image in William Butler Yeats's poem, "Sailing to Byzantium": "Sick with desire / And fastened to a dying animal."[16]

Without outward signs of decay and death, we'd easily forget we're not at our final destination. As I'm fond of saying, "Age conspires with God to take away our temporal hope."[17] (Can you imagine if, instead, we stayed forever young in our body and never had any warning that this life comes to an end?) Moreover, we don't take anything from this life into the next, so we make a huge mistake in our investment strategy if we spend too many of our resources curating materially comfortable lives for ourselves here. Suffering—and anything that doesn't go our way in this life—serves as a vital check, reminding us to invest in the infinite, invisible treasure of a relationship with God above all else.

One can go to an inappropriate extreme with this, assuming an antimaterialist mindset. This too is a mistake. It's not *wrong* to buy a house or accumulate belongings or enjoy a good meal or time with your kids or grandkids, just so long as your hope and joy don't depend on them (and, of course, so long as your actions don't harm others). This created world, in all its beauty and richness, is not an end in itself; again, its beauty and pleasures point beyond to the Creator. God's gifts aren't given to satiate us; rather, they demonstrate that we're objects of his love, and we can accept them with appreciation while responding in worship and praise.

OUR SPIRITUAL HOME

Eternal glory is our destiny. Our imaginations are insufficient for envisioning that destination, but we know for certain it will surpass our greatest visions and expectations. Besides being weighty and eternal, what does this glorious future entail?

The picture God gives in Peter's first epistle is that of a spiritual home. This is not a home of bricks and mortar, but an active body of people—"living stones"—that God himself is building on the chief cornerstone of Jesus: "As you come to him, the living Stone—rejected by humans but chosen by God and precious to him—you also, like living stones, are being built into a spiritual house to be a holy priesthood" (1 Peter 2:4-5).

The word for "house" in verse 5 (*oikos*) can refer to a building or structure, such as a house or a temple, but it is used here in a figurative sense to describe the universal community of believers, who together compose the new temple or "spiritual house" of God. By extension the term *oikos* often refers not just to a building but to its inhabitants—that is, the members of a household, a family, or a lineage.

Like Peter, Paul also uses this imagery of the household in his letters, for example:

> God's *household*, which is the church of the living God, the pillar and foundation of the truth . . . (1 Timothy 3:15, emphasis added)

> Consequently, you are no longer foreigners and strangers, but fellow citizens with God's people and also members of his *household*. (Ephesians 2:19, emphasis added)

The Ephesians passage echoes 1 Peter 2:11 ("foreigners and exiles"), similarly reminding believers of our pilgrim status, and that we're not home yet. Peter's phrase "living stone" is cognate with Paul's reference to believers as "temples of the Holy Spirit" (1 Corinthians 6:19). God dwells in us, and we in him. This is true individually as well as corporately.

All of this language—houses, temples, and stones—is metaphorical, illustrating something real but spiritual. It's important to note that Jesus did not tell us to go and build church buildings; he told us to make disciples. If we're not careful, we'll conflate the organization of a local church body with the organism. This is dangerous because the visible should never supplant the invisible. The organization should always serve the organism, not the other way around.

Remember the churches in China whose leaders expressed *gladness* at the loss of their church buildings? Because of persecution, they had to adjust their organization, and the resulting fellowship within the organism was much richer than it had been before; they didn't want to return to the old way. Buildings can be a wonderful asset for the body of Christ—don't get me wrong—but they're not the church itself: God's people, in all our unity *and* diversity, make up the church. We're the ones who are to serve as royal priests, sacrificing our lives in service to God and others.

Returning to the idea of a spiritual house, the idea of home can be a greatly comforting one, especially to those who are suffering or experiencing feelings of alienation or unsettledness on earth. But the idea can be frightening to those who have come from broken homes and difficult family relationships. We're almost unable to conceive of a deeply happy place where we're not only allowed in but warmly welcomed—a safe, secure place, where we'll be loved forever, unconditionally. But this is what home *should* be, and those who haven't experienced this on earth can take comfort that it's a promise to all believers.

The parable of the prodigal son, and its father figure in particular, is helpful for understanding the reception we'll get in our eternal home. Despite the younger son's rebellion, disrespect, and squandering of his inheritance earlier in his life, the father didn't hold these sins against him when his son repented and returned home. The father *ran* to greet his once-lost son "while he was still a long way off" (Luke 15:20). Even more, he gave the prodigal son royal treatment, putting the best robe on him and throwing him a giant celebratory feast (vv. 22-23).

This scene is immortalized in Rembrandt's monumental painting *Return of the Prodigal Son,* displayed at the Hermitage Museum in St. Petersburg. The painting captures the simultaneous magic and solemnity of that moment. It depicts the warm, tender embrace of the repentant younger son, whose relationship with his father goes from one of alienation to one of love and acceptance in an instance.[18] It also points to the grand homecoming we can all anticipate on the day we meet our heavenly Father face to face:

> God's dwelling place is now among the people, and he will dwell with them. They will be his people, and God himself will be with them and be their God. . . .
>
> It is done. I am the Alpha and the Omega, the Beginning and the End. To the thirsty I will give water without cost from the spring of the water of life. Those who are victorious will inherit all this, and I will be their God and they will be my children. (Revelation 21:3, 6-7)

If ever there were a vision to motivate us during our earthly journeys (especially when that pilgrimage becomes arduous), this is it: the idea of a permanent, spiritual *home,* where joy, intimacy, and a sense of belonging will be complete.

MOTIVATION AND REWARDS

As motivating as a spiritual home is, it can still be a difficult vision to catch. Besides being with brothers and sisters in Christ, what *exactly* are we looking forward to? What does the Father's "house"—this glorious place he's preparing for us—look like, and why should we be eager and motivated to get there? Let's face it, we're a concrete people, and we like visuals.

Years ago Gary Larson depicted well the concept of heaven and eternity as many people (wrongly) imagine it in two different cartoons. One cartoon shows a line of those who have just entered heaven. An angel is welcoming each person and doling out harps to each one. (The lower part of the cartoon humorously shows a demon in hell doling out accordions to those who enter.) In another cartoon, Larson shows someone sitting on a cloud in heaven, wings and halo intact, but clearly bored. "Wish I'd brought a magazine," the thought bubble reads. The poor fellow is missing his harp!

I think many of us envision our spiritual home with imagery far too similar to a Larson cartoon: arriving at the front door, receiving our little heavenly kit (personal cloud, halo, harp, and so on), and then being sent off to have a nice time singing and plucking away—forever. Our imaginations are truly anemic, for even if we played a harp with magnificence, I agree it would be a crashing bore if that is all there is to eternal life. Instead, I think Scripture suggests that, in addition to the fellowship of God and his people, we will enjoy endless creativity, without frustration, to the glory of God. Activity will be energizing, not enervating. We will not be bored but continually stimulated.

There will also be rewards—and let me assure you, the prizes will be a whole lot better than a harp! Consider James 1:12: "Blessed is the one who perseveres under trial because, having stood the test, that person will receive the crown of life that the Lord has promised to those who love him." Now, don't draw an imaginary Larson cartoon in your mind at this point of a hero of the faith being ceremoniously crowned with an Olympic-type wreath on their head. Remember, our imaginations are inescapably limited. This crown of life is a symbolic description of something too wonderful to comprehend. Here are two other similar passages clearly intending to motivate us and appeal to our desires, especially in the moment of testing:

> Do not be afraid of what you are about to suffer. I tell you, the devil will put some of you in prison to test you, and you will suffer persecution for ten days. Be faithful, even to the point of death, and I will give you life as your victor's crown. (Revelation 2:10)

> Blessed are you when people insult you, persecute you and falsely say all kinds of evil against you because of me. Rejoice and be glad, because great is your reward in heaven, for in the same way they persecuted the prophets who were before you. (Matthew 5:11-12)

When many of us read verses about reward, especially in the New Testament, we may see them as automatically applying to all believers. We have been so well trained in the doctrine of grace—the sole basis of our entrance into heaven—that we balk at any hint of the idea of reward for works or faithfulness. And yet there's no way around it: Scripture does speak of degrees of reward in heaven, as well as degrees of punishment in hell (see Matthew 11:21-24; Luke 12:47-48; Revelation 20:12).

In two parables, those of the faithful and unfaithful servants (Matthew 25:14-30) and the minas (Luke 19:11-27), Jesus specifically teaches that rewards will be given by the Father not on the basis of

gifts and abilities or on our level of productivity, but on the basis of
our faithfulness to the assets and opportunities he has given us.[19]
We cannot control the circumstances we're dealt, but we can control
our reaction to them, and passages such as 1 Corinthians 3:12-13,
John 12:25-26, and Revelation 22:12 (among others) lead us to
conclude that our faithfulness and obedience in these circumstances will have a direct bearing on the *quality* of our lives in
heaven.[20] Those circumstances, of course, include adverse ones.
Thus, the degree to which we persevere and faithfully minister to
others out of our own difficulties will have an impact on our
eternity. This is not mercenary—God is not appealing to our greed—
nor is he unfairly doling out favors; rather, the reward is in proper
proportion to the occasion and is not based on anything that he
hasn't given us or hasn't equipped us to do.

What are the nature and content of these rewards? The Bible
gives little detail—probably because our own minds and language
are insufficient for grasping the real nature of these heavenly rewards. However, there do seem to be four general areas related
to rewards.

1. The level of our responsibility (or authority) in the kingdom
   of heaven (Luke 16:10-12; 19:17-19)

2. The degree to which we reflect or display the glory and
   character of God (Daniel 12:2-3; 1 Corinthians 15:40-41;
   2 Corinthians 3:13-18)

3. The nature and depth of our relationships with people in
   heaven (1 Thessalonians 2:19-20; 4:13-18)

4. Our capacity to know and experience God (implied by
   Daniel 12:3)

The day of reckoning and of determining these heavenly rewards may seem far off, but Scripture assures us it will come like

a thief in the night (2 Peter 3:10). We would do well to order our lives with that day in mind, including in how we respond to our "light and momentary troubles" (2 Corinthians 4:17). This isn't meant to induce fear or to prompt a return to law-based living; it should simply flow freely from a growing love and devotion to our Lord and Savior. The more we fix our eyes on the "rewarder of those who seek Him" (Hebrews 11:6 NASB), the less we'll stomp our feet when the comforts and pleasures of this life elude us or slip out of our hands. Consider Jesus' own words: "Look, I am coming soon! My reward is with me, and I will give to each person according to what they have done" (Revelation 22:12).

OUR GLORIOUS FUTURE

I'll close this chapter with one final image, which I referenced briefly in chapter five: a gorgeous tapestry. This familiar metaphor is too good not to use. God is weaving a beautiful tapestry from our lives right now; he's been weaving from the day you were conceived—indeed, even before that (Psalm 139:16)! He may, at times, use some combination of threads that appear discordant or chaotic. From the bottom, the work-in-progress looks like a tangled mess. But on this side of heaven, we only see the underside, while God sees both the top of the tapestry in progress *and* the final outcome all at once. He knows the finished piece will be stunning, but he won't turn the garment over for us until we stand before Jesus.

My suspicion is that the most beautiful patterns in the tapestry of our lives will have been woven in times of adversity and suffering, not in times of ease. In this way, as Elisabeth Elliot once said, nothing—no thread, no seam, no corner of fabric—will be wasted. For now, we see a knotted jumble, and we can't imagine how it'll come out looking good on the other side. But rest assured, it will, because our God does all things well (Mark 7:37; Ecclesiastes 3:11).

As Elisabeth wrote, "The sovereignty of God is not fate but a dynamic unfolding of a design which includes all of our circumstances, conditions, heredity, and environment; the time in which we live, the things beyond our control—and our decisions, every willed choice. God knows how to make even the wrath of man to praise Him."[21]

His eternal glory for every believer will truly be *beyond* anything we can imagine. As we await its full consummation, God himself promises to strengthen and establish us (1 Peter 5:10).

11

A CLEAR CALLING

After you have suffered a little while, [God] will himself
restore you and make you strong, firm and steadfast.

1 PETER 5:10

L IFE HAS CHANGED SINCE I began putting this book together,
and my wife, Karen, and I are learning to cling less tightly to
our plans. I've encountered new trials and challenges in my ministry (along with some exciting developments) as well.

Meanwhile, in the surrounding culture, materialism, sensuality,
corruption, and blatant anti-Christian attitudes continue to run
more rampant. Evil is called good, and good, evil. Spurning authority and anything labeled objective truth, people do as they see
fit in their own eyes (Judges 21:25). On many controversial issues,
citizens from a variety of professions—from pastors and civil servants to college professors and scientists—who take a moral stand
risk their relationships and employment or more. In general, association with Christianity is viewed in a more negative light in
America today than when I was growing up and even than it was

a couple of decades ago. This is not true everywhere, of course, but it's largely true in academia, in a growing number of workplaces, and in other arenas.

I do not mean to sound alarmist or pessimistic; I am generally an optimistic person. And the fact is, great gains have been made in the past fifty to one hundred years: strides in the areas of racial injustice, rights and opportunities for women, medicine and health care, technology, and so on. There are also many heroic and inspiring stories of those who do great good for others even to the point of sacrificing their own lives and comfort; these, of course, don't make for good headlines, so we don't hear about them as often and can therefore get a distorted view of the state of our world.

Modern life, then, is not all bad news. Many aspects of life are better than when I was growing up. But we also need to be realistic and discerning. And if we as believers ignore the warning signs around us today, we do so at our own peril. The pace at which our society is becoming a modern-day Rome is accelerating exponentially. Solomon reminds us that we're not witnessing anything *truly new* at the core—"there is nothing new under the sun" (Ecclesiastes 1:9); evil and sin are still the same old story, played out in different ways and to differing degrees. But I am convinced that there *is* something new and unprecedented about today's age. Digital technology has amplified the opportunities for the flesh to a degree never seen before, and these temptations start from very young ages. Never until recently has it been the case that nine- and ten-year-olds have had nearly unlimited access to the kind of material they can access without a parent's (or anyone else's) knowledge, and filters are only so helpful since children often know more than their own parents about these technologies and can do end runs around the controls. A substantial proportion of the population (children and adults alike) is fully immersed in this "alternate world." This technology is not bad in and of itself; it certainly can be (and has been) leveraged for good, but it's problematic when it becomes a substitute for authentic connections and relationships—the heartbeat of our lives with God and his body. People are less and less embodied.

Besides the changes brought about by digitization, we're seeing an increasingly intense clash of ideologies and a growing asymmetry in the ideas that are tolerated in the public square versus those that are squelched. The division and conflict caused by today's identity politics are the face of a new brand of Marxism—a subtler version than we saw in the twentieth century but equally dangerous, as it goes beyond economics and invades the spaces we inhabit daily, from home to school to work. A collective intolerance now marks our public and private dialogue.

LIVING IN TWENTY-FIRST-CENTURY BABYLON

Yet here we are, agents of light in Babylon. It's easy to feel daunted, beat down, fearful—like retreating or hunkering down might be the best option. I don't think that is what our Lord or the apostle Peter would have us do, though. It's not what countless other followers of Christ have done in much worse conditions—from martyrs like Jim Elliot and the Coptic Christians beheaded in Libya to faithful servants such as Amy Carmichael, Bishop John Rucyahana, and Esther Ahn Kim.

Jesus said we're the light of the world (Matthew 5:14-16), and this is true regardless of the state of the world. Our light isn't intended to be hidden but to radiate. We're called to be humble, respectful, and wise, but we're *never* to be ashamed of our Savior and Lord, who promises, "Whoever acknowledges me before others, I will also acknowledge before my Father in heaven. But whoever disowns me before others, I will disown before my Father in heaven" (Matthew 10:32-33).

When Jesus sent out his disciples in the New Testament, he didn't urge retreat but preparation so his followers wouldn't be caught unaware or misinterpret the circumstances they encountered (see Luke 10:1-16). This is also the purpose of 1 Peter: to equip, prepare, and spur us on to follow Jesus more closely, undergirded by a hope and a joy that the world can't take away, no matter what life throws our direction. Adversity is real and to be expected; but Jesus has overcome the world, and he has *promised* that his people (the church) will prevail (Matthew 16:18).

Although we've been focusing on the writings of Peter as our main text, unsurprisingly, Paul's letters (written earlier than Peter's) have significant parallels. One particular passage in Paul's letter to the Philippians encapsulates our calling as believers in the midst of a difficult cultural context, much as the readers of 1 Peter were facing:

> Do everything without grumbling or arguing, so that you may become blameless and pure, "children of God without fault in a warped and crooked generation." Then you will shine among them like stars in the sky as you hold firmly to the word of life. And then I will be able to boast on the day of Christ that I did not run or labor in vain. (Philippians 2:14-16)

These verses encompass the message of 1 Peter, outlining four areas that all relate to our response and perspective in the context of suffering (past, present, and future):

- Our character ("blameless and pure")
- Our culture ("warped and crooked")

■ Our calling ("shine among them like stars in the sky as you hold firmly to the word of life")

■ The coming of Christ ("the day of Christ")

Let's look at each of these four Cs (character, culture, calling, and coming of Christ) in light of what I've already discussed.

CHARACTER

The formation of Christlike character in us is the goal of the sanctification of believers. As we look forward to being home with the Lord, while we're still in the body we're to be "blameless" and "pure" (innocent), "without fault" (or "above reproach" as some translations say). Peter puts it this way: "As obedient children, do not conform to the evil desires you had when you lived in ignorance. But just as he who called you is holy, so be holy in all you do" (1 Peter 1:14-15). In other words, we're to submit to God, just as Jesus did, and conform our will and ways to his.

Notice that there are no caveats on this command. We aren't called to submit to him *only* when life is to our liking or going well and then get a pass when life becomes difficult. Even when troubles abound, either within or without, we're to entrust ourselves to the One who loves and cares for us, and who has ultimate authority over all things. When we do this, over time we'll develop a compelling character that displays virtues such as charity, honesty, and gentleness; we'll become winsome and attractive people rather than repulsive. We'll be the kind of people to whom others are drawn because of the love of Christ in us. Because people can't resist being loved and served, they'll sense the transcendent God in and through us and wonder what makes us different. At that point, we're to be ready to respectfully and gently "give an answer to everyone who asks . . . the reason for the hope that [we] have" (1 Peter 3:15).

This quality of character is very often forged in and through suffering, whether that suffering comes in an inward or outward form. Courage, for example, develops in times of trial and testing, not in times of ease (otherwise, what need would we have for it?). Patience sprouts not when life is going our way but when we face setbacks (otherwise, again, there would be no need for patience). And perseverance emerges out of situations in which the object of our desire is not coming as easily as hoped.

In his poem "If," Rudyard Kipling wrote of the character-shaping aspect of suffering. In effect, the whole poem explains how God throws out the props of our lives in order that he might enter in and that we might live by faith instead of by sight. When all the props are still on the stage, we'll be tempted to live by sight, trusting and hoping in what we can see. But as the things of earth are stripped away from us and we meet with disillusionment, ill treatment from others, disaster, or loss, we can welcome these events as opportunities (though it be forced upon us) to grow, hold on, and persevere:

> If you can force your heart and nerve and sinew
>   To serve your turn long after they are gone,
> And so hold on when there is nothing in you
>   Except the Will which says to them: "Hold on!" . . .
> Yours is the Earth and everything that's in it,
>   And—which is more—you'll be a Man, my son![1]

Kipling is emphasizing that our *response* to obstacles leads to our character formation—a process we never enjoy at the time (Hebrews 12:11), but the product of which we'll appreciate later. This message isn't unlike the declaration of the apostle Peter when many of Jesus' disciples began to desert him on earth as soon as they realized that being a Christ follower would be a hard calling that demands our all: "'You do not want to leave too, do you?' Jesus asked the Twelve. Simon Peter answered him, 'Lord, to whom shall we go? You have the words of eternal life'" (John 6:66-68).

In this character-forming world, it's only the Lord to whom we can go to find true meaning and significance in our lives. Furthermore, at our low points he's especially able to form a single-minded devotion and growing desire for Christlikeness in us—because all props are gone, and only he remains. C. S. Lewis affirmed this in his *Screwtape Letters* (which, remember, is written from the perspective of junior and senior demons talking to one another about their "Enemy," that is, God):

> He [God] relies on the troughs even more than on the peaks; some of His special favourites have gone through longer and deeper troughs than anyone else. . . . Our cause is never more in danger than when a human, no longer desiring, but still intending, to do our Enemy's will, looks round upon a universe from which every trace of Him seems to have vanished, and asks why he has been forsaken, and still obeys.[2]

In summary, the blameless and pure character we're called to exhibit is nothing less than a character in the image of Christ—the one who pressed on to the end, even when he sensed alienation from his Father because of taking on the sin of the world. This character is formed slowly but surely as we submit to the Lord, obeying him even in the middle of adversity, even when we can't understand what he's doing or when all evidence of him appears gone.

CULTURE

The context in which we live out our character is a "warped and crooked" generation or culture (the second C). Today in America (as well as other countries), we followers of Christ find ourselves more and more separated from our culture in terms of our values and beliefs. Our time is, in fact, more than ever like the culture 1 Peter's first audience was immersed in.[3] Increasingly it's the case that we'll either pay a dear price for our faith or we'll accommodate the culture. And many Christians and even whole churches have indeed accommodated (nearly all of us are guilty of this at least to some degree). We watch things we'd never have watched twenty years ago. (I don't only mean inappropriate content but also inordinate amounts of inane, trivial content.) We spend more time each day on our technological devices, staring at a screen, than we do cultivating relationships with the immortal God and people. Philosophies of secularization, privatization, and pluralization have thoroughly invaded our thinking; beyond postmodernism, we're now postreason. The comfort in this is that even when we fail, God is faithful and ready to lovingly coax us back to life in him, to a vision of flourishing that is trained on eternity rather than on the things of this world.

Os Guinness, in his book *Dining with the Devil*, notes that Christians tend to be culture blind; that is, we're shortsighted and have a hard time distinguishing where our principles end and the culture's begin.[4] For this reason, it's essential that we gain a broader understanding of church history, studying and reading about how Christians from all eras (not only our own) have lived out their faith in the midst of difficult cultural and societal situations.

Nowhere is the decline of culture more evident than in our political arena. If you're over age fifty (or simply into politics or history), you may remember the Moral Majority, a movement that began in the 1970s and sought to further a conservative religious agenda by pressing for legal allowance of prayer in schools, antiabortion laws, and similar legislation. Despite their good intentions, the Moral Majority, in my view, committed the Constantinian error of seeking a political solution to issues that are at root moral and spiritual. Remember, persecution decreased when Emperor Constantine legalized Christianity in the Roman Empire in the early fourth century, but as an unintended consequence the lines between the world and the church began to blur from then on. As the church grew in power and prestige, it and the world soon became bedfellows in the pursuit of power, wealth, and pleasure— hence the Protestant Reformation to correct course.

That mindset of seeking political solutions to our moral and spiritual problems in society still lingers today, and both left- and right-leaning groups commit this error. Don't get me wrong: persecution is not something to seek out, and I'm all for laws that align with biblical morality, promote religious liberty, and do not target Christians (*or* people of any other faith, for that matter, since belief should be a matter of free choice, not compulsion). But too often we put our hope in returning our society to Christian mores and then despair when the opposite seems to be occurring. We do exactly what Peter says we're not to do: get surprised, perhaps indignant, and think the "fiery ordeal" that has come upon us is strange, even an outrage, rather than the normal course for a follower of Jesus (1 Peter 4:12). Author and scholar James Davison Hunter warns of the danger when we begin to see our cultural and political institutions as the primary means for spiritual and moral renewal:

> All social organizations exist as parodies of eschatological hope. And so it is that the city is a poor imitation of heavenly community; the modern state, a deformed version of the ecclesia; the market, a distortion of consummation; modern entertainment, a caricature of joy; schooling, a misrepresentation of true formation; liberalism, a crass simulacrum of freedom; and the sovereignty we accord to the self, a parody

of God himself. As these institutions and ideals become ends in themselves, they become the objects of idolatry.[5]

The time of line-blurring between Christianity and culture is largely over in America, as it has been for the rest of the world for most of history. The distinction between a follower of Jesus and a nonbeliever has begun to sharpen again. This is good, though it's not easy, which is why God's promise in 1 Peter 5:10 to make us "strong, firm and steadfast" is so reassuring. We're not alone, he is with us, and he will strengthen us, not allowing the flames of the fiery ordeal to consume us. The God of Daniel and of Shadrach, Meshach, and Abednego is still alive and well, abiding in his people and protecting us from ultimate destruction.

The Christian message doesn't change with the culture, and it's always countercultural. We may be immersed in a "warped and crooked" culture just as Paul and Peter were in first-century Rome, but we don't need to wring our hands: you and I are called to understand the times (Esther 1:13) and to flourish in twenty-first-century Babylon as "strangers and exiles" who belong to another country.

CALLING

The end of the story is sure, and we know it's not only *good* but *the best* (far beyond what our anemic imaginations can conceive). One day, we'll arrive at "a great city that has expected our return for years," as poet W. H. Auden put it. But in the time being, we're called to follow the One who is the "way and the truth and the life" (John 14:6). Auden eloquently expresses this calling with a clear reference to John 14:6:

He is the Way.
Follow Him through the Land of Unlikeness;
You will see rare beasts, and have unique adventures.

He is the Truth.

Seek Him in the Kingdom of Anxiety;

You will come to a great city that has expected your return
    for years.

He is the Life.

Love Him in the World of the Flesh;

And at your marriage all its occasions shall dance for joy.[6]

As we await the Marriage Supper of the Lamb—the day we'll
"dance for joy" in God's presence—we're to live out our character,
rooted in kingdom values, in the context of our culture. As Paul
says, we're to "shine among [nonbelievers] like stars in the sky as
[we] hold firmly to the word of life" (Philippians 2:15-16). Like
Esther, we're to speak and live our faith fearlessly, knowing God
has called us for "such a time as this" (Esther 4:14).

Each of us is sovereignly embedded in various communities—
households, local churches, neighborhoods, hobby groups, and
workplaces—none of which are by accident. These spheres may
be small or large; size doesn't matter so much as fidelity to Christ
in each. As believers, we carry the aroma of Christ, the very
presence of God, into each of our spheres and wherever we go.
Our integrity (the matching up of our words with our actions)
will then "silence the ignorant talk of foolish people" in those
arenas (1 Peter 2:15).

Our character—and the behavior that flows from it—should
be so Christlike that those around us can't help but see the bearers
of the good news in a positive light: "live such good lives among
the pagans that, though they accuse [us] of doing wrong, they
may see [our] good deeds and glorify God" (1 Peter 2:12). When
asked to give an account for the hope within us, we do so out of
a motivation of love, gently and respectfully; and without fear or

shame as Peter exhibited at his denials before the resurrection (1 Peter 3:13-15).

George Herbert offers a perspective on our calling much like Auden's, rooted in John 14:6. His words in his poem "The Call" reiterate the vitality we have in following Christ.

> Come, my Way, my Truth, my Life:
> Such a Way, as gives us breath:
> Such a Truth, as ends all strife:
> Such a Life, as killeth death.
>
> Come, my Light, my Feast, my Strength:
> Such a Light, as shows a feast:
> Such a Feast, as mends in length:
> Such a Strength, as makes his guest.
>
> Come, my Joy, my Love, my Heart:
> Such a Joy, as none can move:
> Such a Love, as none can part:
> Such a Heart, as joys in love.[7]

The parallelism in Herbert's poem reveals a gradual crescendo: standing firm in truth ends strife (within our otherwise divided hearts and minds), providing clarity to our lives. That clarity (light) illuminates the feast (feeding on Christ), which in turn gives strength. Finally, joy from our life in Christ transcends our circumstances and brings us to love. True desire and fulfillment find joy in love—the two Great Commandments. No adversity can separate us from this love, which comes from God himself, and "moves the sun and the other stars" (that is, *everything*), as Dante put it.[8]

COMING OF CHRIST

God is setting the stage for the next act: the second coming of Jesus. This is the great end goal and purpose of the Christian life, our *telos*. As 1 Peter 4:7 says, "The end of all things is near." When Christ returns, as promised, he'll come back not as he did the first time, as the Suffering Servant and Man of Sorrows, but as a reigning and victorious King. That day is no myth or fairy tale; it's a reality, and it's nearer now than when Peter wrote. We're foolish and shortsighted if we don't heed Jesus' warnings to be prepared and alert for that day.

Both our circumstances and our culture can lull us into compromising our character and forgetting our call. If we're not on guard, we'll be susceptible to those swapped price tags. We may also be tempted to forget our identity as a pilgrim, a wayfarer, and a stranger; we may become bitter and disillusioned, especially when suffering comes our way. But adversity can be the very stuff of redemption, reminding us of our true identity and goal, and serving as a vehicle that brings us to rely more fully on the "awful grace of God" (to borrow Aeschylus's phrase again). Adversity (experiencing it ourselves and witnessing it) can awaken us out of our worldly daze and call us to a better and living hope, one that will never die.

When we entrust ourselves to our loving Father just as Christ did, then when the impurities are finally gone and the gold of glory emerges, no doubt will linger whether we ran in vain. Looking back from the glory of our unbounded future, we'll see that all our adversities were light and momentary by comparison, and well worthwhile. Any pain, loss, relational brokenness, financial difficulty, career problems, health issues—we'll see that every one of these things did in fact work *together* for our good.

The story will not end, but it will continue on in our permanent home, where there will be "'no more death' or mourning or crying or pain, for the old order of things [will have] passed away" (Revelation 21:4). C. S. Lewis described what that day might be like in the final scene of the final book in the Chronicles of Narnia, *The Last Battle*:

> And for us this is the end of all the stories, and we can most truly say that they all lived happily ever after. But for them it was only the beginning of the real story. All their life in this world and all their adventures in Narnia had only been the cover and the title page: now at last they were beginning Chapter One of the Great Story, which no one on earth has read: which goes on forever: in which every chapter is better than the one before.[9]

May you and I both live today in light of that day—standing fast in the grace of God—just as Peter and the first-century believers did (1 Peter 5:12).

ACKNOWLEDGMENTS

F IRST, WE WISH TO EXPRESS OUR GRATITUDE to those whose lives and stories contributed invaluably to this manuscript—both those known personally to us and those whose stories we learned about secondhand. Thank you especially to the family of the late Barry Morrow and to Lois Westerlund for giving us permission to share your encounters and experiences with suffering in a more extensive manner. Thanks too to Glenn Sunshine for pointing us to some of the lesser-known stories of faithful Christians of the past who suffered well.

Second, we offer our profound appreciation to those who read early drafts of this manuscript, especially Michael Stewart and David Robinson as well as the team at InterVarsity Press (particularly Al Hsu). Their insights and suggestions were critical to the shaping of the final manuscript. Michael Stewart's editorial input from start to finish of the book was especially vital. Finally, I (Ken) thank the men who attend my Wednesday morning Bible study; as with the previous book (*Life in the Presence of God*) in this unofficial trilogy, they again provided the first audience for the content that was ultimately shaped into this manuscript. Their clarifying questions and comments enhanced both my teaching and the book's writing.

APPENDIX 1

HOW CAN A GOOD GOD ALLOW EVIL AND SUFFERING?

A Brief Theodicy

T HE BIBLE TEACHES THAT "GOD IS LIGHT; in him there is no darkness at all" (1 John 1:5). He is the absolute standard of goodness. And as the sovereign Lord, he is both all-knowing and all-powerful. If these things are true, however, then why is his creation so full of evil and suffering? He planned the universe, yet the world abounds with destruction and misery. Is God ultimately to blame?

I will briefly summarize a biblical response to this question here; for a more in-depth treatment, please see chapter five of my book *God, I Don't Understand* (from which much of this appendix material was condensed).[1]

THE NATURE OF EVIL, SIN, AND SUFFERING

Evil is traditionally divided into two basic types: natural evil and moral evil. The first is the "natural disease and death environment," encompassing both natural events leading to loss of human life (earthquakes, floods, plagues) and sickness and suffering with no apparent cause (birth defects, disease, and the like). In this realm of natural evil, both the righteous and the wicked seem indiscriminately attacked (not to mention the whole area of animal pain and suffering). The second type of evil, moral evil, consists of both people's rebellion against God and people's cruelty toward other people.

According to the Scriptures, people's sin (defined as anything contrary to the character of God) has devastating results. The question that logically arises is, Couldn't God prevent both kinds of evils (natural and moral) if he really wanted to? And the logical follow-up question is, Since he does not prevent both types of evil and suffering, how can we believe that he's perfectly good? Another way to ask this question with respect to moral evil is, If God knew that certain of his creatures were destined to an eternal sentence in hell, why did he create them at all? In other words, even if we acknowledge that people are directly responsible for pain and destruction due to their sin, we may view God as ultimately responsible since, after all, "he planned it this way."

INADEQUATE SOLUTIONS

The Bible clearly teaches that evil exists though God is omnipotent and good. The question of how this can be true is the problem of evil. Many attempts over the years have tried to solve this problem by minimizing God's goodness or omnipotence, or by denying the reality of evil. These inadequate solutions have appeared because people are rarely willing to let God's wisdom be greater than theirs. Some may really desire to justify God by defending him, but in their zeal to help they sometimes water down the Bible's truths. Others have no desire to defend God and their questions are merely rhetorical—an attack.

Here are six frequently proposed "solutions" that fall short of solving the problem of evil and suffering (each is developed more fully in *God, I Don't Understand*):

1. God's goodness is different from man's goodness. (This meaningless argument amounts to redefining the word *good* and ultimately denies God's goodness.)

2. All evils are punishments for sin. (This is unsatisfactory and unbiblical for a couple of reasons, not the least of which is the fact that Christ himself gave examples of people suffering because of another's moral evil and because of natural evil [see chap. 6 of this book]).

3. God is somehow "beyond" good and evil; he created both. (This is similar to the first solution because it ultimately denies that God is good in the ordinary sense of the word.)

4. The problem of evil is exaggerated. (This reduces the problem to an issue of quantity rather than quality—it only alleviates the problem of evil and suffering but doesn't solve it.)

5. Evil is only an illusion. (This is the solution of pantheists and, in the West, of the Christian Scientists; it forces us to deny the validity of our own senses and thoughts.)

6. God is struggling against evil, but he is not omnipotent. (In this view, promoted in Rabbi Harold Kushner's book *When Bad Things Happen to Good People*, God is not to blame for evil because he's not powerful enough to overcome it. This solution of finite theism distorts the Scriptures; diminishes the power, majesty, and glory of God; and removes any assurance that God will ever overcome evil.)

THE DIVINE SOVEREIGNTY-HUMAN RESPONSIBILITY ANSWER

Only the Bible offers a satisfactory solution. That solution lies within the divine sovereignty-human responsibility mystery. Even though God is omnipotent and sovereign, he created creatures with genuine freedom to make real moral choices. These creatures could and did willfully rebel against God and deserve full blame for the evil that resulted. Though God is sovereign, he did not make any creature sin. Everything that came from his hands was originally perfect and sinless.

There's no question that God knew what would happen when he created beings with free will. He knew that Satan and humans would introduce evil into a perfect creation as a result of their willful rebellion against their Creator. The real mystery here is that God incorporated sin and evil in the outworking of his plan without being responsible for its commission.

Failure to believe both truths in this biblical mystery can lead to one of two basic extremes. The first is that God never expected sin to exist in his creation. But God's eternal plan, which included the sacrifice of his Son on behalf of sinful humanity, proves that God preplanned for sin. The second extreme is far more common and is a frequent objection by non-Christians to the biblical picture of reality. This is the view that pins the ultimate responsibility for sin on God, sometimes in an attempt to lighten the burden of human true moral guilt. This second extreme overemphasizes divine sovereignty to the virtual exclusion of human responsibility. But does divine sovereignty really make God the author of sin? The answer is that God is the designer of a plan that included sin, but he is *never* responsible for committing the sin. We must distinguish design from execution. Evil is caused by the free acts of God's creatures, not by God himself.

Even though God doesn't approve of sin, it's here by his permission. In his omniscience he knew that the plan he chose, even though it included evil, would bring the greatest ultimate good.

While God has not seen fit to reveal all his reasons for allowing evil to come into his perfect creation, at least one of them is clear. Because evil now exists, God can show forth the glory of his grace not only as the Creator of all things but also as the Redeemer. That redemption process is exactly what this book is all about.

The reality of sin made it necessary for God to send his Son to overcome the power of sin and of death. The crucifixion and resurrection of Jesus Christ were the greatest possible display of God's love, mercy, and holiness to humans and angels. God chose the plan that would allow him most completely and effectively to demonstrate the splendor of his attributes.

RESPONDING TO SOME OBJECTIONS

A natural question to ask at this point is, "To whom is *God* responsible?" The answer is simple: no one (see Isaiah 40:13-14; Job 40:2). His character is the absolute standard for good (Mark 10:18), the changeless criterion for right versus wrong. God is free to do the whole counsel of his will, which, by definition, will lead to the greatest good. Many have objected to this, claiming the God of the Bible isn't good, at least in terms of society's standards. But society's moral standards have no foundation apart from the revelatory base of the Bible. Those who refuse to believe that God is good have no basis for morality at all.

So God didn't directly create evil and suffering, but he did allow them to be a part of his plan. An important objection arises out of this biblical solution: Couldn't God have made creatures who would always have chosen to do right? Some say no, that our free will makes sin a necessity. I disagree. In *God, I Don't Understand,* I point to two pieces of evidence—(1) the unfallen angels (see Revelation 5:11-14); and (2) resurrected believers (who will not sin)—that demonstrate that there *can* be free will without the necessity of sin. Divine sovereignty will coexist with the creatures' freedom for eternity. Thus, God *could* have kept his creatures from sinning without interfering with their free will—indeed, this is precisely what will happen in heaven.

This brings us back to the divine sovereignty-human responsibility mystery. Am I answering the problem of evil and suffering with a mystery? Yes, in a way I am. But remember that the truths of a mystery are not contradictory. They only appear to be that way to human comprehension. It doesn't take away the fact that the biblical solution to the problem of evil is a *self-consistent explanation* based on the original assumption that God has revealed himself to people, and that revelation is the Bible. No matter what God was *able* to do about free will and sin, he is never to blame for the execution of sin if it occurs. As to the question of why God freely chose to include evil in his plan, we must answer that God cannot deny himself; it *must* be the best possible reality. This isn't the best of all possible worlds, but it is the best way to bring about the best of all possible worlds.

GOD'S SOLUTION FOR EVIL: THE WORK OF CHRIST

From beginning to end, the Bible consistently says that while evil and suffering are real, God is nevertheless omnipotent and good. Moreover, God is thoroughly aware of people's troubles and needs, and in his love he has done something about them. He sent his own Son to die and pay for sin. Jesus Christ came to face and overcome evil as the sinless God-man (1 John 3:8). Though humans brought death through their rebellion, God came to earth to give life, not willing to let sin, disease, and death have the last word. In this way he proved he loved us (Romans 5:8; 1 John 4:9-10).

Moses says, "The secret things belong to the LORD our God" (Deuteronomy 29:29). We don't know all of God's purposes for including evil in his plan, but the Bible does indicate some of them—the principal one being to display the riches of his glory to creatures who can willingly respond. Because of Christ's blood, God can transform sinful rebels into the image of his Son perfectly.

No one can see the whole picture as God sees it. From our perspective many things appear out of God's control. But we must place our trust in him. God has revealed that he is guiding everything toward a glorious and purposeful consummation. When we finally see what he's been doing, *we will be satisfied*. We'll learn how divine sovereignty and human responsibility can both be true and there will be no suffering or problem of evil. God's justice will be vindicated, and all creatures will bow to his holiness (Philippians 2:9-11).

FOR FURTHER READING

In addition to my book *God, I Don't Understand*, I recommend these works to further understand the problem of evil and suffering:

- Ken Boa and Larry Moody, *I'm Glad You Asked* (Colorado Springs, CO: David C. Cook, 1995), esp. chap. 9: "Does God Make Sense in a World Full of Suffering?"
- C. S. Lewis, *The Problem of Pain* (New York: HarperOne, 2015).
- Ravi Zacharias and Vince Vitale, *Why Suffering?* (New York: FaithWords, 2014).
- Timothy Keller, *Walking with God Through Pain and Suffering* (New York: Penguin Books, 2015).
- Philip Yancey, *Where Is God When It Hurts?* (Grand Rapids: Zondervan, 2002) and *Disappointment with God* (Grand Rapids: Zondervan, 1997).
- William Dembski, *The End of Christianity: Finding a Good God in an Evil World* (Nashville: B&H Academic, 2009).

TEN INTERCESSORY PRAYER TIPS

T O MAKE OUR INTERCESSORY PRAYER FOR OTHERS (as well as petitionary prayer for ourselves) more effective during times of adversity or anytime, use the following biblical principles, all of which are united by a one-word theme: ask.

1. Ask. (Matthew 7:7-8; Philippians 4:6; James 4:2)

2. Ask in the will of God. (James 4:13-17; 1 John 5:14)

3. Ask in faith. (1 John 5:15; James 1:6-7; Mark 11:22-24)

4. Ask specifically. (Mark 10:51; Luke 6:12-13; 2 Corinthians 12:8)

5. Ask with thanksgiving. (Hebrews 13:15; Philippians 1:3-4; Colossians 1:3-4, 11-12)

6. Ask in the Spirit. (Romans 8:26–27; Ephesians 6:18; Jude 20)

7. Ask in fellowship. (John 15:7; James 5:16; 1 John 3:21-22)

8. Ask frequently. (1 Chronicles 16:11; Colossians 4:2; 1 Thessalonians 5:17; Luke 18:1)

9. Ask with others. (Matthew 18:19-20; Romans 15:30)

10. Ask in Jesus' name. (John 14:13-14; 16:24; Ephesians 3:11-12; Hebrews 10:19-22)

POWERFUL PRAYERS FOR YOURSELF AND OTHERS

WHEN PRAYING FOR OURSELVES OR OTHERS, we often resort to requests focused on temporary needs and happiness, or on relief or resolution to a particular difficulty. The following prayers based on Scriptures of Peter and Paul offer samples for how we can elevate our prayers and ensure they're framed by an eternal perspective. Each uses an adapted version of the NASB translation.

THREE HOPE-FILLED PRAYERS BASED ON 1 PETER

May you greatly rejoice in your salvation, even though now for a little while, if necessary, you have been distressed by various trials. May these trials prove your faith to be more precious than gold, which is perishable, even though tested by fire; and may your faith be found to result in praise and glory and honor at the revelation of Jesus Christ; and though you have not seen Him, you love Him, and though you do

not see Him now, but believe in Him, may you greatly rejoice with joy inexpressible and full of glory, that you may
obtain as the outcome of your faith the salvation of your
soul. (1 Peter 1:6-9)

The end of all things is near; therefore, may you be of sound
judgment and sober spirit for the purpose of prayer. Above
all, may you keep fervent in your love for others, because
love covers a multitude of sins. May you be hospitable to
others without complaint. As you have received a special gift
from God's Spirit, employ it in serving others as good
stewards of the manifold grace of God. When you speak, may
you do so as one who is speaking the utterances of God; when
you serve, may you do so by the strength which God supplies;
so that in all things God may be glorified through Jesus Christ,
to whom belongs the glory and dominion forever and ever.
Amen. (1 Peter 4:7-11)

May you humble yourself under the mighty hand of God, that
He may exalt you at the proper time, casting all your anxiety
on Him, because He cares for you. May you be of sober spirit
and on the alert. Your adversary, the devil, prowls around
like a roaring lion, seeking someone to devour. May you
resist him, firm in your faith, knowing that the same experiences of suffering are being accomplished by your fellow
brothers and sisters in Christ throughout the world. After
you have suffered for a little while, may the God of all grace,
who called you to His eternal glory in Christ, perfect, confirm,
strengthen and establish you. To Him be dominion forever
and ever. Amen. (1 Peter 5:6-11)

PAUL'S FOUR LIFE-CHANGING PRAYERS

I ask that the God of our Lord Jesus Christ, the Father of glory, may give to you a spirit of wisdom and of revelation in the knowledge of Him. I pray that the eyes of your heart may be enlightened, so that you will know what is the hope of His calling, what are the riches of the glory of His inheritance in the saints, and what is the surpassing greatness of His power toward us who believe. (Ephesians 1:17-19)

May the Father grant you, according to the riches of His glory, to be strengthened with power through His Spirit in the inner man, so that Christ may dwell in your hearts through faith; and that you, being rooted and grounded in love, may be able to comprehend with all the saints what is the breadth and length and height and depth, and to know the love of Christ which surpasses knowledge, that you may be filled up to all the fullness of God. (Ephesians 3:16-19)

And this I pray, that your love may abound still more and more in real knowledge and all discernment, so that you may approve the things that are excellent, in order to be sincere and blameless until the day of Christ; having been filled with the fruit of righteousness which comes through Jesus Christ, to the glory and praise of God. (Philippians 1:9-11)

I ask that you may be filled with the knowledge of His will in all spiritual wisdom and understanding, so that you will walk in a manner worthy of the Lord, to please Him in all respects, bearing fruit in every good work and increasing in the knowledge of God; strengthened with all power, according to His glorious might, for the attaining of all steadfastness and patience; joyously giving thanks to the Father, who has qualified us to share in the inheritance of the saints in Light. (Colossians 1:9-12)

APPENDIX 4

PSALMS OF LAMENT

THE PRACTICE OF LAMENT IS AN ART that contemporary Christians, especially in the West, have largely lost. To lament means "to express sorrow, mourning, or grief." Psalms of lament, in fact, make up one-third of the entire book of Psalms. All share a common structure, moving from a complaint or expression of sorrow (negative) to praise (positive). Use the psalms below when you or your church body are going through a hard or painful time to help you cry out to God. You can also suggest these psalms to friends who are suffering. (Of course, there are many more psalms of lament than are listed here.)

FOR INDIVIDUAL LAMENT

Psalm 3

Psalm 6

Psalm 13

Psalm 22

Psalm 28

Psalm 44

Psalm 56

Psalm 57

Psalm 71

Psalm 77

Psalm 86

Psalm 142

FOR CORPORATE LAMENT

(during times of communal distress, including natural disasters or national oppression)

Psalm 44

Psalm 60

Psalm 74

Psalm 79

Psalm 80

Psalm 85

Psalm 90

SCRIPTURE FOR AN ETERNAL PERSPECTIVE ON SUFFERING

FOLLOWING ARE VERSES FOR COMFORT, hope, and joy in times of loss or adversity. (Nearly all of them are my own translation, but several are NIV.)

> If someone dies, will they live again?
>> All the days of my hard service
>> I will wait for my renewal to come. (Job 14:14)

> I know that my redeemer lives
>> and that in the end he will stand upon the earth.
> And after my skin has been destroyed,
>> yet in my flesh I will see God;
> I myself will see him
>> with my own eyes—I, and not another.
>> How my heart yearns within me! (Job 19:25-27)

> As for me, I will see Your face in righteousness;
>> when I awake, I will be satisfied with your likeness.
>> (Psalm 17:15)

No one who waits for you
   will be ashamed,
but those who are treacherous without cause
   will be ashamed.
Show me your ways, O Lord,
   teach me your paths;
lead me in your truth and teach me,
      for you are the God of my salvation,
      and my hope is in you all day long. (Psalm 25:3-5)

I would have lost heart unless I had believed
      that I would see the goodness of the Lord
      in the land of the living.
I will hope in the Lord and be of good courage,
      and he will strengthen my heart;
      yes, I will hope in the Lord. (Psalm 27:13-14)

Then [the thief on the cross] said, "Jesus, remember me when you come into your kingdom." Jesus answered him, "Truly I tell you, today you will be with me in paradise." (Luke 23:43)

Do not let your hearts be troubled. You believe in God; believe also in me. My Father's house has many rooms; if that were not so, would I have told you that I am going there to prepare a place for you? And if I go and prepare a place for you, I will come back and take you to be with me that you also may be where I am. You know the way to the place where I am going. (John 14:1-4)

I have told you these things, so that in me you may have peace. In this world you will have trouble. But take heart! I have overcome the world. (John 16:33)

I have hope in God, that there will be a resurrection of both the righteous and the wicked. In view of this, I strive always to keep my conscience blameless before God and men. (Acts 24:15-16)

I rejoice in my tribulations, knowing that tribulation produces perseverance; and perseverance, character; and character, hope. And hope does not disappoint, because the love of God has been poured out into my heart through the Holy Spirit who was given to me. (Romans 5:3-5)

I consider that our present sufferings are not worth comparing with the glory that will be revealed in us. (Romans 8:18)

Eye has not seen,
    ear has not heard,
nor have entered the heart of man
    the things that God has prepared for those who love
        him. (1 Corinthians 2:9)

God both raised the Lord and will also raise me up through his power. (1 Corinthians 6:14)

Now I see dimly, as in a mirror, but then I shall see face to face. Now I know in part, but then I shall know fully, even as I am fully known. (1 Corinthians 13:12)

I know that he who raised the Lord Jesus will also raise me with Jesus and present me in his presence. (2 Corinthians 4:14)

I do not lose heart; even though my outward man is perishing, yet my inner man is being renewed day by day. For this light affliction which is momentary is working for me a far more exceeding and eternal weight of glory, while I do not look at the things which are seen but at the things which are unseen. For the things which are seen are temporary, but the things which are unseen are eternal. (2 Corinthians 4:16-18)

I know that if my earthly house, or tent, is destroyed, I have a building from God, a house not made with hands, eternal in the heavens. For in this house I groan, longing to be clothed with my heavenly dwelling, because when I am clothed, I will not be found naked. For while I am in this tent, I groan, being burdened, because I do not want to be unclothed but to be clothed, so that what is mortal may be swallowed up by life. Now it is God who has made me for this very purpose and has given me the Spirit as a guarantee. (2 Corinthians 5:1-5)

I make it my ambition to please the Lord, whether I am at home in the body or away from it. For we must all appear before the judgment seat of Christ, that each one may receive what is due for the things done while in the body, whether good or bad. (2 Corinthians 5:9-10)

My citizenship is in heaven, from which I also eagerly await a Savior, the Lord Jesus Christ, who will transform my lowly body and conform it to his glorious body, according to the exertion of his ability to subject all things to himself. (Philippians 3:20-21)

We should not be ignorant about those who fall asleep or grieve like the rest of mankind who have no hope. For if we believe that Jesus died and rose again, even so God will bring with him those who have fallen asleep in Jesus. According to the Lord's own word, we who are alive and remain until the coming of the Lord will not precede those who have fallen asleep. For the Lord himself will come down from heaven,

SCRIPTURE FOR AN ETERNAL PERSPECTIVE

with a loud command, with the voice of the archangel, and with the trumpet of God, and the dead in Christ will rise first. Then we who are alive and remain will be caught up together with them in the clouds to meet the Lord in the air. And so we will be with the Lord forever. (1 Thessalonians 4:13-17)

By God's grace I want to live to the end in faith, knowing that I will not receive the promises on earth, but seeing them and welcoming them from a distance, I confess that I am a stranger and a pilgrim on the earth. Instead, I long for a better country, a heavenly one. In this way, God will not be ashamed to be called my God, for He has prepared a city for me. Like Moses, I esteem reproach for the sake of Christ as of greater value than the treasures of this world, because I am looking to the reward. (Hebrews 11:13, 16, 26)

Here I do not have an enduring city, but I am seeking the city that is to come. (Hebrews 13:14)

Blessed be the God and Father of my Lord Jesus Christ, who according to his great mercy has given me new birth into a living hope through the resurrection of Jesus Christ from the dead, and into an inheritance that is incorruptible and undefiled and unfading, reserved in heaven for me. (1 Peter 1:3-4)

And the God of all grace, who called you to his eternal glory in Christ, after you have suffered a little while, will himself restore you and make you strong, firm and steadfast. (1 Peter 5:10)

Now I am a child of God, and what I shall be has not yet been revealed. I know that when he is revealed, I shall be like him, for I shall see him as he is. And everyone who has this hope in him purifies himself, just as he is pure. (1 John 3:2-3)

God is able to keep me from falling and to present me before his glorious presence faultless and with great joy. (Jude 24)

I heard a loud voice from the throne saying, . . . "He will wipe every tear from their eyes. There will be no more death' or mourning or crying or pain, for the old order of things has passed away."

He who was seated on the throne said, "I am making everything new!" . . .

"It is done. I am the Alpha and the Omega, the Beginning and the End. To the thirsty I will give water without cost from the spring of the water of life. Those who are victorious will inherit all this, and I will be their God and they will be my children." (Revelation 21:3-7)

STUDY GUIDE

THIS GUIDE INCLUDES FOR EACH CHAPTER:

- Questions to prompt personal or group reflection

- Application exercises to help you put the truths and commands of God's Word into practice in your life

- A related verse from 1 Peter for meditation or memorization

CHAPTER 1: THE CRUCIBLE OF SUFFERING

Questions

1. What trials have you endured or are you currently enduring?

2. Has adversity made you "bitter or better"?

Application

Read through the epistle of 1 Peter. Mark (or on a separate piece of paper, make a note of) every verse that references suffering (or any of its synonyms). As you note these verses, make a list of some of the attitudes, perspectives, and responses Peter urges his readers to have toward suffering. How is the list similar to or different from what you've believed or heard taught (even in church or by other believers)?

Meditation

"In all this you greatly rejoice, though now for a little while you may have had to suffer grief in all kinds of trials." (1 Peter 1:6)

CHAPTER 2: THE ALCHEMY OF GRACE

Questions

1. Think about the difficulties you face right now or have recently faced. What impurities do you think God is trying to skim off the top of your life through the means of these trials so he can forge Christlike character in you?

2. If you're in a trial and find yourself bitter or angry, what obstacles are causing you to resist God's work in and through this hardship?

Application

Think of a follower of Christ you know personally whose life displays the "alchemy of grace" at work and who has shown a willingness to talk about the suffering she or he has endured (it can be a result of persecution or any other type of adversity). Ask that person to share what she or he learned through the trial and how God used difficulties to change her or him. (For context, you can read 1 Peter 1:6-7 to the person first.) Focus on listening and restrain from giving advice or input.

Meditation

"These [trials] have come so that the proven genuineness of your faith—of greater worth than gold, which perishes even though refined by fire—may result in praise, glory and honor when Jesus Christ is revealed." (1 Peter 1:7)

CHAPTER 3: A LIVING HOPE

Questions

1. We all have longings and hopes on earth. What are yours for yourself and your loved ones?

2. Are your earthly hopes "living" or "dead" from the perspective of eternity—that is, which will go on, and which will not last beyond this lifetime?

3. What shifts in thinking or action do you need to make to actively transfer your hope from the temporal to the eternal?

4. What's the difference in hoping *for* and hoping *in* something?

Application

Find some time (preferably an hour or more, so you can linger) to go outside and observe nature. Once surrounded by the created order, notice the signs of the season: death and barrenness if it's winter, new life if it's spring, and so on. What evidences of each season do you see, hear, smell, and feel? What beauty do you notice (such as an intricate flower or graceful bird) alongside ugliness (for example, a dead animal, decaying leaves, a decrepit tree trunk)? Reflect on how one is necessary for the other. What can you learn about the cycles of suffering and death followed by restoration, hope, and glory, from the way God created the visible world?

Meditation

"Praise be to the God and Father of our Lord Jesus Christ! In his great mercy he has given us new birth into a living hope through the resurrection of Jesus Christ from the dead." (1 Peter 1:3)

CHAPTER 4: A PRESENT JOY

Questions

1. If you'd been in Paul and Silas's situation, unjustly imprisoned in a Roman jail for an indefinite amount of time, would you have had the same reaction as they did? Why or why not?

2. What's the difference between happiness and joy?

   Can you describe a time when you had one without the other?

3. In her book *Keep a Quiet Heart* (Vine Books), Elisabeth Elliot said, "The secret is Christ in *me,* not me in a different set of circumstances." What circumstances are you in right now that you'd like to change or be rid of?

   How does (or would) inviting Christ's presence into those circumstances change how you view them?

Application

Listen to a hymn or praise song that lifts your sights to the hope and joy of heaven (two suggestions: "The Solid Rock" or "In Christ Alone"). Focus on the words and then pick a line or two to chew on throughout your day. Consider listening to or singing this song whenever you're down, discouraged, or in a painful set of circumstances.

Meditation

"Though you have not seen him, you love him; and even though you do not see him now, you believe in him and are filled with an inexpressible and glorious joy." (1 Peter 1:8)

CHAPTER 5: PREPARING TO SUFFER

Questions

1. Has suffering ever caught you off-guard?

2. What are a few of the ways we can prepare for suffering, according to Peter's letter (and this chapter)?

3. If a significant trial came your way tomorrow, would you be ready for it? If not, what could you do differently today to make sure you're prepared—to "moor yourself to the Rock of Ages," as Charles Spurgeon put it?

Application

Act on the answer you gave for question 3. Maybe it's memorizing a particular Scripture, committing to being in prayer and in God's Word on a regular basis, or finding an accountability partner (someone who will encourage you in your relationship with God in the good times and bad). If you're unsure what to do, focus on building your foundation on the rock of Christ by studying God's character. Consider a study of Genesis and Exodus (a chapter a day), Psalm 78, or Hebrews 11; you can also read a book like A. W. Tozer's *The Knowledge of the Holy* (or another book on God's attributes). As you study, consider keeping a running list of the ways God has shown himself faithful to his people in the past and how he's proving himself faithful to you in the present.

Meditation

"Dear friends, do not be surprised at the fiery ordeal that has come on you to test you, as though something strange were happening to you." (1 Peter 4:12)

CHAPTER 6: IMITATING CHRIST

Questions

1. What are the three ways Christ suffered (and we are called to imitate)?

2. Thinking about current challenges and pain in your life, what are some specific, practical ways that you can follow Jesus' example in your response to these difficulties?

3. When it comes to enduring injustice, mistreatment, or similar forms of suffering, there's often tension between mercy and justice, between forgiving as Christ forgave us while holding others accountable for sin (not condoning wrongdoing). How have you seen this tension played out? (This may be an account from your personal life, the life of someone you know, or the life of a well-known believer from modern-day life or history.)

4. What does Jesus' example teach us about how to respond in these situations?

Application

Read and meditate on Isaiah 53 (a passage foreseeing what Jesus, the Suffering Servant, would endure on earth for God's glory and our good).

Meditation

"To this you were called, because Christ suffered for you, leaving you an example, that you should follow in his steps." (1 Peter 2:21)

CHAPTER 7: SUBMITTING TO GOD

Questions

1. What does it mean to submit to God in our suffering? How is this different from fatalism?

2. How does seeing yourself as both an agent and a victim relate to submission to God?

   How will this view help *you* submit to him?

3. Romans 8:28 is an oft-quoted verse (sometimes somewhat carelessly) to those who are suffering. How did this chapter change or enhance your view of this verse?

Application

For a couple of years now I've used a small card when I wake up in the morning that has several pairs of words on it. One pair is *Submit and Depend.* It's a reminder to me to submit myself and my day to God—placing myself under his authority—and to depend on him to order my priorities and my time. I urge you to take a small, colored piece of paper or index card and write these same words on it. Place it by your bedside and look at it before you get out of bed, or place it strategically so you see it when carrying out another routine morning habit (such as brushing your teeth or showering). Make the words a prayer to God, asking his special assistance for submitting to him even in the difficulties that come your way that day. Over time, you won't need the card anymore, but it's good to keep at hand as a regular reminder.

Meditation

"Humble yourselves, therefore, under God's mighty hand, that he may lift you up in due time." (1 Peter 5:6)

CHAPTER 8: SUBMITTING TO AUTHORITY

Questions

1. Review the four spheres of authority and submission described in 1 Peter. In which sphere do you struggle to submit the most? Why do you think that is?

2. In light of the epistle's original audience, why do you think
   Peter spent so much time talking about submission to human
   authority?

   How is it related to the central theme of this epistle—suffering?

Application

One of the best ways to prepare ourselves for the day of suffering
when it visits us is to read accounts of people who have suffered.
Testimonies of believers undergoing "trials of various kinds"—
including those who've been persecuted for their faith—provide
an eternal perspective on our own lives. Pick a book (or film) that
will help you get an inside look into someone's suffering. As you
read (or watch), ask God to help you empathize with the person's
situation and to use it to prepare you for whatever suffering will
come your way.

Some recommendations:

- *If I Perish* by Esther Ahn Kim

- *China Cry: A True Story* by Nora Lam with Ruth Lam

- *A Grace Disguised* by Jerry Sittser

- *Amy Carmichael: Beauty for Ashes* by Iain H. Murray; also
  Elisabeth Elliot's *A Chance to Die* is a wonderful, longer
  read on Carmichael

- *Every Bitter Thing Is Sweet* by Sara Hagerty

- *Joni: An Unforgettable Story* or *Heaven* by Joni Eareckson Tada

- *The Hiding Place* by Corrie ten Boom

- *Bonhoeffer: Pastor, Martyr, Prophet, Spy* by Eric Metaxas

- *Shadow of the Almighty* or *A Path Through Suffering* by
  Elisabeth Elliot

- *In the Presence of My Enemies* by Gracia Burnham with Dean Merrill

- *Tracks of a Fellow Struggler* by John R. Claypool

- *The Gulag Archipelago* by Aleksandr Solzhenitsyn, three volumes

- *The Book Thief* by Markus Zusak (also a film)

- *Chariots of Fire* (film)

- *Schindler's List* (film)

Meditation

"Submit yourselves for the Lord's sake to every human authority: whether to the emperor, as the supreme authority, or to governors, who are sent by him to punish those who do wrong and to commend those who do right." (1 Peter 2:13-14)

CHAPTER 9: MINISTERING TO OTHERS

Questions

1. In chapter 6, three s-words are mentioned in connection with Jesus' example: sinless, silent, and substitutionary. A fourth s (discussed in this chapter) is sympathy; this is one more way we imitate Christ in our relationships. How well do you sympathize with others who are suffering, especially those who are going through something you can't relate to very well?

   How can you imitate Jesus better in this way?

2. Who in your life do you know who's suffered and ministered to *you* out of their own difficulties? How?

3. What are the two priestly roles described in this chapter?

Do you think you're guilty of leaving either of these roles too much to "the professionals" (such as paid pastors or others in formal ministry positions)? Explain.

Application

Any one of us can love, serve, and pray for others. Based on ways you've suffered personally, discuss with God how he wants to use your experiences of suffering to minister to others in these three ways. Then act on what he shows you.

Meditation

"Each of you should use whatever gift you have received to serve others, as faithful stewards of God's grace in its various forms." (1 Peter 4:10)

CHAPTER 10: AN ETERNAL GLORY

Questions

1. Atheists are fond of accusing Christians of making up heaven as a kind of wish fulfillment or emotional crutch. How would you (and Peter) counter this charge?

2. What are some of the "patches of Godlight"—tastes of heaven—you've experienced on earth? (If it helps, think in terms of the three categories of beauty, intimacy, and adventure.)

3. What's your vision of eternity like?

   How similar (or dissimilar) is it to the Gary Larson cartoons mentioned in this chapter?

4. Has there been a time when adversity in this life amplified your desire for heaven? If so, try to put into words what it is you were longing for at that moment.

Application

Take a moment to imagine being the thief on the cross crucified next to Jesus—the one who asked Jesus to remember him when he entered his kingdom. What would Jesus' words have meant to you when he said, "Today you will be with me in paradise" (Luke 23:43)? Now imagine yourself standing before God, and ask him to fill you with eternal joy in his presence (Psalm 16:11). If you're so inclined, place the words of Psalm 16:11 somewhere prominent to remind yourself of the access you have to God's "eternal pleasures" even now.

Meditation

"And the God of all grace, who called you to his eternal glory in Christ, after you have suffered a little while, will himself restore you and make you strong, firm and steadfast." (1 Peter 5:10)

CHAPTER 11: A CLEAR CALLING

Questions

1. What were the four *c*'s gleaned from Philippians 2:14-16?

2. Describe in a sentence or two how these relate to 1 Peter and its theme of suffering.

3. This chapter asserts that the boundary lines seem to be sharpening between Christians and the surrounding American culture. Do you agree? Why or why not?

4. In what specific arenas or personal circumstances has this chapter (and the book as a whole) challenged you personally to live (or to continue living) with Christlike character?

Application

If you're a follower of Christ, then you're an agent of the King, and you're on the way home, where everything will be better—relationships and fellowship, beauty and adventure. But as long as you have life and breath, there are two things you can do on earth that you'll never have a chance to do again in heaven. Both are encompassed in our clear calling as believers: (1) Share the gospel with the lost, and (2) serve people in need. Take time to invest in doing each of these things today (and every day or whenever the opportunities present themselves). Remember, you can live out this calling fully even if you yourself are walking a difficult road—in fact, God may even use your suffering to touch others even more powerfully. Pray that, in the process, people will see Christ in and through you.

Meditation

"In your hearts revere Christ as Lord. Always be prepared to give an answer to everyone who asks you to give the reason for the hope that you have. But do this with gentleness and respect." (1 Peter 3:15)

NOTES

INTRODUCTION

[1] A brief theodicy is provided in appendix 1 along with some suggested authors and books that deal with this topic more extensively.

[2] A few recommendations for books on coping from a biblical viewpoint—all from an inside perspective (those reflecting on recent or ongoing personal suffering)—are C. S. Lewis, *A Grief Observed* (New York: HarperCollins, 1996); Jerry Sittser, *A Grace Disguised: How the Soul Grows Through Loss* (Grand Rapids: Zondervan, 2004); and John R. Claypool, *Tracks of a Fellow Struggler: Living and Growing Through Grief* (Harrisburg, PA: Morehouse, 2004).

[3] Consider, for example, the innocent and inward suffering of David in the Psalms, which showcases honest expressions of inner turmoil over persecution at the hand of his enemies. We also find there instances of David's own self-inflicted, inward pain and regret as a result of failing to trust God (a suffering we also witness in the author of 1 Peter in his own famous example of denying Christ). Examples abound of the outward suffering of the innocent, in both torture and death, the prime example being Christ our Lord, followed by martyrs of the faith such as Stephen, James, and other disciples (Peter too would meet this fate, as predicted by Jesus in John 21:8-19). For self-inflicted, outward suffering, consider the Corinthian church, which let pride and selfishness corrupt the observation of the Lord's Supper—a moment that should have focused on worship and fellowship. Paul revealed that this disobedience was the cause of physical illness of several individuals, even leading to the death of some.

[4] The guide is available in print form at kenboa.org and as a mobile app at presence.app.

[5] Linda Lowry, "11 Christians Killed Every Day for Their Decision to Follow Jesus," Open Doors USA, March 13, 2019, www.opendoorsusa.org/christian-persecution/stories/11-christians-killed-every-day-for-their-decision-to-follow-jesus.

[6] Julian of Norwich, quoted in *Devotional Classics: Selected Readings for Individuals and Groups*, ed. Richard J. Foster and James Bryan Smith (San Francisco: HarperSanFrancisco, 2005), 73.

1. THE CRUCIBLE OF SUFFERING

[1] Barry Morrow, quoted with permission from Anna Morrow Braund's eulogy of her father at his memorial service. The C. S. Lewis quote is from a letter he penned to Sheldon Vanauken, author of *A Severe Mercy*, shortly after Vanauken's wife died.

[2] "Dropping a Romans 8:28 bomb" is from a talk by John Stonestreet at a youth conference on June 24, 2018, in Charlottesville, Virginia.

[3]Aleksandr I. Solzhenitsyn, *The Gulag Archipelago, 1918–1956* (New York: Harper & Row, 1975), 2:617.

[4]The early church almost universally acknowledged the apostle Peter as the author of 1 Peter, and no internal or external evidence has arisen since then to confidently suggest otherwise; others have refuted doubts as to Peter's authorship promoted by critics such as Bart Ehrman (for example, in his book *Forged*). Thus, I assume the traditional view of Peter as author. The likely time of writing was AD 63, about a year prior to the outbreak of the first of ten waves of persecution that would occur over three centuries.

[5]The historian Tacitus, *Foxe's Book of Martyrs*, and others have laid the blame at Nero's feet.

[6]William Byron Forbush, ed., *Foxe's Book of Martyrs* (Grand Rapids: Zondervan, 1969), 5.

[7]Forbush, *Foxe's Book of Martyrs*, 5.

[8]Only Christ was 100 percent without sin, and thus his suffering was always for the sins of others, never for his own. Suffering for doing wrong, in the sense that Peter uses it, is referring to a more direct consequence of disobedience.

[9]"A grace disguised" comes from Jerry Sittser's excellent book by the same title, which I'll discuss more later.

2. THE ALCHEMY OF GRACE

[1]Joni Eareckson Tada, "Reflections on the 50th Anniversary of My Diving Accident," *Gospel Coalition*, July 30, 2017, www.thegospelcoalition.org /article/reflections-on-50th-anniversary-of-my-diving-accident.

[2]Tada, "Reflections."

[3]Tada, "Reflections."

[4]Tada, "Reflections."

[5]Aeschylus, *Agamemnon*, lines 179-183, in *The Greek Way*, trans. Edith Hamilton (New York: W. W. Norton, 1993), 61. Note that the word *despair* in this passage is translated by Hamilton as *despite*; however, that translation is debated, and other translations use *despair*. We have gone with the version that makes the most sense in the context.

[6]Lois is a friend of my coauthor, Jenny, and these quotes are shared with her permission.

[7]For help on this front, I recommend my books *Life in the Presence of God* (Downers Grove, IL: InterVarsity Press, 2017) and *A Guide to Practicing God's Presence* (Atlanta, GA: Trinity House, 2018). The latter contains exercises designed to help you in the moment of temptation.

3. A LIVING HOPE

[1]Jerry Sittser, *A Grace Disguised: How the Soul Grows Through Loss* (Grand Rapids: Zondervan, 2004), 40, 41, 64.

[2]Sittser, *Grace Disguised*, 70.

[3]Sittser, *Grace Disguised*, 71, 66, 88.

[4]William Styron, *Darkness Visible: A Memoir of Madness* (New York: Random House, 1990), 62.

[5]Joseph T. Hallinan, "The Remarkable Power of Hope," *Psychology Today*, May 7, 2014, www.psychologytoday.com/us/blog/kidding-ourselves/201405/the-remarkable-power-hope.

[6]Ravi Zacharias, "The loneliest moment in life is when you have just experienced that which you thought would deliver the ultimate and it has just let you down," July 18, 2013, 10:01 p.m., https://twitter.com/RaviZacharias/status/358089129713598466.

[7]Sittser, *Grace Disguised*, 164.

[8]Sittser, *Grace Disguised*, 164.

[9]John R. Claypool, *Tracks of a Fellow Struggler: Living and Growing Through Grief* (Harrisburg, PA: Morehouse, 2004), 41.

[10]Claypool, *Tracks of a Fellow Struggler*, 38-39.

[11]Claypool, *Tracks of a Fellow Struggler*, 40, 44.

[12]Claypool, *Tracks of a Fellow Struggler*, 38.

4. A PRESENT JOY

[1]This retelling of Acts 16:16-25 is embellished for the sake of story while staying true to the original account as well as known historical details.

[2]From Acts 9:16. We don't know if Paul actually recalled these words at this moment, or even if Ananias relayed these words to Paul (then Saul). However, that Paul knew he would suffer much for the name of Christ is clear from all of his writings, so this is not beyond the realm of possibility.

[3]Corrie ten Boom with Jamie Buckingham, *Tramp for the Lord: The Story That Begins Where* The Hiding Place *Ends* (Fort Washington, PA: CLC Publications, 2011), 126.

[4]Van Jones, "CNN: Van Jones Responds to First Emanuel Service since Charleston Shooting," *CNN*, June 21, 2015, www.youtube.com/watch?v=MWsq9BvNUXQ.

[5]Martyn Lloyd-Jones, *Life in Christ: Studies in 1 John* (Wheaton, IL: Crossway, 2002), 28.

[6]Lloyd-Jones, *Life in Christ*, 30.

[7]Jerry Sittser, *A Grace Disguised: How the Soul Grows Through Loss* (Grand Rapids: Zondervan, 2004), 89.

[8]Sittser, *Grace Disguised*, 90.

[9]Sittser, *Grace Disguised*, 169.

[10]Henry J. M. Nouwen, *Out of Solitude* (Notre Dame, IN: Ave Maria Press, 2004), 53-54.

[11]C. S. Lewis, *Surprised by Joy: The Shape of My Early Life* (New York: Brace & World, 1955), 17-18.

[12]Lewis, *Surprised by Joy*, 18.

[13]Lewis, *Surprised by Joy*, 220.

[14]Ruth Whippman, "Happiness Is Other People," *New York Times*, October 27, 2017, www.nytimes.com/2017/10/27/opinion/sunday/happiness-is-other

-people.html. Whippman was a recent transplant from the United Kingdom to the United States. The article is a surprising and welcome departure from the usual blind positivism of our individualistic, self-help culture.
[15]Edward Mote, "The Solid Rock," 1834.

5. PREPARING TO SUFFER

[1]Barbara G. Baker, "Egypt Seeks International Help Against IS After 21 Christians Beheaded," *World Watch Monitor*, February 16, 2015, www.worldwatch monitor.org/2015/02/egypt-seeks-international-help-against-is-after-21 -christians-beheaded.

[2]Linda Lowry, "In Egypt, Families of 21 Martyrs Beheaded by ISIS Feel 'Inner Peace' After Remains Returned," Open Doors USA, May 16, 2018, www .opendoorsusa.org/christian-persecution/stories/in-egypt-families-of-21 -martyrs-beheaded-by-isis-feel-inner-peace-after-remains-returned; "Egypt: Families of Beheaded Copts Finally Reunited with Remains of Loved Ones," *Christian Headlines*, May 16, 2018, www.christianheadlines.com /blog/egypt-families-of-beheaded-copts-finally-reunited-with-remains-of -loved-ones.html.

[3]Lowry, "In Egypt, Families of 21 Martyrs Beheaded."

[4]Daniel Goleman, "A Rising Cost of Modernity: Depression," *New York Times*, December 8, 1992, www.nytimes.com/1992/12/08/science/a-rising-cost-of -modernity-depression.html.

[5]One study showed a 52 percent increase in major depression symptoms among twelve- to seventeen-year-olds and a 63 percent increase among eighteen- to twenty-five-year-olds over a ten- to twelve-year period. Tara Bahrampour, "Mental Health Problems Rise Significantly Among Young Americans," *Washington Post*, March 16, 2019, www.washingtonpost.com /local/social-issues/mental-health-problems-rise-significantly-among -young-americans/2019/03/14/5d4fffe8-460c-11e9-90f0-0ccfeec87a61_story .html?utm_term=.e233b76e9218.

[6]Rebecca Ahrnsbrak et al., "Key Substance Abuse and Mental Health Indicators in the United States: Results from the 2016 National Survey on Drug Use and Health," Substance Abuse and Mental Health Services Administration, September 2017, www.samhsa.gov/data/sites/default/files/NSDUH -FFR1-2016/NSDUH-FFR1-2016.htm.

[7]For example, see Greg Koukl, "Line in the Sand," *Stand to Reason* (blog), October 31, 2014, www.str.org/publications/line-in-the-sand-solid-ground -november-2014#.W9yE9JNKhPY.

[8]Russell Shaw, "Persecution," *Arlington Catholic Herald*, June 3, 2015, www .catholicherald.com/Opinions/Columnists/Russell_Shaw/Persecution.

[9]The last of these examples has occurred in many places, including, for example, the University of California, Berkeley, in fall 2018. Multiple news articles reported the incident, such as Crystal Woodall, "UC Berkeley Christian Student Senator Faces Major Backlash for Defending Biblical View of Gender," *CBNNews.com*, November 12, 2018, www1.cbn.com/cbnnews

/us/2018/november/uc-berkeley-christian-student-senator-faces-major-backlash-for-defending-biblical-view-on-gender.

[10]Lysa TerKeurst, "Finding Strength in the Midst of Disappointment (Part 1 of 2)," Focus on the Family Broadcast, www.focusonthefamily.com/media/daily-broadcast/finding-strength-in-the-midst-of-disappointment-pt1. More of her story is told in her book *It's Not Supposed to Be This Way: Finding Unexpected Strength When Disappointments Leave You Shattered* (Nashville: Thomas Nelson, 2018).

[11]Esther Ahn Kim, *If I Perish* (Chicago: Moody Press, 1977), 145-46. Kim's given name was Ei Sook, but upon moving to America after her time of persecution, she assumed the American name Esther Ahn Kim.

[12]Noël Piper, *Extraordinary Women and Their Extraordinary God* (Wheaton, IL: Crossway, 2005), 134.

[13]Piper, *Extraordinary Women*, 133.

[14]Kenneth Boa, *Conformed to His Image: Biblical and Practical Approaches to Spiritual Formation* (Grand Rapids: Zondervan, 2001), 105-6.

[15]Edward Mote, "The Solid Rock," 1834.

[16]Jerry Sittser, *A Grace Disguised: How the Soul Grows Through Loss* (Grand Rapids: Zondervan, 2004), 27.

[17]Eric Vess, "Three Ways Chinese Christians Are Responding to Persecution in China," Advancing Native Missions, November 7, 2018, https://advancingnativemissions.com/persecution-in-china-three-ways-the-church-is-responding.

[18]"Spurgeon and the Hurricane of 1878," *Spurgeon Center* (blog), August 29, 2017, www.spurgeon.org/resource-library/blog-entries/spurgeon-and-the-hurricane-of-1878.

6. IMITATING CHRIST

[1]Dallas Willard discussed this topic in his discipleship-focused book *The Divine Conspiracy* (New York: Harper, 1998). In addition, some today, including students of Willard's such as James Bryan Smith, have taken this original discipleship concept seriously through means such as the Apprentice Institute.

[2]John Piper, "Our Captain Made Perfect Through Sufferings," *Desiring God*, June 2, 1996, www.desiringgod.org/messages/our-captain-made-perfect-through-sufferings.

[3]Os Guinness, *In Two Minds: The Dilemma of Doubt and How to Resolve It* (Downers Grove, IL: InterVarsity Press, 1976), 264, 284.

[4]James M. Houston, ed., *The Mind on Fire: Faith for the Skeptical and Indifferent* (Colorado Springs, CO: Victor Books, 2006), 23.

[5]Blaise Pascal, "A Prayer of Pascal Asking God to Use Sickness in His Life Appropriately," quoted in Houston, *Mind on Fire*, 281-83. In his editor's note, Houston estimates that Pascal likely penned this prayer around 1660 (two years before he died). The prayer is over 3,700 words and well worth reading in full.

[6]George Eliot, *Middlemarch* (Middlesex, UK: Penguin Books, 1965), 896.

[7]Rachael Denhollander, "In Her Own Words: Nassar's Victim's Emotional Statement," *Detroit News*, January 24, 2018, www.detroitnews.com/story /news/local/michigan/2018/01/24/rachael-denhollander-larry-nassar -statement/109781984.

7. SUBMITTING TO GOD

[1]This story is told in more detail in The Voice of the Martyrs, *Hearts of Fire: Eight Women in the Underground Church and Their Stories of Costly Faith* (Bartlesville, OK: VOM Books, 2015). I am summarizing parts of that retelling.

[2]Ling's sentence wound up being commuted to only two years.

[3]Voice of the Martyrs, *Hearts of Fire*, 223-24.

[4]Voice of the Martyrs, *Hearts of Fire*, 216.

[5]Darlene Zschech, "The Potter's Hand," 2003. It's only fair to reveal to the reader that (as explained in the introduction) within days of finishing the first draft of this manuscript, Jenny learned she was expecting her first child. And yet the pain of infertility has shaped her, and she can honestly say she would never trade the lessons she learned through her suffering.

[6]C. H. Spurgeon, *The Metropolitan Tabernacle Pulpit* (Pasadena, TX: Pilgrim Publications, 1970), 15:460.

[7]"How Does One Find Faith?" *Firing Line with William F. Buckley Jr.*, episode S0432, September 6, 1980, https://youtu.be/o6gB4GXP4kA.

[8]Amy Carmichael, quoted in Iain H. Murray, *Amy Carmichael: "Beauty for Ashes"* (Edinburgh, UK: Banner of Truth Trust, 2015), 97.

[9]Murray, *Amy Carmichael*, 97.

[10]Murray, *Amy Carmichael*, 98.

[11]Murray, *Amy Carmichael*, 102.

[12]Samuel Rutherford, quoted in Amy Carmichael, *Gold by Moonlight: Lessons for Walking Through Pain* (Fort Washington, PA: CLC Publications, 2017), 7, 48. The line, Carmichael notes, was penned by the Scottish minister Samuel Rutherford in a letter to a friend in 1637.

[13]Murray, *Amy Carmichael*, 112.

[14]*Zoē* is used in some contexts to mean physical or biological life, but here I'm using it to refer to spiritual or supernatural life, which is how the term is used in a majority of cases in the New Testament.

[15]Others have explored this tension in great depth. For more on this topic, consider the collection of essays found in *Suffering and the Sovereignty of God*, ed. John Piper and Justin Taylor (Wheaton, IL: Crossway, 2006).

[16]Some victimizers have so brainwashed their victims that those victims begin to genuinely believe they're at fault. In fact, an entire syndrome describes a pattern of behavior in which a person denies wrongdoing, capitalizes on the resulting confusion, and then paints the other person as the problem or offender. This behavior is called DARVO (alternately called gaslighting), which stands for deny, attack, and reverse victim and offender. Such relationships need a supernatural breakthrough to function properly again. They affirm

the truth of Jeremiah 17:9, "The heart is deceitful above all things and beyond cure."

[17]I'm indebted to Timothy Keller for pointing me to this letter in his book *Walking with God through Pain and Suffering* (New York: Penguin Books, 2013), 266-67.

[18]Os Guinness, *In Two Minds: The Dilemma of Doubt and How to Resolve It* (Downers Grove, IL: InterVarsity Press, 1976), 284.

[19]In his book *Not the Way It's Supposed to Be* (Grand Rapids: Eerdmans, 1996), Cornelius Plantinga defines sin as a culpable disturbance of *shalom*. There is some merit to this definition if the disturbance includes both our vertical and horizontal relationships as well as our relationship with ourselves and the creation (the four alienations that occurred at the fall of humankind).

[20]This quote is attributed to Michelangelo, but the original source and authenticity are unknown.

[21]Jerry Sittser, *A Grace Disguised: How the Soul Grows Through Loss* (Grand Rapids: Zondervan, 2004), 204.

[22]Sittser, *Grace Disguised*, 205.

[23]Sittser, *Grace Disguised*, 206.

8. SUBMITTING TO AUTHORITY

[1]Glenn Sunshine, "Christians Who Changed Their World: Chiune Sugihara (1900–1986)," *Breakpoint*, March 1, 2013, www.breakpoint.org/2013/03/chiune -sugihara-1900-1986.

[2]Sunshine, "Christians Who Changed Their World: Chiune Sugihara."

[3]The verse goes on to add the words "as the weaker partner," which likely refer to the real, biological differences between men and women. That men are stronger physically is true in one respect *in general*, but not in all respects. For example, women tend to outlive men worldwide, and the vast majority of the oldest living people in the world are women (Rachel Nuwer, "Keeping Track of the Oldest People in the World," *Smithsonian.com*, July 8, 2014, www.smithsonianmag.com/science-nature/keeping-track-oldest -people-world-180951976). Differences do exist, contrary to the current claims of our culture, and God clearly created two sexes, both male and female, according to Genesis, but we have to be careful not to homogenize certain statements to an extent that Scripture itself doesn't do.

[4]Rick Rood, *Our Story . . . His Story* (Maitland, FL: Xulon Press, 2014), 62-63.

[5]Rood, *Our Story*, 150-51.

[6]Larry Crabb writes at length on this topic in his book *A Different Kind of Happiness* (Grand Rapids: Baker, 2016).

[7]Linda Graf, "About Me," *From Bitterness to Abundant Life* (blog), accessed June 12, 2019, https://lindagraf.org/about-me; see also Linda Graf, "My Story of Bitterness, Grace, and Repentance, Part 1," Bitter Truth Conference, CrossLife Community Church, April 9, 2016, https://vimeo.com/162751266.

8. Linda Graf, "My Story of Bitterness, Grace, and Repentance, Part 2," Bitter Truth Conference, CrossLife Community Church, April 9, 2016, https://vimeo.com/162858098.

9. You can read more of Linda's insights and journey at her blog *From Bitterness to Abundant Life*, https://lindagraf.org.

10. Martin Luther, quoted in Eric Metaxas, *Martin Luther: The Man Who Rediscovered God and Changed the World* (New York: Viking, 2017), 216. Some question whether Luther really said the words beginning with "Here I stand"; regardless, the spirit of them was certainly present in his testimony.

11. Kellsye M. Finnie, *William Carey: By Trade a Cobbler* (Kent, UK: STL Books, 1986), 32.

12. Glenn Sunshine, "Christians Who Changed Their World: William Carey (1761–1834)," *Breakpoint*, December 12, 2011, www.breakpoint.org/2011/12/william-carey-1761-1834.

13. Finnie, *William Carey*, 31.

14. For instance, some church leaders today believe the age of the earth is an issue of biblical authority, while others believe it's only a matter of interpretation.

9. MINISTERING TO OTHERS

1. The Rwandan genocide was also tragic on another level in that, as Timothy Paul Longman points out in his book *Christianity and Genocide in Rwanda*, the church in Rwanda (as a whole) did not condemn the violence and thus is often accused of being complicit in the events that occurred.

2. "History of Mission: John Rucyahana," Traveling Team, accessed June 12, 2019, www.thetravelingteam.org/articles/john-rucyahana.

3. "History of Mission: John Rucyahana."

4. John Rucyahana, *The Bishop of Rwanda* (Nashville: Thomas Nelson, 2007), xvi.

5. Rucyahana, *Bishop of Rwanda*, xviii, xv. In addition to sharing this in his book, he has shared this in other forums as well, such as in an interview with Bob Abernethy of PBS's *Religion & News Weekly*, April 17, 2009, www.pbs.org/wnet/religionandethics/2009/04/17/april-17-2009-rwandan-reconciliation/2708.

6. Rucyahana, *Bishop of Rwanda*, xvi. If you'd like to learn more about the amazing testimonies and reconciliation that came out of the tragedy of the Rwandan genocide, see Catherine Claire Larson, *As We Forgive* (Grand Rapids: Zondervan, 2009), which was also released as a documentary by the same title.

7. George Müller, *The Autobiography of George Müller* (Louisville, KY: GLH Publishing, 2015), 171.

8. Several months later, after surgery and thirty-five rounds of radiation, she was given the good news that her scans were clear—the treatment worked. The day after Easter 2019 she wrote, "I mean look. I know that one day I'm gonna die of somethin.' It's the way of all flesh. No one's gettin' out of here

alive. But for now, for today, I'm not dying of cancer; maybe in the future, but not now. I'm breathin' good. And it's why last Sunday when we sang of the resurrection: 'up from the grave He arose . . . no guilt in life, no fear and death, this is the power of Christ in me,' I was praisin' the Lord for being the air that I breathe." Joni Eareckson Tada, "My Lungs Are Okay," *Joni and Friends Blog*, April 23, 2019, www.joniandfriends.org/my-lungs-are-okay.

[9]*Empathy, sympathy*, and *compassion* are cognate terms. *Empathy*, however, refers to an ability to imagine another's pain, while *sympathy* refers to a more active entering into (or personally relating to) that pain. *Compassion* carries an element of action; not only do we feel someone's pain, but we feel the desire to see it alleviated.

[10]Jerry Sittser, *A Grace Disguised: How the Soul Grows Through Loss* (Grand Rapids: Zondervan, 2004), 176-77.

[11]John R. Claypool, *Tracks of a Fellow Struggler: Living and Growing Through Grief* (Harrisburg, PA: Morehouse, 2004), 83.

[12]Claypool, *Tracks of a Fellow Struggler*, 82-83.

[13]Note that this role is different from that of a prophet, who actually speaks for God in the present, versus teaching the laws and truths God has already spoken.

[14]Alex J. Webster, ed., *Refuge of My Weary Soul: Selected Works of Anne Steele* (Birmingham, AL: Shazbaar Press, 2017), iv.

[15]Anne Steele, "Dear Refuge of My Weary Soul," 1760.

[16]Steele, "Dear Refuge of My Weary Soul."

[17]Kenneth Boa, *Conformed to His Image* (Grand Rapids: Zondervan, 2001), 311.

[18]R. A. Torrey, *How to Pray* (Chicago: Moody, 2007), 63.

[19]Torrey, *How to Pray*, 64.

[20]You can download this booklet, *Think on These Things: Perspectives on Prayer*, for free in digital form at https://kenboa.org/perspectives-on-prayer or purchase a print copy at https://kenboa.org/product/think-on-these-things-perspectives-on-prayer.

[21]Rusty Russell, "Mueller's Persistent Prayer," *FaithLife Sermons*, accessed June 12, 2019, https://sermons.faithlife.com/sermons/120117-mueller's-persistent-prayer.

[22]Constance K. Walker, *Adolphe Monod*, Bitesize Biographies series (Darlington, UK: EP Books, 2013), 54.

[23]Adèle Babut, quoted in Walker, *Adolphe Monod*, 59-60.

[24]Walker, *Adolphe Monod*, 65.

[25]Adolphe Monod, quoted in Walker, *Adolphe Monod*, 67.

[26]Authors such as Greg Ogden and Glenn Sunshine have made similar points in their writings, but the charge to finish the "unfinished business" of the Reformation (as Ogden puts it in his book by the same title) has gone largely unmet on a broad scale.

[27]See, for example, Ed Stetzer, "Survey Fail—Christianity Isn't Dying," *USA Today*, May 14, 2015, www.usatoday.com/story/opinion/2015/05/13/nones-americans-christians-evangelicals-column/27198423.

[28]"Competing Worldviews Influence Today's Christians," Barna Group, May 9, 2017, www.barna.com/research/competing-worldviews -influence-todays-christians; "The State of the Church 2016," Barna Group, September 15, 2016, www.barna.com/research/state-church-2016. Note too that Pew and Gallup polls have shown a decades-long decline in one of the biggest indicators of spiritual commitment: church attendance.

[29]For further reading on how God uses suffering to bind brothers and sisters in Christ together in fellowship and to minister to a broken world, see Paul Borthwick and Dave Ripper, *The Fellowship of the Suffering* (Downers Grove, IL: InterVarsity Press, 2018).

[30]"A Decade After Amish School Shooting, Gunman's Mother Talks of For-giveness," *NPR Morning Edition*, September 30, 2016, www.npr .org/2016/09/30/495905609/a-decade-after-amish-school-shooting-gunman-s -mother-talks-of-forgiveness.

[31]Colby Itkowitz, "Her Son Shot Their Daughters 10 Years Ago," *Washington Post*, October 1, 2016, www.washingtonpost.com/news/inspired-life /wp/2016/10/01/10-years-ago-her-son-killed-amish-children-their-families -immediately-accepted-her-into-their-lives/?utm_term=.82fabb8e9f12; "Amish Forgiveness," *PBS Religion and Ethics Newsweekly*, September 21, 2007, www.pbs.org/wnet/religionandethics/2007/09/21/september-21-2007 -amish-forgiveness/4295.

[32]"Amish Forgiveness."

[33]"A Decade After Amish School Shooting."

10. AN ETERNAL GLORY

[1]Various resources, including Elisabeth Elliot's own books and newsletters, serve as sources for this information.

[2]Elisabeth Elliot, *Loneliness* (Nashville: Oliver Nelson Books, 1988), 55.

[3]Elisabeth Elliot, *A Lamp unto My Feet: The Bible's Light for Your Daily Bible*, Day 18 (Ventura, CA: Regal, 2004), 33.

[4]Jennifer Lyell, "What I Learned from Elisabeth Elliot in Her Last Years," *Gospel Coalition*, June 25, 2015, www.thegospelcoalition.org/article /what-i-learned-from-elisabeth-elliot-in-her-last-years.

[5]George Eliot, *Middlemarch* (Middlesex, UK: Penguin Books, 1965), 896.

[6]When Paul considered suffering and glory as weighed against one another, he may have had in mind a Hebrew term for glory, *kābôd*, a word that carries the idea of heaviness or magnitude. In the negative sense, it was used to convey a burden, but used in the positive sense it refers to a thing of splendor or glory.

[7]C. S. Lewis, *The Weight of Glory and Other Addresses* (New York: Touchstone, 1996), 26.

[8]Lewis, *Weight of Glory*, 26.

[9]Lewis, *Weight of Glory*, 26.

[10]Tony Campolo, *Who Switched the Price Tags?* (Nashville: Thomas Nelson, 2008), 13-14.

¹¹Lewis, *Weight of Glory*, 26.
¹²Lewis, *Weight of Glory*, 28.
¹³Lewis, *Weight of Glory*, 28.
¹⁴Lewis, *Weight of Glory*, 38.
¹⁵C. S. Lewis, *Letters to Malcolm: Chiefly on Prayer*, letter 17, accessed July 21, 2019, https://gutenberg.ca/ebooks/lewiscs-letterstomalcolm/lewiscs-letter stomalcolm-00-h.html.
¹⁶William Butler Yeats, "Sailing to Byzantium," 1928.
¹⁷This quote isn't original with me, but I've never been able to locate the original source.
¹⁸This is the meaning of the concept of *propitiation*—a change of attitude toward us by God.
¹⁹For a lengthier discussion on rewards, see chap. 11, "Motivated Spirituality: Love, Gratitude, and Rewards," in Kenneth Boa, *Conformed to His Image* (Grand Rapids: Zondervan, 2001), 138-42; also, see chap. 28, "Rewards," in Kenneth Boa, *Leadership in the Image of God* (Atlanta: Trinity House, 2015), 278-86.
²⁰Other verses on the rewards promised to believers who remain faithful include 1 Corinthians 9:25-27; Philippians 3:14; and 2 Timothy 4:7-8. Verses such as James 3:1 and 2 Timothy 2:12 speak to the ability to be disqualified from certain rewards due to lack of faithfulness.
²¹Elisabeth Elliot, "The Sovereignty of God," *Elisabeth Elliot Newsletter*, January-February 2001, www.elisabethelliot.org/newsletters/2001-01-02.pdf.

11. A CLEAR CALLING

¹Rudyard Kipling, "If—," 1895, www.poetryfoundation.org/poems/46473/if—.
²C. S. Lewis, *The Screwtape Letters* (Grand Rapids: Zondervan, 2001), 40.
³In 2005 I did a presentation called "The Decline of Nations" on this very topic, highlighting ten ways in which the US culture now mirrors the culture of Rome at its decline. The comparison would be even closer now, with changes occurring not at a steady rate but exponentially.
⁴Os Guinness, *Dining with the Devil: The Megachurch Movement Flirts with Modernity* (Grand Rapids: Baker, 1993).
⁵James Davison Hunter, *To Change the World: The Irony, Tragedy, and Possibility of Christianity in the Late Modern World* (New York: Oxford University Press, 2010), 234-35.
⁶W. H. Auden, "For the Time Being: A Christmas Oratorio," 1944. This is the concluding chorus of Auden's poem. The genuineness of Auden's conversion to Christianity has been debated; his views were certainly not entirely orthodox. By quoting him, I am in no way endorsing him or his views in their entirety.
⁷George Herbert, "The Call," from *The Temple*, 1633, www.ccel.org/h/herbert/temple/Call.html.

[8]Dante Alighieri, "Paradiso 33," *The Divine Comedy*, in Teodolinda Barolini, "Paradiso 33: Invisible Ink," Commento Baroliniano, Digital Dante (New York: Columbia University Libraries, 2014), https://digitaldante.columbia.edu/dante/divine-comedy/paradiso/paradiso-33.

[9]C. S. Lewis, *The Last Battle* (New York: Collier Books, 1975), 184.

APPENDIX 1

[1]Ken Boa, *God, I Don't Understand* (Colorado Springs, CO: David C. Cook, 2007).

ABOUT THE AUTHORS

Dr. Kenneth Boa is engaged in a ministry of relational evangelism and discipleship teaching, writing, and speaking. He holds a BS from Case Institute of Technology, a ThM from Dallas Theological Seminary, a PhD from New York University, and a DPhil from the University of Oxford. Ken is engaged in a wide variety of ministry activities. He is founder and president of Reflections Ministries, Omnibus Media Ministries, and Trinity House Publishers. On a local level, he teaches four studies a week and leads seven small discipleship groups on a monthly basis. He is also engaged in one-on-one discipleship, mentoring, and spiritual direction. On a national and international level, Ken speaks and teaches throughout the United States and in various countries. He lives in Atlanta with his wife of more than fifty years, Karen.

Jenny Abel is editor and publications development manager for Omnibus Media Ministries, founded by Dr. Boa in 2018. Having sat under Dr. Boa's teaching since she was a teenager, she began working for him and his Reflections Ministries in 2013 and continues to serve as editor of the monthly *Reflections* teaching letter. She cowrote *A Guide to Practicing God's Presence* with Dr. Boa and edited *Life in the Presence of God*. She holds a BS in mathematics with a concentration in Latin American studies from Furman University, is a graduate of the Focus on the Family Leadership Institute, and has spent her entire career in communications. She is the editor of *The Panoramic Bible: The Storyline of Scripture* (William Hollberg, 2018). She and her husband, Ben, live in Charlottesville, Virginia, with their young daughter, Heidi.

REFLECTIONS MINISTRIES

Dr. Boa founded Reflections in 1995. Its mission is to encourage, teach, and equip people to know Christ, follow him, become progressively conformed to his image, and reproduce his life in others. The ministry accomplishes this mission through local studies, special outreach events, conferences, and numerous written, audio, visual, and video resources (http://kenboa.org).

OMNIBUS MEDIA MINISTRIES

Founded by Dr. Boa in 2018, Omnibus Media Ministries expands on Reflections' mission with a focus on the digital arena. Omnibus Media seeks to multiply disciples who invest the Word of God into the lives of others. It fulfills this vision by generating transformative media across multiple platforms, ranging from apps and websites to audiobooks and curricula. See some of its current offerings at presence.app and praytoday.com (http://omnibusmedia.com).

SOCIAL MEDIA

www.facebook.com/KennethBoa
www.instagram.com/ken.boa
twitter.com/kennethboa
vimeo.com/user10496586

OTHER BOOKS BY KEN BOA

AVAILABLE FROM IVP

Faith Has Its Reasons

Life in the Presence of God

Passionate Living: Praises and Promises

Passionate Living: Wisdom and Truth

Rewriting Your Broken Story

ALSO BY KEN BOA

20 Compelling Evidences That God Exists

Augustine to Freud

Conformed to His Image

God, I Don't Understand

A Guide to Practicing God's Presence

Handbook to Leadership

Handbook to Prayer

Handbook to Renewal

Handbook to Scripture

I'm Glad You Asked

A Journal of Sacred Readings

Leadership in the Image of God

Talk Thru the Bible